How Peace Came to the World

How Peace Came to the World

*edited by Earl W. Foell
and Richard A. Nenneman*

The MIT Press
Cambridge, Massachusetts
London, England

Second printing, 1986

© 1986 by The Christian Science Publishing Society

This book was set in Baskerville by Achorn Graphics and printed and bound by The Murray Printing Company in the United States of America.

Library of Congress Cataloging-in-Publication Data
Main entry under title:

How peace came to the world.

Based on entries to The Christian Science Monitor's Peace 2010 contest.
    1. Peace—Addresses, essays, lectures.   I. Foell, Earl W.
II. Nenneman, Richard A.   III. Christian Science Monitor.
JX1963.H738   1985   327.1'72   85-24130
ISBN   0-262-06100-7

To the 1300-plus people who entered the Peace 2010 contest and to peacemakers around the globe.

Contents

How Peace Came to the World

1

Introduction

Turn to the index of any general history book. Page after page, the listings for wars leap to the eye: War of Jenkins' Ear, War of the Spanish Succession, War of 1812, Punic Wars, Peloponnesian War, War of the Roses. . . .

Or battles: Agincourt, Tsushima Strait, Thermopylae, the Siege of Peking, Pripet Marshes, Omdurman, Alamo, Yalu River. . . .

We hate war. We say it is hell. We repeatedly take the pledge that the current war is the one to end all wars. We go cold turkey against our addiction and create detoxification machinery: the Congress of Vienna in 1814, the League of Nations in 1919, the United Nations in 1945, the Kellogg-Briand Pact, and assorted SALTs to control weapons just in case.

But after the great European powers met in Vienna to set up what was supposed to be a perfect peaceful balance of power, the world still witnessed 103 more wars over the next ninety-nine years. The first war, Napoleon's 100-day return from Elba, occurred before the Vienna parley had ended. The ensuing post-Napoleonic era—the glittering Victorian-Edwardian age, the ascent to the Belle Epoque in France, the birth of modern Italy and Germany—culminated after Sarajevo in one of the most senseless carnages in history carried on by well-educated rationalists and backed by a generally well-informed public.

But surely World War II, the only slightly delayed sequel, would end all that by creating enduring repugnance against genocide, buzz bombs, incendiary fire storms, and above all the threat of Hiroshima to the nth power. Large-scale nuclear war, yes—so far so good. But alas, not small-scale war. The world has engaged in 130 wars, small and not so small, in the forty years since World War II ended.

Is the situation, then, hopeless? Are those behaviorists who say that humans are a warring species whose territorial instincts or aggressive nature is a genetic trait correct?

The purpose of *The Christian Science Monitor*'s Peace 2010 contest and of this book is to explore the opposite possibility—at a time in human history when the answers to those two questions are of vital importance to all who are living today. Namely, that it is possible to move past the watershed in which war *had* been an open option—when all else failed. This book assumes that that is indeed possible. The writers of some 1300 essays assumed that it was possible. And by forcing these writers to look forward twenty-five years and at least partially embroider the outlines of the process by which the world had moved ahead to such a state, we compelled each writer to pick a scenario, one approach by which a peaceful world could be attained.

A part of the *Monitor*'s announcement of its contest read:

Peace is a condition all the world's statesmen say they yearn for. Every individual would like to live in peace. The Beatitudes call the peacemakers "the children of God."

Instead of only reacting to each new international crisis, let's think instead about what conditions could prevail that would bring about a substantially altered climate of world opinion.

Your essay will be judged for its literary qualities, but it will be judged even more on the basis of the feasibility of the ideas it contains. Essays will be expected to show a knowledge of the framework of international relations in the world today and the process by which those relations are bettered.

The edifice of a lasting peace will have many building blocks. You may wish to emphasize economic factors, the role of moral leadership, or a need to control world armaments.

Halfway through the period of the contest the *Monitor* noted (in a column) that the contest was not meant only for statesmen and professors.

Try to think your way through to a cohesive strategy. Face the practical questions: How would you fund your plan? Would you use existing institutions, or are new ones needed? What about political opposition? How permanent is the solution? How do you persuade other leaders, other nations to agree?

Those are practical questions any decisionmaker must deal with. After that, you—and we—face one overriding question: Isn't it naive, even presumptuous, for amateurs to try to fix up the world?

We wrestled soberly with this criticism. After all, soliciting reader essays about realistic peace plans isn't quite like asking for reader ideas on making safer cars or tastier cakes.

In the end we felt a strong duty to proceed. The chief reasons are closely related:

(1) Active citizens—whether so-called average, or professionals involved in peace planning—can stimulate their leaders to be more bold in finding peaceful solutions to disputes.

(2) When leaders do take such bold steps, they need realistic backing from informed citizens if their plans are to succeed.

The use of the word "realistic" in the previous sentence is important. There is an old axiom that applies to peacemaking of all kinds. It reads: Be open-minded about possibilities, tough-minded about evidence. Doves are good about the former, sometimes vague about the latter. Hawks often err in the opposite direction.

It should be noted at this point that there was a lack of unanimity over the comprehensiveness of the definition of peace. If a better relationship between the superpowers was a starting point, it was clear that some essayists saw peace almost entirely in terms of a lack of armed conflict, others saw it as a progressively interactive exchange among the nations of the world, and some related it in the end to the peace of the individual that is felt first in his or her family and then radiates outward. Although the call to the *Monitor*'s contest did imply that there must be a resolution of the superpower arms race, the *Monitor*'s editors and hundreds of writers for the contest are aware that peace is a more complex subject than just the arms race.

Some of the writers, such as one of the three winners, Thomas Fehsenfeld, doubted that peace as a kind of permanent harmony among all mankind is even attainable. But he did feel that the containment of conflict was a distinct possibility and in his essay talked in terms of the resolution of the conflicts that will inevitably occur among human beings and their political structures—at least so long as they do not all serve identical political goals.

The four judges of the *Monitor*'s contest were Dr. Kurt Waldheim, Admiral Stansfield Turner, Dr. Lincoln Bloomfield, and Dr. Curt Gasteyger. Kurt Waldheim served two terms as the elected secretary-general of the United Nations—from 1972 to 1982. He is currently president of Interaction, an international policy group of former heads of government from around the world. Admiral Turner served as director of the American Central Intelligence Agency from 1977 to 1981, was commander-in-chief of NATO forces in southern Europe, and was formerly president of the US Naval War College. Dr. Bloomfield, who is Professor of Political Science at the Center for International Studies, Massachusetts Institute of Technology, was in charge of global issues at the National Security Council in the White House from 1979 to 1980 and has done extensive research on arms control, policy planning, global interdependence, and computerized conflict-minimizing systems. Dr. Gasteyger is director of the Program for Strategic and International Security Studies at the Graduate Institute of International Studies in Geneva.

The two European judges—Kurt Waldheim, who is Austrian, and Curt Gasteyger, who is a German Swiss—commented on the relative lack of entries that looked on peace as much more than the cessation of the generation-old cold war between the two superpowers. This, the editors explained, was because the announcement of the *Monitor*'s contest implied that peace between the super-powers was paramount. In discussing the issue further, we still feel that the emphasis in the contest and in the entries was a correct one, because nothing threatens the world today as much as the 50,000-plus nuclear warheads that stand in a state of near-readiness.

It is correct, of course, that a genuine world peace by the year 2010 will require much more than an improvement in the superpowers' relationships. It is even possible that an improvement in the superpower relationship will be the catalyst for something else's seeming to come unglued elsewhere in the world. The European judges felt that there was more potential for conflict between the North and South of the world than between the East and West. If, within the next ten years, let us say, several Third World countries come to possess the nuclear bomb, can we be so sure that they will be as reluctant to use it as both the United States and the Soviet Union have been? Even without resort to that weapon, the causes for economic and social strife between the rich and the poor nations already exist in abundance in a North-South framework: the poor nations' debt to the banks of the United States, Europe, and Japan; the relations of the oil-producing countries to those dependent on oil; the willingness of the OECD (Organization for Economic Cooperation and Development) nations to take the primary wealth of continents such as Africa without undue concern for the development and future of the countries from which they extract that wealth. There even exists the potential for one more struggle in which religion is at least a partial cause, as the Islamic (largely poor) part of the world feels its culture threatened by the post-Christian culture of much of the OECD area. The Arab-Israeli dispute has a particular poignancy because it crosses so many of the division points of this age: religion, Europe versus an older Middle East, cultural modernism versus tradition.

Without the North-South friction points, other causes remain that could also be tackled in a peace contest. One of the judges told us that if we were to ask the average Swiss or German what most concerns him or her today, it would not be the potential for war but the ruination of the forests of central Europe. Ecological questions pose problems right within the borders of many individual nations. They pose more serious problems to peace when the cause of pollution drifts through the air or flows through the rivers to other countries. The mention of environmental dangers to the earth, however, brings us full circle to the greatest environmental danger of all—extinction by massive use of nuclear explosives and the nuclear winter that could result. Carl Sagan and the World after Nuclear War group of scientists have raised the level of public consciousness about this problem. For 1985 and the foreseeable immediate future, this means that containing the distrust between the Soviet Union and the United States is still the greatest challenge and therefore the appropriate subject for most of the essays included here.

Each of the next seven chapters of this book reflects the main approaches to peace taken by the writers of the essays. But in another sense there were not seven approaches to peace but only two: those starting with governments alone or through intergovernmental organizations, such as the United Nations, and those starting with individuals. Some writers began with government actions, produced either by normal diplomatic and military bargaining, such as that now going on in Geneva, or by the cataclysm of disaster. Others proceeded basically from the action, at first, of individuals. The two approaches are not actually mutually exclusive, and in some of the essays we have excerpted, we have done a partial injustice to the writer by excerpting what was to us the essay's core thought. All governmental actions are initiated in the end by some individual. And most governments are at least indirectly responsive to the most pressing intellectual currents of the thinkers in their societies. The final chapter of this book examines practical ways in which such private ideas may be translated into government action.

On the other hand, the essays that are built around the individual and what actions he or she may initiate go further than trying to influence only governments to act. Many of them envision a change of consciousness within the individual—ultimately within enough individuals—to change the definition of the problem. Each reader of this book must decide how realistic such an approach is. Bluntly stated, if the enemy is no longer seen as the enemy, does this new insight change the reality of the situation or are the seers fooling only themselves?

Since peace ultimately depends on the actions of many nations, a change of consciousness among even millions of people in one country or in the NATO area or the larger OECD area would not necessarily bring peace—unless that change of consciousness was matched by changing perceptions and actions inside those nations that are potential adversaries.

The writers of many of these individual approaches to peace are idealistic. Many belong to action groups that hope to influence foreign policy by their views. Many of the readers of the *Monitor* are themselves Christian Scientists and, although few identified themselves or their approaches to peace in any kind of denominational sign language, we know from an analysis of the newspaper's readership that many of the essays must have come from Scientists. Although Christian Scientists would not feel that their religion is adequately defined by calling it simply idealistic, it would be broadly accurate to say that many of its adherents gain from its study a sense of idealism that they take as their individual responsibility to see fulfilled in practical solutions to the problem at hand. There were also several essays identifiably linked to Quaker groups, who are well recognized for their long-standing devotion to nonmilitant solutions of disputes.

The power of ideas is, of course, one of those perennial subjects that historians continue to debate among themselves. To Americans, the broad ideals of individual freedom and political equality explain a substantial part of the development of their nation. On the other hand, to Marxists the inevitability of the historic process, the class struggle, the determinism suggested by economic processes explains the greater part of history. Yet even Marxists might admit that their bagful of ideas constitutes a kind of ideology that has been useful to them in trying to gain power around the world. Most practitioners of the art of history would probably come down somewhere in between, admitting the power of a new idea but also firmly believing that the weight of history in any society cannot be completely ignored or even overcome in a short time interval.

Whatever the ultimate power of ideas, one must recognize that a particular idea or human ideal can be either good or evil. National socialism in prewar Germany gained much of its initial support from an appeal to idealism, which runs high in the German character. Roderick Stackelberg, in his 1981 book, *Idealism Debased* (Kent State University Press), writes that

the disaffection of some idealists from Nazism should not lead us to underestimate the idealist content of National Socialism

nor the capacity for ruthlessness of those who prided themselves on their idealism. The fanatical implementation of ideals
usually leads to the violation of these ideals in practice, for he
who regards himself as the instrument of higher forces feels
himself freed of worldly scruples.

The writer of one long essay envisioned improving the
world's organizational framework through an expansion
of the system of ideas embodied in the US Constitution.
This expansion involved the widening of the political
structure of the United States to include all the world,
whose nations would join up in some kind of Judeo-
Christian framework. The concept of this essay was a
daring one, in the sense of moving toward a united world
by way of what is at once one of the dominant historical,
cultural, and religious threads of the past 3000 years. On
the other hand, the Judeo-Christian approach, essentially
a matter of morality and metaphysics, became intertwined with an advocacy of democratic capitalism, which
is the outcome in certain countries of an alliance of history, culture, and stage of economic development that
may not be universally applicable.

Most of those who envision an ultimate family of humanity see a tapestry woven of more intricate threads,
needing to contain what is worthwhile from the traditions
of all races, cultures, and continents. One question for
readers of this book to consider in their own minds is to
what extent an ideal, or a whole set of ideals, can be
separated from the institutions or organizations that have
been most closely identified with its promulgation or
practice in the past. It would almost seem as if an idealism
that would be acceptable on a global scale would be one in
which the ideas are persuasive enough—and manifestly
universal enough—to exist without the institutional setting that may have supported them in an earlier age. The
reference to nazism is apropos. German philosophical
ideals of the eighteenth and early nineteenth centuries
were among the loftiest, but they had not been tested in

centuries of political experimentation and development, as in either England or France, and ultimately were susceptible to being stolen and misused by Hitler. Communism under Stalin similarly was able to misappropriate early Christian communitarian ideals and mislead some Westerners as to the true nature of the Soviet system.

Sir Laurens van der Post in his latest book, *Yet Being Someone Other* (Morrow, 1983), expresses the heartfelt sense of universal brotherhood that could be acceptable around this whole globe. He senses a vision of a united mankind that many of the essay writers saw as being able to override the political divisions of the world of 1985. Van der Post writes from an elevation which sees meaning in history beyond what many historians have found. In writing about the England of the 1930s, for instance, he says:

I had become increasingly impatient with history as I was taught it. It seemed to me more and more a superficial catalogue of external events and a mobilization of statistics of time and change which ignored a deeper something seeking to accomplish itself and increase the meaning of life through men and their societies.

In a later section of the book, as he describes his passage on the last sailing of regular passenger service between South Africa and England in the 1950s, van der Post sees in the crowd that gathers at Cape Town for the farewell how a sense of higher purpose or destiny overcame even for a brief moment the division that already existed among his native South Africans.

The diversities which normally set us apart were erased for an instant by an eruption from this patient, brooding and ultimately irresistible urge gathering in the unconscious of the world, namely the power to assert one day, and for good, the values of the family of man on our journey ahead, however roundabout the route—just as our ship was bound for home. That sight of black, coloured, white, Indians, Pakistanis, Afrikaners and English, single and at one *because the right occasion was there to reflect this concealed potential* [italics added], still remains as a candle in the dark of what has followed on since. It remains, too, a reproach to the bankruptcy of a world that seems incapable of producing other and more positive evocations of the meaning of history, to make the manifestation of our latest human singleness not random and spasmodic but permanent. (p. 344)

"The values of the family of man" he refers to were on the *Monitor*'s mind during the summer of 1985, when at the height of the hostage crisis after the hijacking of TWA Flight 847, it published an editorial entitled "Brothers' keepers" (June 26, 1985):

Ever since the legendary murder of his brother Abel, Cain has had the company of a considerable number of mankind on his side, asking, "Am I my brother's keeper?"

Over the centuries, groups of people have been learning to enlarge their concept of just who their brother, and sister, is. Loyalty to family and tribe gradually gave way to a concern for a wider environment of human beings. For half a millennium the nation-state has been the outer limit of one's loyalties, although in certain parts of the world, such as Western Europe, there has been a slowly growing pride in what one area of the world has come to stand for in terms of civilization and culture. Perhaps less known to the West, that same kind of pride has existed in the Islamic crescent, arcing from Morocco to Indonesia and encompassing all of the Middle East.

The advent of the most modern means of transportation—jet aircraft and spaceships—and of ever newer forms of communication is forcing a global sense of brotherhood on mankind. Who is ready for it? TV shots of militant Shiites shouting epithets against the West certainly don't indicate a sense of brotherhood there.

Is the sense of brotherhood, however, much greater here in the Western world? How many of us even care to read about the beliefs of another worldwide religion, Islam, or the beliefs of one of its many subgroups, the Shiites, or the concerns of individual Shiites, who more often than not represent the poor of their countries?

Before a realized brotherhood there must be understanding. And that understanding can come only through love, from a sense of compassion, or at least concern, for the lives of those who seem so different from what we in the Western world take as the norm.

None of this makes a crime such as hostage-taking any less a crime. But in the *Angst* of the moment, one easily forgets that in this age of modern technology it is not going to be business as usual. The world has been made one because it is inevitably traversing a path from separation and division to one in which all men have an interest in the welfare of all others.

It is doubly hard to think this way at a time when the West— at least the United States—is being openly taunted and is seemingly without effective weapons. But acknowledging concern for our brother, which Cain did not do, is a constant need. It is not only the implantation of a Western-type society, Israel, in the midst of the Islamic Middle East that challenges mankind to outgrow old concepts, or the reports of strife between Sikhs and Hindus in India that compel us to attempt to understand what we might prefer to consider an internal rivalry in the world's most populous democracy. It is also the knowledge, through television, trade, and travel, of what life is like for mankind all over the globe that forces us to deal with injustices and inequities that we once thought were only the concern of someone else's brother. No longer. We are now that brother.

We also think it appropriate, in ending this introduction to quote from Mary Baker Eddy, the founder of *The Christian Science Monitor,* some words that are familiar to every editor of the paper and which they think form a useful guide to whatever lofty idealistic aims mankind is trying to achieve.

One infinite God, good, unifies men and nations; constitutes the brotherhood of man; ends wars; fulfils the Scripture, "Love thy neighbor as thyself;" annihilates pagan and Christian idolatry,—whatever is wrong in social, civil, criminal, political, and religious codes; equalizes the sexes; annuls the curse on man, and leaves nothing that can sin, suffer, be punished or destroyed. (*Science and Health with Key to the Scriptures,* p. 340)

EDITORS' NOTE: Each of chapters 2–8 begins with our introductory remarks, followed by a rule signaling the beginning of the essay section of the chapter. The essayist's name, which appears in italics in our text, follows the essay.

2

Awakening through Disaster

Poor Santayana. Of all his philosophical musings, only one sentence has been remembered by hordes of speech writers and essayists—and it is a sentence about forgetting: "Those who cannot remember the past are condemned to repeat it." Alas, we are condemned to repeat the aphorism once more here, for it is the perfect description of the much noted war/peace cycle in history. That cycle exists, according to many scholars of the history of war, because humans do not remember wars with sufficient intensity to make sure peace becomes permanent.

Some who are pessimistic about mankind ever breaking the cycle and establishing an era of unshattered peace argue that the leaders of the world and/or their peoples have never been frightened enough by war to renounce it for more than a generation or so—much less permanently.

The gist of the pessimists' case is this: Leaders and peoples make war, scare themselves into stratagems for preventing future wars, then become either apathetic or overconfident enough to slip into war again. Tribes and nations have experimented with an extensive repertory of war-prevention ideas in the immediate aftermath of wars. But, say the pessimists, all strategies have failed the test of time.

There are two logical counterarguments to this implacable view of history. One asserts that a break in the war/peace cycle is not only possible but also probable in an age that is both sobered by nuclear risk and tied together by instant worldwide communication—an age, moreover, that is influenced as never before by a worldwide change of thought about the inevitability of war. Social scientists are wary of crediting any power to such abstract ideas as a "yearning" for peace or a persistent "search" for more peaceful ways of solving disputes. When pressed, however, many will admit that such power exists and can have an impact on leaders and their policies.

A second, quite opposite argument posits that some drastic catastrophe will finally so frighten everyone that no leader or society will ever again break Santayana's commandment.

The first of these two theses, the optimistic one, is explained by a simple metaphor almost in the cliche category: Achieving success at keeping the peace is compared to breaking free of earth's gravity. Before mankind knew how to fly, the argument goes, few believed flying possible. Many experiments ended in failure. But that didn't preclude the right—Wright—experiment from succeeding. And once we got the hang of it, it was a fairly simple matter to go from 6.8 mph at Kitty Hawk to 24,000 mph when rocketing free of gravity and off to the moon.

For thousands of years, says this thesis, both the war cycle and earthboundness seemed inevitable. Looking back at earthboundedness post 1903, we wonder why da Vinci's vision wasn't implemented earlier. Someday we will likewise look back at the conflict-solving machinery that lifted mankind out of its history of settling conflicts by war and wonder why it took so long, just as we now take for granted conflict-solving machinery for settling business disputes or labor/management collisions.

Proponents of the second school of argument are what might be called optimists-through-pessimism. They do not believe that the war/peace cycle is immutable. They believe that flying is possible—that international conflict-solving machinery is achievable. But they do not see it arriving because of an inventive breakthrough or a gradual evolution of popular thought. They argue that only a disaster—perhaps a cataclysm—can change world thinking, including the thinking of leaders. Their approach is equivalent to arguing that driver training is OK, but having an accident or near-accident is what makes a really safe driver.

Many of the essays submitted to the *Monitor* contest followed this line of logic. One of the three winners, *Richard Lamm,* the governor of Colorado, used a particularly grim disaster scenario, involving a nuclear war between India and Pakistan. The war, whose starting point was obscured by the ashes, involved the detonation of about twenty bombs, killing uncounted millions in that heavily populated bulge of the Eurasian continent. The crucial factor, pointed out by Lamm, was that the destruction was reported live and moment by moment on hundreds of millions of television sets throughout the world.

Governor Lamm wrote:

In those moments, with a horrified world glued to its television sets in homes or in windows of stores, . . . came the horror of modern weapons. . . . Thus wisdom came not through treaty but through tragedy. The goal of peace was no longer something left to politicians, but became the demand of every citizen. If "war was too important to be left to generals," in Clemenceau's famous phrase, peace became a ground swell that swept over politicians and nationalities. . . .

Unlike Carthage, whose destruction was witnessed by few, the Great Annihilation was witnessed by all. . . .

No formal arms control agreement followed the holocaust. . . . Both the Soviet Union and the United States simply stopped building new weapons and missiles. These were not weapons but suicide devices. Man had at last invented a doomsday machine. . . . Peace was not negotiated. It burst on a stunned mankind. . . .

Governor Lamm later reported that deep down he did not feel such a disaster was inevitable. He said it was his hope that dramatizations of nuclear disaster such as the one about which he had written would themselves serve as catalysts to force progress—thus avoiding in real life the scene he had so grippingly created in fiction.

Robert Aronstein, of Falls Church, Virginia, derived his essay from his unpublished novel *Witness,* in which Chicago is destroyed by nuclear attack. The crisis begins with a revolt in East Germany leading to West German intervention, followed by American moves in Eastern Europe. A Soviet ultimatum is ignored, and tit-for-tat salvos destroy Chicago and Kiev. Aronstein's essay is written in the form of a letter from a Soviet technician to his son in the peaceful December of 2010. The Russian is working on a joint Soviet-American agricultural project in Ethiopia.

Lamm dramatized his Indo-Pak nuclear Götterdämmerung; Aronstein used his tale of the destruction of two cities mainly to set the scene for an elaborately detailed peace settlement between the United States and the Soviet Union. New Zealander *Vernon F. Wilkinson* presented yet another variation on the nuclear theme: a close call but no detonation. A 1987 crisis created by a lightning Solidarity strike and the assassination of the leader of Poland leads to an eyeball-to-eyeball confrontation of the superpowers. Then a faulty computer aboard a Soviet submarine sends a missile screaming on a trajectory toward Manhattan. Tragedy is averted. Details can be found in Wilkinson's essay.

Other essayists drew on nonnuclear disaster themes for their Grim Awakener. Some saw a global *economic* crisis forcing cooperation. Others focused on a widespread *ecological* disaster. Several chose a more science-fiction-style Awakener: the threat of invaders from another solar system.

Professor J. Edward Barrett, of Muskingum College, New Concord, Ohio, took the economic crisis path to jolt the world to its senses.

It was not catastrophic nuclear war nor was it conversion to sweet reasonableness that brought us peace. But during the last twenty-five years a constellation of events has occurred that constitutes a peaceful world. . . .

That constellation included patient determination to hold successful nuclear arms control'talks. But a key change came about in the economic sphere.

Already . . . the Western economy was truly international, but exclusive of the Soviet bloc. The average American might enjoy coffee from Central America, shave with a razor from the Netherlands, wear a shirt made in Korea, own a watch made in Singapore, drive a Toyota made in Japan, fueled with gasoline from Saudi Arabia. . . . Yet, while international business had taken on a prosperous life of its own . . . international banking was undergoing traumatic shock waves of default. . . . Foreign money, which had poured into the United States in the 1980s because of high interest rates was withdrawn in the 1990s because of fear that the economic bubble in the United States would collapse. This, of course, contributed to its collapse. By 1995 it was clear that whatever future course recovery might take, it would leave everything different from before. . . .

For decades American policy had been to contain and isolate the Soviety economy. Now, pressure from two sources forced that policy to be abandoned. The first was the need of the international banking system itself. With dozens of nations in default, the Soviet offer [to deal with East European debt] meant partial but practical relief. And bankers know how to bring effective pressure on national leaders. The second was the decades-old problem of farmers in the United States. American farmers . . . needed long-term agreements to sell grain to the Soviet Union. In 1985, two 20,000-ton freighters loaded with grain left the United States for Russia every day.

By 1995, that amount was multiplied fivefold. For the first time, the international economy was truly global, influenced but not controlled by any one superpower.

Disaster of ecology, rather than economy, concentrated minds in the scenario submitted by Rudolf Jackli, of Zug, Switzerland.

Looking back, it is striking how much was contributed to peace by people who simply and soberly did the sensible thing without using the word "peace" and sometimes probably without even thinking of peace.

A lot went wrong in 1986 and 1987: Most of central Europe's forests simply vanished. Bald patches appeared equally in northwest North America. In 1988 a satellite photograph showed a barren area the size of Switzerland in the Amazon basin, where uncontrolled use of pesticides and defoliants had wrought havoc. Every year more fish disappeared in the Adriatic and the Baltic. Some of the groundwater resources in the United States were found to be literally poisoned by both heavy metals and organic substances. The "greenhouse effect" became noticeable: the mean level of oceans rose, albeit just measurably. . . . Scientists had been predicting all this, and many others had taken up their prophetic call to stop laying waste to the earth before it was too late. . . . Scientists all over the world held up a mirror to man and man did not like what he saw. . . .

It was as if newspaper people, university presidents, the Red Cross, church leaders, and many others had only been waiting for the time when the large powers would be driven together by a common menace forcing them to cooperate. If ever a dark cloud had had a silver lining it was the brown acrid fumes of pollution. These women and men knew that they had a new opportunity for fostering peace. . . .

Other essays dealt with an Awakener that is both nuclear and environmental: the fear of nuclear winter. Professor Louis René Beres, of Purdue University, Lafayette, Indiana, used that theme in an essay that commenced by quoting poet Theodore Roethke: "In a dark time, the eye begins to see." Not only the threat of nuclear winter but also the economic damage done by the arms race lead an American president to be courageous enough to make some concessions on arms control. These are matched by Moscow, and gradually the process of defusing distrust leads to a reduction of both arsenals and budget drain.

But most of the scenarios in which world leaders learn from disaster do not envision a change brought about by rational examination of the possibility of tragedy. A majority of the authors envisioned at least a token slip over the brink:

A Soviet missile accidentally fired at an American city.

A bluff in which Libya's one nuclear warhead is placed in the Egyptian desert and detonated, after which blackmail threats are made to explode further (nonexistent) A-bombs in Egyptian cities.

A conventional naval battle between Soviet and American fleets in the Norwegian Sea.

The last scenario here was developed by *Robert Hunt Sprinkle,* a Dallas, Texas, doctor. He penned a spare, dramatic narrative in which Moscow, concerned about moves toward German reunification and a cryptic Chinese claim to all of Mongolia, arranges a naval show of force in the English Channel. The American president, Jack Kemp, counters with a US naval presence. (Readers who keep score on political prognostication may be interested to know that such real figures as Congressman Kemp, Secretary of Transportation Elizabeth Dole, and neoconservative author Midge Decter appear as US presidents in various essays—as do a host of fictional characters with catchy names that Pat Caddell would envy.)

The navies clash. Ineptitude, disaster, dud weapons, and tragic casualties result, but no escalation to wider nuclear war. Kemp, who is pictured as bold and somewhat impetuous at first, is portrayed as creative and statesmanlike in the crunch. And his attitude helps draw out the statesmanship in Soviet President Ulyanov. The peace deal they strike is aided by improved arms control verification gadgetry.

For students and scholars engaged in war- and peace-gaming, these dramatic scenarios that require a purgatory before humanity can reach a state of peace may seem both dramatic in plot and colorful in detail. But in an age that has left Dante and his era's theology behind, purgatories and infernos (poetic or nuclear) seem an anachronism to many writers of peace scenarios. We shall hear their ideas in the chapters that follow.

Excerpt from "A History of the Twentieth Century," *By Cornelius Barnes. Boston: Houghton-Mifflin.* *2010.*

When we released the energy from the atom, everything changed except our way of thinking. Because of that, we drift toward unparalleled disaster. We shall require a substantially new manner of thinking if mankind is to survive.

Albert Einstein's prophetic words foreshadowed the Time of Peace; 1994 was the year of the ultimate war and the year that a lasting peace finally arrived on earth.

History shows periods of peace to be the exception rather than the rule. Since the dawn of history, neighbor has fought neighbor, tribe has fought tribe, religion has fought religion, nation has fought nation. The history of man is partially written in blood: construction giving way to destruction; peace and stability turning into war and chaos. Wars have been as inevitable to history as storms are to weather.

Violence and terrorism increased dramatically as the twentieth century, already history's most destructive century, lurched to a close. In the 1970s and 1980s, violence seemed to reach a crescendo. By the late 1980s, Russia and the United States both instituted "launch on warning" nuclear systems. A myriad of local wars, revolutions, incidents of religious and sectarian strife, terrorism, and random acts of violence were made even more frightening by the rapid growth of the nuclear club. Peace was a stranger. Man seemed to have lost his capacity for shock, inundated as he was—wherever he lived—by daily news bulletins and TV reports of wars, terrorism, and violence.

One American wit, Woody Allen, seemed to sum up the dilemma:

More than any other time in history, mankind faces the crossroads . . . one path leads to despair and utter hopelessness, the other to total extinction. I pray we have the wisdom to choose wisely.

The flash point came, with history's usual irony, in the least expected place. Although India and Pakistan had fought three wars (1947, 1965, and 1971), an uneasy truce had existed between them. Despite their legacy of hate and distrust, no significant increase in tensions is known to have preceded the devastating nuclear exchange. None of history's usual causations seemed to trigger the conflagration: no jihad, no territorial dispute, no recent reason for revenge. History's most bloody war was apparently caused by some minor miscalculation. Like the War of Jenkins' Ear, the cause, while lost in the radiated ashes, was so insignificant as to conjure up Hannah Arendt's phrase, "the banality of evil." No international threat or declaration from either country harbingered the holocaust. It just happened.

The morning of November 29, 1994, dawned clear and cool over the Indian subcontinent. The harvests had been sparse, but adequate. The border between India and Pakistan, long filled with minor incidents, had been exceptionally quiet.

Granted, the religious differences were as strong as ever, but no known incident or aggravation was present. November 29 was like so many similar days—alive with pungent smells, buzzing women on the way to market, mischievous children, men sweating in the fields. True, the Hindus worshiped a myriad of gods, while the Muslims worshiped one; the Muslims eschewed pork and were quiet in their worship, while the Hindus proscribed beef and had music in their worship. Both shared a legacy of religious strife and conflict that defied even a peacemaker such as Gandhi and resulted in the partition of a continent. But nothing in the mind or imagination of man could have justified or explained a spasm of hate equal to The Great Annihilation.

Simply put, one moment tens of millions of people were going about their daily routines and the next moment they were ashes. For historical accuracy, it must be pointed out that satellite pictures confirm that India was attacked first, but American satellites monitoring radio traffic over the Indian subcontinent recorded that the Indians had a sudden, unmanageable fear that the Pakistanis had mobilized and were prepared to launch their recently acquired, supposedly obsolete, American-purchased cruise missiles. So India sent its rockets, just purchased from Russia, on a preemptive strike. Analysts later agreed that there must have been a computer failure in New Delhi. But in the end, it is impossible to assign "blame"; even the concept seems irrelevant to the horror that followed.

What is important to note is the unpredictability of events and how easily one minor event led to another, with increasing speed and significance, until a human chain reaction caused a nuclear chain reaction. The twentieth century had seen a world of isolated, independent events become an interdependent global village. Just as an assassination in Sarajevo started a chain of events, one following inevitably after another, it is likely that on the Indian subcontinent some slight error led to an insult; an insult to an incident; an incident to an outrage; and an outrage to a holocaust. Events soon passed beyond all human control. The "Guns of August" became the "Missiles of November."

"If the iron dice must roll, may God help us," anguished Theobald von Bethmann-Hollweg on August 1, 1914. Eighty years later the nuclear dice rolled—on a scale that eclipsed even the destruction of two world wars. But the rolling dice did something else more important: It made absurd such concepts as "winners" or "losers" in modern warfare. President Dole, in her characteristic way, put it succinctly: "Winning a nuclear war is like saying, 'Your end of the boat is sinking!' "

The total devastation of modern weapons is seen in the absence of reports from either Pakistan or India. Few were left to carry the word. The first news came from US and Russian satellites that reported a nuclear exchange involving at least twenty detonations. There were no "stop the presses" telegrams from Sarajevo, no cacophony of reports from Pearl Harbor. The first sound of this war was silence.

Chilling eerie silence.

When reports did come, they were of "multiple blinding flashes seen to the northwest," as radioed from Colombo, Sri Lanka. A radio operator in Bangalore, India, reported "large mushroom clouds rising from Bangalore and Madras." Seismic recorders around the world registered multiple shocks in both India and Pakistan.

If one could pinpoint the beginning of The Time of Peace, it would be December 1, 1994, when the first television reports burst upon a world that had thought itself beyond shock. The initial images were pictures taken from the air by American network news organizations in leased airplanes hurriedly flown to India from Sri Lanka and Thailand. The first images were sweeping panoramas of a moonlike landscape. Nothing stood but charred rubble. News reports repeated Robert Oppenheimer's observation at the first successful atomic test five decades earlier, when he recalled the Bhagavad-Gita: "I have become Death/Destroyer of Worlds!" Here was a world destroyed.

In those moments—with a horrified world glued to its television sets in homes or in windows of stores with TV sets—came the horror of modern weapons. Craters where cities once stood. A myriad of people struck blind whose only mistake had been to look at the fireball. Into every world capital, country, town, village, barrio, ghetto, fravello, and most huts, the universality of suffering was dramatically played out before shocked eyes. Nuclear war, like Medusa, consumed all who looked it in the face.

Thus wisdom came not through treaty but through tragedy. The goal of peace was no longer something left to politicians, but became the demand of every citizen. If "war was too important to be left to generals,'' in Clemenceau's famous phrase, peace became a ground swell that swept over politicians and nationalities. The demonic horror of the Indian subcontinent brought home to everyone the universality, not of brotherhood, but of the vulnerability of man. Man looked into the abyss and he was horrified beyond words. No religious or national goals could justify destruction and desolation on this scale. War was mutual suicide. The message went not only to the head but to the heart. As Aeschylus had said:

Even in our sleep
Pain that we cannot forget
Falls drop by drop upon the heart
Until in our own despair
Against our will
Comes wisdom
Through the awful grace of God.

One is cynically tempted to cite Tacitus: ''When they made a desert, they called it Peace.'' The aphorism would seem appropriate if restricted to the survivors of India and Pakistan. Those two countries were left with a desert, their people too exhausted and traumatized to fight. They could only suffer. Hundreds of millions of refugees in both countries rushed to escape the fallout. Survival was determined by the caprice of the winds.

But this ''desert'' aphorism misses the symbolic value of the horror. It ignores the vividness of the pictures sent around the world. Unlike Carthage, whose destruction was witnessed by few, the Great Annihilation was witnessed by all. Grim pictures of the widespread suffering were transmitted to the end of the globe. Children died who were guilty of no sins save those of their fathers. The whole world could clearly see that in a nuclear war, the survivors would envy the dead. In a thousand languages and dialects, people of different faiths recognized, ''There, but for the grace of God, go I.''

As if to drive the point home came the Years Without Summer. The nuclear explosions and resulting fires put large quantities of fine dust and soot into the atmosphere and changed the climate of the entire Northern Hemisphere. Actually, everyone outside the Indian subcontinent was fortunate, even though all suffered through three successive summers that were 10 to 15 degrees below normal, with resulting crop losses that were barely overcome by emptying America's gigantic grain storage bins. But if it had been fifty bombs instead of twenty, the "nuclear winter" would have destroyed all life on earth.

Tests showed that, in addition, the atmosphere's ozone, which shields man from the carcinogenic ultraviolet radiation, had been permanently damaged. Man learned unequivocally that a depletion in the stratospheric ozone by nuclear explosions would dangerously increase solar ultraviolet radiation. Nuclear war was Hydra headed: first the catastrophe of the blast; then the devastation of the fallout; then the climatic disaster of the nuclear winter; and, finally, after the soot and dust had settled out, the continuing curse of ultraviolet radiation.

No formal arms control agreement followed the holocaust. Politicians continued to find barriers to treaties. As always, technical problems and difficulties of ensuring compliance were solemnly cited. But peace is neither the absence of war nor the presence of a disarmament agreement. Peace is a change of heart. Both the Soviet Union and the United States simply stopped building new weapons and missiles. These were not weapons but suicide devices. Man had at last invented a doomsday machine.

The revulsion came in many forms and in many languages. The nations of the world clearly shared too small a star to allow this to happen again. Peace was not negotiated: It burst on a stunned mankind. Multiple messiahs preached the common theme of peace on earth. "Blessed are the peacemakers," urged Christian ministers. "Never in the world can hatred be stilled by hatred; it will be stilled only by nonhatred—this is the law eternal." quoted the followers of Buddha. A religious leader from China, quoting an old Vietnamese proverb, "If we take vengeance on vengeance, vengeance will never end," gained millions of converts. The ancient simple truths of love and charity were reinforced by the terror of example.

In the words of Shelley:

> Most wretched men
> Are cradled into poetry by wrong;
> They learn in suffering what they
teach in song.

A tidal wave of peace swept the world.

Other factors supplemented the change of heart. Both the United States and Russia were increasingly frustrated by the pouring of resources into the arms race. Each had to match the other, but the cost was high. Both had built the twenty-first-century equivalent of the Maginot line: an awesomely expensive but unusable defense system. This system gave little military security, and that at the expense of economic security. Both nations suffered domestically because of the resources put into arms. Both had lost the economic race while struggling to win the arms race.

By 1994, the United States was allocating 40 percent of its scientists and 9 percent of its gross national product to the military. Its previous role as world economic leader was suffering severely. Once having had the highest per capita income, by 1994 it was down to seventh in per capita income. Once the world-leading exporter, it had become the world's leading importer, with a devastating negative balance of trade. Once the financier of the world, since 1987 it had been a debtor nation. America was an economic giant crippled by the costs of defense and an economy that had lost its magic.

The Soviet Union was similarly beset. Its expensive nuclear arsenal was no help for its real problems. The Russian Bear was beset by multiple problems: a billion Chinese on one border who hated Soviets, an unwinnable war in Afghanistan, a military machine that drained 20 percent of its gross national product, restive national minorities and rebellious satellites, a history of bad harvests, and the highest alcoholism rate in the world.

Like two clumsy, muscle-bound fighters eyeing each other suspiciously, the two superpowers added useless missile upon useless missile while other sectors of their economies suffered and while living standards started to decline. The peace process, once started, also became an economic issue. The wisdom came because the costs of war in economic as well as human terms became manifest.

One additional result completes the picture: the "Adopt a Refugee" program. So many children were orphaned, so many needed extraordinary care, that the developed world agreed to take in these children for treatment and adoption. The one international conference that did succeed was the "Save the Children" conference, organized by Switzerland. At that conference, Russia made a dramatic announcement that it would accept the same number of children that the United States did. All nations took in some of the injured, and as these children spread across the world, they served as a grim reminder of the human costs of breaking the peace.

John Locke observed, "Hell is truth seen too late." In our time, peace was hell seen just in time. Peace came not from the efforts of the actors on the world stage who had failed so often, but through a preview of coming events.

The front line of nuclear war was everyman's backyard. It was neither idealism nor love of mankind that brought peace but the reality therapy of war. It was not the abstract odds of war, but the recognition of the devastating stakes. Man looked into the abyss and saw an irradiated hell and recoiled in horror. Both heads and hearts came to realize that war was mutual suicide that would destroy not only nations but the species.

The cost was high but, in the end, reality was the only effective teacher.

(Governor Richard D. Lamm)

Callafo, 5 December 2010

Dear Petya,

It is your birthday tomorrow and for the first time I will not be home to wish you all that a father can possibly dream for his only child. And as I scan the flat emptiness of this African outpost and behold the trailing colors of a vanishing sun, I cannot help reflect on the events that brought me here and keep me away from you, your mother, and my beloved Moscow.

You know of course that I am helping our Ethiopian friends set up cooperative farms on their land, that I am doing this with a team of American agricultural experts, and that such an effort is a result of the Treaty of Casablanca of 2005.

What you do not know is that this era of peace we have been enjoying now for the past twenty years has been the result of victories painfully won by both sides, working together, forced to work together, accepting finally what the American president aptly called the "burden of brotherhood".

Peace did not come easily. . . . As is usually the case, peace followed war. . . .

Back in the 1990s, while bureaucrats on both sides were trading in megatons and kilotons, CEPs and delivery systems, real history was moving on, with a mind of its own, until one day revolt flared up in East Germany.

The West Germans rushed to the help of their brothers, with American support. Soon we were fighting them all. Berlin fell. The revolt spread to Poland and Czechoslovakia. Poznan was in flames; the Poles were fighting us in Warsaw. And all the while the Americans were driving a wedge through the Warsaw Pact forces, much like their General Patton did in World War II. When they threatened to reach our borders, our leader at the time, Konstantin Ivanovich Vanik, sent an ultimatum to President Brandon: Unless the latter would stop the advance of his troops, cease fighting, and withdraw to safe borders, we would destroy one American city. When Brandon refused to meet his terms, Vanik had no choice but to destroy Chicago, the third largest American city, known to us Russians primarily as a grain center and the home of Al Capone and other notorious gangsters of the 1930s. With the mechanism of retaliation well in place—forty years in developing war plans and strategic target plans gave both sides solid habits to draw upon—it did not take long for Brandon to obliterate our beautiful city of Kiev.

To say that the rest of the world stood paralyzed by fear can hardly describe the sense of rape, mutilation, and danger that pervaded the whole planet once it knew that two thriving cities had been cauterized out of existence. . . .

Faced with their mutual destruction, one city at a time if not all at once, our two countries, through their presidents, arranged a hasty truce. . . .

President Brandon and President Vanik agreed to convene a conference which would set up the building blocks for further discussion on the following topics:

1. Reduction and scaling down in offensive power of the North Atlantic Treaty Organization (NATO) and the Warsaw Treaty Organization (WTO) over a period of ten years, to a level commensurate with mutually agreed defensive needs of both alliances.

2. Conditions necessary to bring about a gradual demilitarization of Western and Eastern Europe and steps to be taken by both superpowers to encourage this process.

3. Possible reunification of East and West Germany within a ten-year framework and conditions needed for a satisfactory evolution of this policy.

4. An increase in communication and exchanges between the people of the United States and the people of the Soviet Union at all levels (political, governmental, cultural, technical, professional, educational, tourist).

5. Possibilities for increased trade between the two countries.

6. Possibilities for joint programs of technical and economical help to Third World countries.

7. Possibilities for joint programs for the exploration of space.

8. Creation of a permanent committee for the exploration of potential and actual sources of conflict between the two superpowers and creation of ad hoc commissions to deal with such problems.

9. Creation of a Center for Ideological Studies (CIS), where Marxist-Leninist and Western political and economic thought can be examined jointly.

The United States and the Soviet Union further committed themselves to the following key points . . . :

1. Consultation with each other on all questions affecting the balance of power between the two nations and a peaceful resolution of said issues.

2. Voluntary suspension of an increase in the nuclear arsenal of both countries for a period of two years, after which a discussion would take place on the possible gradual dismantling of existing stockpiles on both sides.

3. Suspension of the militarization of outer space for a period of three years (excluding military surveillance), after which means would be explored between technical bodies of both countries for the possible application of military space research to peaceful purposes.

4. Acceptance and recognition of certain "areas of legitimate concern" on the part of the other country, such areas to be delineated during the course of discussions to be started within the next twelve months.

5. Consultation with each other on matters related to political, social, and military developments in other countries, with a view to avoiding possible military or covert intervention and an escalation of conflict.

The Soviet Union agreed to the following:

1. Acceptance of some degree of emigration for their people, the quotas to be established by a Russian commission to be convened to that effect. This commission would also study the implementation of quotas for immigration to the Soviet Union by citizens from other countries and the gradual implementation of such a policy.

2. On-site verification of arms control agreements by teams drawn from countries not belonging to either NATO or the WTO.

The United States agreed to the following:

1. Respect and acceptance of the territorial integrity of the Soviet Union as defined at the time of the treaty of Brest-Litowsk (1918).

2. Renunciation of the use of overt and/or covert operations aimed at altering the structure, balance, and political character of the Soviet Union. . . .

These were only the key issues, my dear Petya, but we all hoped that, through this framework of resolution and consultation, we would finally achieve the peace that had eluded us for forty-five years. The following years were not easy, for any of us: Beyond the terror of renewed nuclear warfare and our aspirations for a safer world lay the frailty of human intentions and the temptations of power. There were moments of tension: the Syrian-Israeli war of 1993, the Chilean revolution of 1994. Again, it took the skill of our diplomats and the strength of our determination to avoid further escalation.

We all rejoiced when, after four years of hard work, lengthy discussions, and tough bargaining, President Brandon and President Cherilenko [Vanik's successor] signed in Vienna in 1996 a Memorandum of Agreement that solidified the results already obtained and paved the way for more formal and wide-ranging discussions.

We stayed on course and painfully dealt with all the issues raised by the Geneva Initiative, and then some, until, in the fall of 2005, we signed the Treaty of Casablanca, ratifying objectives already achieved and paving the way for others to follow:

1995   Creation of the Western European Union

1998   Creation of the United States of Germany (USG)

2001   Creation of the Eastern European Union

2003   Simultaneous dissolution of NATO and the WTO

I wish I could tell you that we have enjoyed the fruits of our labor for the past five years, but I do not want to convey to you that peace, once achieved, can be stashed away. It must be cajoled, pampered, nurtured, and treated seriously. And it can be maintained only by constant work, by constant vigilance. As we and our American friends are continuously finding out, without the excuse of external danger we must pay more attention in our own countries to internal grievances, perennial injustices, human rights, and all the vagaries of our human condition. But we do continue, we do persevere, my dear Petya, because after having tasted our own Hiroshima, we can no longer continue to afford the luxury of hate.

My most fervent wish is that you may continue to grow in a peaceful world.

Happy Birthday, dear son, from

your

Papa

(Robert Aronstein)

0528 hours, January 1, 2010 A.D. says my bedside calendar and I turn away to escape beneath the bedclothes to the unreal world of the half-sleep. Then I fall to wondering which is the reality—the nuclear nightmare under which my generation tossed and turned for the greater part of their youth or the dream of peace which has enfolded us for almost two decades now. Still too vivid to be forgotten is the memory of that obscene mushroom cloud with its message of fantastic destruction which drove many among the most advanced species of life on this planet to abandon hope. Then at last I awake and see again that truth is always clear and real.

Yet even in those nuclear days not everything was dark and ominous. People went about their daily life as they have always done and always will, seemingly unconcerned about a nuclear fate, an indifference really born of an inability to grasp the sheer size of the potential for destruction. Deep down was insecurity, which whispered, "Eat, drink, and be merry, for tomorrow. . . ."

So many tried to drown their sense of the human tragedy in various ways—drug and alcohol abuse, sexual hedonism, the gratification of greed and lust, a passion for material goods, even a desperate search for comfort and reassurance through new, and often false, gods. They seemed to be secretly yearning for their old faith, which had become clouded by knowledge undissipated by the light of wisdom and responsibility.

Well, there is a limit to the amount of philosophy younger readers can absorb, so it is time to look into the events, and the undercurrents of national feeling behind them, that brought civilization to the brink in the late twentieth century.

After World War II, the United States of America and Soviet Russia, proud, powerful, and exultant in victory, exchanged an uneasy alliance for bitter hostility. Ideology so reinforced their natural chauvinism that in the forty years during the most crucial period of the world's history, their original, mutual suspicion and fear intensified rather than abated.

Truth was an inevitable casualty of the cold war, as both countries fell into the trap of believing their own lies and half-truths about the other. Those who preached tolerance and understanding as part of the Christian message of love found themselves treated with suspicion or worse.

Cycles of confrontation, crisis, and détente marked their relationships. The first cycle ended in the Cuba crisis and the second in the positioning of American intermediate-range nuclear weapons in Europe. In between, a period of détente raised hopes temporarily, but while it was based on deterrence alone without genuine attempts to reach a settlement or even to actively understand each other, it was bound not to last.

Deterrence was based on the supposition that either country could survive a nuclear first strike with enough strength left to inflict unacceptable damage on the aggressor. It is easy to see how an arms race would accelerate as each country overensured its ability to survive and retaliate. The danger was that one side, fearing that a technological breakthrough was putting the other in a position of overwhelming superiority, might then decide in desperation to strike first. Another possibility was the acquisition of a nuclear capacity by an irresponsible leader, such as Amin or Gadaffi, and a third, which almost did happen as we shall see, was computer accident.

In the early 1980s people were still apathetic or resigned enough to leave the issue of peace and war to their governments, who persisted in relying on a policy of deterrence because they knew no other. . . .

This may have been a defensible proposition even in 1939, but some "hawks" still adhered to it in the 1980s. They were reluctant to admit that responsible scientific research was proving that nuclear war might be so utterly destructive that neither side could afford to adopt a policy which might lead to it. Only when the theory of a "nuclear winter" became widely accepted did they concede that the worst-case consideration in their strategy was now unacceptable. Instead of millions dying that billions might live, it was a distinct possibility that billions would die and no one might live.

However, long-established patterns of thought do not change overnight. President Reagan was preoccupied with restoring American pride, which had suffered blows at home and abroad. His habit of rattling his saber at the Russians may have appealed to national jingoism but alarmed his allies, dismayed the hungry of the Third World, and drove the Russian bear into a dangerously sullen mood.

In his second term he muffled his saber, and internal prosperity encouraged another period of détente. The president visited Moscow and was greeted by hope and cheering crowds. . . .

This time détente was even shorter lived. Prosperity brought renewed demand for oil, and the price jumped again leading to another recession. Libya, Pakistan, and Iran collaborated on the development of an Islamic bomb, adding a new sense of doom to the prevailing gloom, and an American technological breakthrough which made it possible to pinpoint Soviet nuclear-armed submarines aroused Moscow's suspicions that the Americans might be planning a first strike. . . .

A series of incidents, comparatively insignificant but blown up by the media, increased friction. Then in June 1987 came the worst crisis of all.

The assassination of the Polish head of state, a lightning strike by Solidarity, and a menacing buildup of Soviet troops on the borders all happened within a week. President Reagan demanded a guarantee of nonintervention. The Soviet reply was to issue a "launch-on-warning" notice to its armed forces. . . .

A faulty computer on a Soviet "Typhoon" class submarine triggered the dispatch of a nuclear missile toward Manhattan. Detecting it immediately, the American Supreme Headquarters ordered its Initial Retaliation Salvo (IRS) unit to fire within fifteen minutes. The Soviet High Command, also instantly aware of the malfunction, flashed details of the exact course of the missile to the Americans. The new American electromagnetic cannon destroyed the missile, and the order to the IRS was countermanded with three minutes to spare. The Duke of Wellington would have described it as "the nearest run thing you ever saw."

. . .The televised display of the pyrotechnics which followed the destruction of the missile convinced even the most skeptical that the human race could scarcely expect to escape twice its Götterdämmerung so narrowly.

After the initial shock, the reaction changed to a mixture of relief and anger. Billions poured into the streets demanding that something be done somehow. In Britain a million women marched on Greenham Common, and in Berlin the Wall was demolished by infuriated crowds on both sides.

The superpower leaders were quick to respond. In a joint announcement they pledged the cessation of all nuclear weapons testing without any restrictions on verification. In the United States the two presidential candidates promised a bipartisan approach to foreign policy, so that it would not be a political football in their campaigns. In Moscow . . . Potachev, one of the younger breed of Soviet politicians but hitherto suspect in certain quarters as too "doveish," became General Secretary. He was known to be friendly with Edward T. Bryce, which was probably a factor in the latter's election to the presidency. A more certain one was Mrs. Bryce's leadership in the peace movement.

Two months after his inauguration Bryce met Potachev at Tashkent, in their first heads-of-state meeting. They agreed to have regular informal and media-free discussions in the future.

Out of this first meeting came the momentous Tashkent Declaration, a statement of noble aspirations mixed with practical decisions and friendly gestures. It acknowledged that world peace largely rested on the relationship between the superpowers, pledged them to foster mutual tolerance and trust, and formally rejected the adversary principle in future negotiations. As a token they promised to dismantle one-fifth of their intercontinental ballistic missiles within six months. They also agreed to facilitate full inspection of their ICBM sites, a concession involving some diminution of sovereignty. It was a significant change of attitude.

The final paragraph was a guarantee by the two parties to abide by the principles of a "revitalized United Nations." This and a proposal to hold a World Security Summit conference early in 1990 at last convinced the other members of the United Nations that the two powers were determined to come to terms.

They were not disappointed. . . .

For seventeen years ambassadors from the two powers had been quietly meeting in Vienna to negotiate "mutual and balanced force reduction." The talks had been conducted in an atmosphere of genuine friendship and trust, but both sides knew that they were low level and that any decisions reached—and the military and civilian envoys who attended were confident they could soon reach agreement on most vital issues—would be vetoed by politicians back home as being "politically unacceptable." Bryce and Potachev decided that making use of this somewhat neglected peace conference would be equivalent to a fresh start and immediately raised the level of representation. They relied on the retreat from chauvinism in their two countries to prevent any further local political interference.

They wisely invited the new UN Secretary-General, Wang Chow, formerly the respected Chinese Foreign Minister, to take the chair at the Vienna peace talks. This linked the Vienna Conference and the United Nations and brought China into the top level of decision making.

Six months later Bryce and Potachev announced that such progress was being made that a timetable had been drawn up for a 90 percent reduction in nuclear and conventional arms by 1999. As though this laconic statement was not impressive enough, they added that their joint policy included the establishment of a permanent UN police force. . . .

Full consultation with the other powers, both great and small, took place before and during the Security Summit and dissipated any cynical speculation that the two superpowers intended to divide the world into spheres of interest. . . .

A second summit was planned for 1995 and another for 1999.

The informal meetings between Bryce and Potachev, the three summit conferences, and the refurbished United Nations kept public attention on progress toward peace. Certainly, given the will to understand each other's point of view, in five years the two powers made more progress toward disarmament than in the forty years of confrontation. . . .

These spectacular gains in multilateral disarmament tended to overshadow solid progress in other fields of human endeavor, without which the seeds of war lie dormant but not dead. . . .

Every large power agreed to contribute a part of what it was now saving in armament expenditure toward assisting countries to stand on their own feet. . . .

Not everything went smoothly of course. For instance, dismantling the armed forces caused local unemployment. Nor did there seem to be any other way of disposing of nuclear weapons without putting future generations at risk, except by dispatching their nuclear contents into space. This was expensive but most agreed that the billions of dollars spent on ridding the world of such time bombs was worth it. . . .

The same desire to reach a consensus was shown in discussions on global problems, such as pollution, shortages, human rights, and others too many to detail. . . . The most important single feature of the 1995 Security Summit was the Soviet willingness to withdraw its troops from Eastern Europe and Afghanistan and to accept the principle of self-determination for the minorities on its borders in return for a guarantee by the former NATO powers that its frontier zones be completely and permanently demilitarized. The iron curtain had been ripped aside at last. . . .

As the shadow lifted from the hearts and minds of men and women we have seen for ourselves one of those great surges of the human spirit which has marked the bursting of the bonds of ignorance, greed, and hate throughout the ages. Our artists, scientists, writers, thinkers, are as surely the children of a new age of greatness as were Socrates, da Vinci, Shakespeare, and Einstein.

We now expectantly await leaders of the same spirit to emerge and express the values of yesterday in the words of tomorrow.

Strangely the words I heard Winston Churchill utter in a time of war sixty-eight years ago apply with even more force to our present condition of peace:

"This is not the end. It is not even the beginning of the end. But it is, perhaps, the end of the beginning."

(Vernon F. Wilkinson)

I spent yesterday afternoon in my garden, fiddling among the pumpkins and the occasional weeds, admiring the former and plucking out the latter with an unabashed sense of dominion. Aside from my elderly leaning-over groans and the common sounds of nature, there was no distress, no disturbance, and, overlooking my horticultural inefficiencies, there was no disorder. All very agreeable. And all very surprising. In my youth, after all, I, in concert with my peers, had feared the future, and I certainly never thought I'd see as much of it as I have.

There was a time in the mid-1990s when the fabric of five billion lives seemed about to unravel. It wasn't the first time, of course, but it had about it that sense of inevitability that distinguishes impending disaster from impending escape. But escape we did, most of us, all but a few of us, all but individuals from among us for whom those days were truly the last days, the final ripping terror-filled days of fire and storm and death. But they were few. Relatively few. One mourns for them as much for their ignorance of the present peace as for their pain in achieving it. Then again, it's a little patronizing to say that peace was "achieved" at all. . . .

I had newly come to the State Department as a specialist in the public health needs of developing nations—an odd fish in a foggy-bottomed pond. I didn't anticipate a career at State. I'd been surprised by their interest in my area and didn't expect it to persist. But, for the time, that's where I was. I was not an important figure; I didn't even have access to State's war shelter, which, by '95, had been expanded to accommodate almost everyone in the department. (It is in the nature of govenment to accept "almost" as "good enough.") My contacts with those in security areas were social for the most part—college friends, largely, but also a few people who worked on the politics of the "strategic poor," those who by accident of geography, resource, or leadership had become more important to us than we had ever been to them. Through their eyes and mine I watched the endangering of our collective lives.

The general nuclear war so long expected in the late twentieth century had not occurred, and, of course, would not occur. But it is crucial to an understanding of the period to remember just how fatalistic we had all become by that time. Our historical models, the two world wars, taught us nothing but despair: Potential military energy always became kinetic military energy. The accumulated risk of war had seemed in the popular mind as well as in the political mind to increase year by year, not exponentially as so many claimed, but at least steadily.

Looking back on it now, I am reminded more of a sense of impotence than a sense of fear. Major economies had become so adapted to the production of hostile goods that their vitality, indeed, the internal social stability of the first- and second-rank powers, was more dependent on the threat of war than on the preservation of peace. The occasional hopeful diplomatic sign, the uncensored friendly glance, the endless "first steps to better relations," always made news but never made a difference. If anybody ever suggested that great nations could get along more easily than not get along, somewhere a well-placed brow would furrow and from a barely opened orifice just south of the brow would proceed a sentence one of whose words would be "inappropriate" or, in a really threatening case, "counterproductive."

The opening crisis was a little eerie. No trip to the map room needed. . . . For the fourth time in 125 years, the world was looking down the barrel of German nationalism. Of course, the scent of anachronism was heavy, but it was misleading. The Germans themselves were not the problem, at least not in our view. We had become friendly to the idea of reunification. The French had not, of course, but they had long seen it coming, and some of the French liked the idea privately—more of a center-stage position for the neo-Gaullists, a return to backyard power politics. It was the Soviets who were most concerned. "Concerned" is a rather flimsy word here. The Soviets were grim. And as the re-unification talks edged beyond the pre-arranged futility to which the Warsaw Pact had agreed, the Soviets became hostile. They demanded an end to the meetings; the East Germans reassured them but continued to attend. For the GDR, the issue was terribly complex. They were comfortable as authoritarian socialists and were resigned to their eastward priorities. But they were not willing to remain unsovereign; they were not willing in this latter day, their reliability beyond the questioning of any self-confident ally, to commit themselves as Germans to the same Slavic subservience they felt natural for Poles.

It was at this very moment, entirely by coincidence as far as any of us knew, that the Chinese, with characteristically ominous good humor, began to discuss their heartfelt unity with "the Mongolian Chinese of our great Asian grasslands." Greater Mongolia, they said (not "Inner" or "Outer," but "Greater"), was now as Taiwan had been till the year before and as Hong Kong would be still until 1997. No one in the West quite knew what they meant by this. Surely, they didn't imply territorial claims in Central Asia. How could they? We daily expected a public clarification. And, we now know, State instantly, almost frantically, sought private clarification. There was none, either publically or privately. And we were very close to Beijing at the time. I can only imagine the mood in the Kremlin.

This might have been a good time for the West Germans to take a holiday. A recess in the reunification talks might have helped a lot. We could have asked Bonn to cool off a bit, but we didn't. Jack Kemp was not that kind of president. His was a foreign policy . . . of momentum, and he saw here an opportunity to score. Kemp had made his career by conforming the world to his vision. He wasn't overly confident in the usual sense. Actually, he was rather cautious, or to use a now meaningless word, "conservative." . . . Kemp understood the heat the Russians felt, sitting to the east of a bad memory and to the west of a bad dream. What he did not seem to understand, or at any rate take seriously, was the unfortunate consequence of applying heat to gunpowder.

The Russians increasingly felt pressed to respond, and they chose to move in the West. I think they chose the West for two reasons. First, they really did not know if the Chinese were up to anything at all. They—the Russian Soviets—had become a minority in their own country and were unenthusiastic about dignifying any external claim to ethnic identity with their non-Russian Soviet countrymen. Second, they feared their Asian future more than their European past and thought they had a better chance of impressing the Chinese by a move in the West than the other way around. Specifically, without consulting East Berlin, they put their few remaining German divisions on alert while announcing the sudden commencement of "war games" in Poland and Czechoslovakia. These games were not Warsaw Pact exercises. They were exclusively Soviet. In fact, Soviet troops were seen maneuvering around their stationary allies throughout Eastern Europe. A week later, the Baltic Sea Fleet was in the North Sea and a week after that two of its carrier task forces were loitering in the English Channel. It was an odd spectacle: French, British, and Turkish workmen finishing the Channel Tunnel while overhead steamed the harbingers of conflict. Members of the House of Commons debated whether it would be more embarrassing to delay the Tunnel's dedication or to go ahead with it. And one member from Inverness urged that the "French Tube" be flooded while there was still time.

As it stood, the situation seemed salvageable enough. German reunification was not an American priority. In fact, we had much more to lose strategically by the demilitarization that would follow than did the Soviets. True, France would surely rejoin NATO, but America's status as a legitimate European land power would end. On the other hand, our greater strength was at sea and, increasingly, in near-earth orbit, and we would find real economic advantage in the withdrawal of our enormous and slothful German-based forces. Besides, East-West trade had become the dominant European reality and stood a greater chance of loosening the Soviet grip in Eastern Europe than did the maintenance of a war-ready army in Germany. Many historians believe that events would have been much different if the American president had explained to the Soviets our ambivalence toward the reunification talks. I've never quite bought that view. A frank, high-level discussion with the Soviets might have helped, but there are many who believe that Kemp tried to make such a contact only to be rebuffed. . . .

My skepticism about the "talking would have worked" theory is based on my doubt about Soviet motivations. They would not stand for German reunification, but they also needed to make a point about what constituted acceptable behavior by non-Russian peoples within the Russian sphere, whether outside or inside Soviet borders. Whatever they did in the West had to be impressive in the East. And it also had to be safe strategically. They could neither waste nor relocate significant numbers of their ground forces and could not afford a Chinese perception that they would be strained by a two-front crisis. And damage to the European economy would simply mean damage to the Soviet economy.

The key to ensuing events was held by the American president. He decided, as was his style, to meet challenge with strength and, in this case, with surprise. The Soviets probably expected some sort of symbolic American response in Europe—the traditional "increased readiness status" or just a cancellation of leave. But they must not have expected what they got.

Both sides had developed a contingency for posturing that avoided the depreciation of expensive real estate: war at sea. Just the thing. Pure combat, no pacification, no occupation, just dueling. The United States played its ordinarily self-satisfying hand: It dispatched a carrier task force. Since the tensions in question were all land based, there wasn't anywhere sensible for the task force to go (the English Channel was not considered sensible), so it tried "to make a show" by precipitating an oft-rehearsed confrontation in the Norwegian Sea. After announcing a minor provocation by an anxious Soviet fleet, the United States challenged and the Soviets responded. Each side committed to the effort much more than it had ever projected, and by the time unreserved combat had been established, the two flotillas were enormously potent.

The Battle of the Norwegian Sea was a great and prolonged disaster for each side. For twenty-three days, counting the early engagements, the world was enthralled by this greatest piece of combative theatre ever staged. These old allies, the United States and the Soviet Union, had finally gone to war, but there was no exchange of ICBMs, no radioactive fallout, no loss of cities, no crossing of borders, no tank battles. Just flame, agony, heroism, and drowning.

Simply from a professional military viewpoint, the Norwegian Sea was a nostalgic revelation. There was a general malfunctioning of the most sophisticated American equipment. All seven of the American carriers engaged were incapacitated early, but none was sunk, lending support to carrier advocates and critics alike. There was wholesale destruction of Soviet submarines. . . . Contributions by land-based air forces were about equal, and the argument for air superiority became moot as both navies perfected their surface-to-air defenses under fire. And, most surprisingly of all, the weight of battle was carried by smaller surface ships, whose ultimate and apparently mutually spontaneous withdrawal signaled the end of hostilities.

The cost of this flashing conventional war was amazing, and neither navy was ever comprehensively rebuilt. There was a period of shocked disappointment that such effort and sacrifice produced absolutely nothing for either side. Not even crosses in a poppy field.

The Battle of the Norwegian Sea is universally oversimplified. It was a military calamity so impressive in its dimensions and even-handedly adverse in its consequences that it acquired something of the reputation of a natural disaster. . . . It now seems to have marked the decline of one set of domineering forces and the preordained rise of another. It does remain more convincingly a marker of change than a cause of change, at least in so far as we note the rise of Brazil and China. . . . But it also caused change and did so to general advantage.

The Soviet and American nations and, for once, their respective leaderships, found themselves unified in grief. Returning sailors and airmen were broadly heard in both nations. They described the usual events of war but did not describe the taking of trenches, towns, or territories, but simply the loss of ships and the loss of their friends. It became known, first in Russia and then in a doubting America, that early orders on both sides had been to kill opposing survivors, however encountered. And it became known as well that later in the conflict individual commanders had overridden those orders and in many cases had foregone offensive opportunities to take aboard their imperiled enemies. There were in fact so many prisoners of battle and so many of them severely burned that their return took a long time. And they returned somewhat less as heroes than as honored victims of a universal tragedy. Very few had had an opportunity to commit the atrocities of land war and none, in fact, was charged by or particularly misused by his captors, though some were court-martialed by their comrades—an awkward reality not remembered in popular histories.

As silly as it sounds now, as historically naive as it may seem to be still, it is literally true that most Americans, shortly after the conclusion of hostilities, could not recall the reasons for the battle. I might guess a similar phenomeneon was noticed in Russia but I can't say for sure. On our side of the pole, public opinion is a business, and it can be shown down to a p-value that most of us really didn't recall what we were doing out there or what it was those thousands of sailors had drowned trying to defend. And whether he couldn't remember either or whether he just preferred to forget, President Kemp came out of this mess as creatively—but not as aggressively—as he went in. Suddenly—it seems to have happened suddenly, looking back on it, but it seemed quite natural at the time—Jack Kemp decided that the two great powers should henceforth offer each other security and nothing else. The Soviets, first President Ulyanov, then the Politburo, then the Supreme Soviet, rumbled up the same sort of rhetoric, more verbose than Kemp's, as was their habit, but much to the same effect.

Kemp went to Murmansk to accompany back the last group of Americans . . . , and Ulyanov, not yet boasting the famous beard so reminiscent of his supposed forebear, performed similarly in Norfolk. He . . . stopped on the way back in Reykjavik to lay a wreath at a memorial raised to all submariners lost throughout the twentieth century.

Ulyanov was really a pivotal figure here. He did very well in public—did very well in the West. And was genuinely liked at home and almost trusted abroad. It was his career as a civil libertarian, as measured by contorted Communist party standards, that more than anything else ensured for his country the foreign tranquility it had never foreseen. It was so much harder for us to fear a man who treated his subjects fairly, even kindly. We still knew they were indeed "subjects," but we came to feel they had a chance to breathe at home, a chance to be safe in their thoughts, maybe even a chance to change their society just a little. It was Ulyanov's unexpected likability and Kemp's even-handed opportunism in playing it up that got things working. And, of course, exquisitely clever disarmament verification gadgetry didn't hurt either. . . . The Germans were allowed to confederate but were required to disarm. . . . The Chinese lost interest in Mongolia after the Red Army (the Soviet Red Army, that is) changed its address from the Elbe to the Amur.

Even if the Battle of the Norwegian Sea had stayed in the training manuals, the term "superpower" was going to lose its shine. It's the kind of word applied to one or two nations at a time, not five or six (counting India and Japan, as most would concede to be necessary anymore). And it's a word that's probably lost its meaning altogether, really, since there's so little chance that any of the half dozen great powers will pick a fight outside its region, though some of us turn a concerned eye toward Asia, overcharged as it is with virility in need of release. There are still the backyard nuclear bombers, as last year's loss of Baghdad reminds us. But I'm not describing the millennium, the amusingly obvious calendric coincidence notwithstanding. I'm just describing a world worthy of its imperfect sovereign species, nothing more, but, at long last, nothing less.

(Robert Hunt Sprinkle)

_____

3

The Superpower Game

Up the gangplank of history they go. Assyria and Egypt. Athens and Troy. Rome and Carthage. Mongols and China. Tatary and Muscovy. Charlemagne's Rome and Byzantium. Napoleonic France and Britain. Imperial Germany and Imperial Britain. And, finally, today's duo: the United States and the Soviet Union. How often have rival powers entered the ark of history two by two!

Great powers have only become "superpowers" with the advent of nuclear warheads and intercontinental missiles. But the theme of two great powers at odds (and often endangering their smaller neighbors) has frequently troubled history. East Africans even have a folk saying to fit: "When the elephants fight, other animals may be trampled."

The enmity of democratic Athens and authoritarian Sparta is so engraved in many a modern politician's book of analogies that it is often cited by those who fear a supposedly monolithic Soviet Union will overwhelm an undisciplined American democracy. What Athens and Sparta are to these American hawks, Rome and Carthage are to their dove opponents. The doves cite Cato the Elder, who tacked onto his answer to any question asked in the Roman senate around 150 B.C. the unvarying tag line: "Carthage must be destroyed." And it was—leveled! Soft-liners worry that Cato's dictum, on which the Roman legions acted, could have a parallel in today's preemptive nuclear strike arguments.

The historian Tacitus, who lived two centuries after Cato, described the kind of peace that follows such a razing in the famous mocking phrase attributed to Galgacus: "They make a desert, they call it peace."

In dual-power eras, the total triumph of one super-opponent over the other often leads to a period of enforced peace. But such one-power peace seldom lasts long, as examples from ancient Mesopotamia to the restless Pax Romana to Hitler's stillborn thousand-year-Reich grimly remind us.

From the Pax Romana point of view, the obliteration of Carthage down to its mosaic floors was a success for the home base, long harried by the marauding Carthaginian general, Hannibal. But other Hydra heads of resistance to the glory of being Roman soon caused casualties in Greece, Gaul, and Illyria. None of the conquered or killed are believed to have been happy to contribute to a wider peace.

Nor does the alternative—a condominium arrangement of some sort to divide and rule the proximate world—appear to fare much better. Rome and Carthage agreed to a peace in which each would rule its shore of the Mediterranean, but they were soon at each other's throats. Spain and Portugal ostensibly had both their Iberian and their worldwide quarrels settled by the remarkable hubris of the Papal Line of Demarcation, which divided much of the southern part of the globe between them. But they soon fell out over what that meant in South America.

It is not surprising, then, in light of this long history of dual-power conflict, that one theme occurs more often than any other in late twentieth-century scenarios for preventing war and ensuring peace: improving Soviet-American relations.

Nor is it surprising that the two superpowers hold center stage in scenarios written for the *Monitor*'s 2010 competition. Their presence so dominated the entries that the judges remarked on the prevalence of East-West conflict resolution to the virtual exclusion of North-South conflict resolution.

The variations that appeared in the essays are mostly familiar: superpower arms control, Soviet-American cultural and scientific exchanges, student exchanges, periodic summit meetings, regular meetings of the two nations' joint chiefs of staff, improved hot lines, joint Mars missions, joint projects in the Third World, and increased East-West trade. (Detailed proposals for student, cultural, and other exchanges are set out in chapter 8.)

In this chapter we examine other ideas that were advanced in Peace 2010 essays for turning the dark US/USSR relationship toward thaw, cooperation, and eventually guarantees of peace for others in the family of nations.

No reader is likely to be surprised to hear that formulas for a superpower turnaround set forth from the vantage point of the year 2010 range from tough-minded skepticism to heady optimism based on the logic of nuclear stalemate, or from the Kremlin and White House cooperating with China and the Third World to the Kremlin and White House becoming a benign duumvirate policing the globe for the benefit of all.

Godfried van Benthem van den Bergh, senior lecturer in international relations at the Institute of Social Studies and chairman of the Netherlands Association for International Affairs, submitted an essay in which world-weary European doubt and exuberant leaps of optimism about superpower leadership mingle. He envisioned two steps that bring about, if not permanent peace, an equilibrium and a framework for tackling future threats to peace. One step is the ratification by the five major nuclear powers of a comprehensive arms agreement. The second step involves a series of regional peace conferences which simultaneously tackle—and solve!—all important regional conflicts. Included in the latter: South Africa, Palestine-Israel, and Cambodia-Vietnam.

The catalysts for this dramatic improvement in the family of mankind are none other than the heretofore dangerous musclemen of the family, the duo from Pennsylvania Avenue and Red Square. "Perpetual peace can never be guaranteed," writes van Benthem van den Bergh. "Yet the unintended benefits of nuclear weapons have now tamed the great powers and have made them at the same time assume the role of 'international sheriffs' that President Roosevelt aimed for at the end of the Second World War."

In his scenario, the two powers' leaders jointly decide to act after Libyan nuclear blackmail against Egypt in 2008 almost sets off a wider war. In fact, two American presidents—Reagan in an earlier decade and an early twenty-first-century occupant of the Oval Office named Jackson—provide the crucial stimuli. Reagan in his time surprises a Berkeley graduation audience by praising the sincerity of the new Gorbachev leadership. Later, Jackson (obviously not another Stonewall) gets the regional conferences going after the aforementioned Libyan crisis draws the superpowers into partnership against such dangerous regional flashpoints.

In a crucial passage, van Benthem van den Bergh makes it clear, though, that the superpowers are *catalysts*, not imperial *dictators* creating a condominium over the world:

The nuclear arsenals of the great powers would be reduced to levels at which durable invulnerability would be guaranteed. Space and counterforce weapons were to be eliminated. In that way nuclear weapons could become a functional equivalent for the central monopoly of violence of the state, at the global level. Their existence—more and more pushed to the background—formed the ultimate guarantee for peaceful conduct of the great powers among each other and for joint peacekeeping actions in situations like the crisis of 2008. But if that would have been all, the world would be faced with a great power condominium.

It is at this point that President Jackson proposes regional conferences to settle major area problems. Chairman Topol (of the Soviet Union) and President Cheng (of China) concur:

The great powers at the same time agreed on the establishment of a standing joint peacekeeping force, eventually to be placed under the authority of the Security Council. . . .

Though human violence can never be completely eliminated, we can now, on January 1, 2010, look forward to a lasting peace. A functional substitute for a world state has developed. Nuclear weapons have tamed the great powers, and the great powers have tamed nuclear weapons. Mankind can now devote itself to eradicating poverty and to a cultural renaissance.

Van Benthem van den Bergh emphasized personal leadership and nuclear agreement, whereas Tom Fehsenfeld, one of the three winners selected by the panel of judges, focused on reversing the way the superpowers dealt with each other from the 1950s through the 1980s. "It seemed to me," Fehsenfeld's narrator says, "that we were working backward. Our government was working very hard to make agreements with a government we didn't like or trust. This was bound to fail."

Fehsenfeld, a business-school-trained executive of a small oil distributing company in Grand Rapids, Michigan, wrote tersely about an international conflict-management system he felt was the pragmatic way to reduce superpower distrust. His narrator starts the ball rolling with an article that outlines "about a dozen low cost steps we could take to improve our underlying relations." Among his ideas: a joint US/USSR trade center with a database to aid in matching products and markets and a jointly financed and operated space station.

Both Fehsenfeld and his narrator, who speaks by means of a worldwide computer network conference, are dryly pragmatic about each step of their unfolding cold-war-to-cold-peace scenario. They end with a world in which conflict management becomes a ubiquitous craft. A world that is more peaceful but not entirely at peace. Military budgets have been drastically reduced. "The incidence of war has dropped to 0.25 wars per year from the twentieth-century level of 1.5 per year." Wars, when they do occur, have fewer casualties—usually fewer than 1000 fatalities—because of prompt conflict resolution action. (The complete Fehsenfeld essay appears in chapter 7.)

As we saw earlier in the van Benthem van den Bergh excerpt, Ronald Reagan, erstwhile anti-Soviet ideologue, makes an irresistible vehicle for surprise peace initiatives in many of the scenarios. In van Benthem van der Bergh's essay, the US leader broke the logjam of superpower relations with a speech at the University of California, Berkeley, that was sympathetic toward the Soviet leaders and their problems. Many other contest entrants cast Reagan in a similar role. And several did the same with the Soviet leader, either Gorbachev (who hadn't actually acceded to Politburo power when the contest deadline passed) or some fictional party general secretary.

One of the more fertile plot sequences utilizing President Reagan was written by Nabil M. Kaylani, a professor of the College of Liberal Arts, Rochester Institute of Technology, New York. Kaylani's Ronald Reagan first creates momentum by staying in character. He was

unwilling to raise taxes beyond a bare minimum needed to prevent a slump in the economy. Only a significant reduction in defense appropriations remained a feasible option. . . . That led an essentially pragmatic Ronald Reagan to adopt a more conciliatory approach toward the Soviet Union at the reconvened arms talks in Geneva. . . . Foreign and economic policies had become inextricably intertwined.

What followed is still astonishing to recall. Only a handful of observers had anticipated so positive a Soviet response to the American initiative, but virtually no one expected the two superpowers to develop mutually reinforcing and sustainable policies that led to the dramatic breakthroughs of the 1990s.

Much had been written during the 1970s and early 1980s about the growing difficulties Soviet leaders had been facing in governing their sprawling empire. By 1985, the Kremlin was in desperate need of trimming down the Soviet defense budget. [But] apart from an obsolescent ideology and the ubiquitous presence of the Red Army, there was little to hold the Soviet empire in eastern Europe together. . . .

Early in 1985 yet another in a series of Soviet offensives against Afghan rebels had ended in failure. . . . It was in these circumstances that the United States and the Soviet Union resumed their arms limitation talks in 1985.

The Kaylani thesis then has the United States secretly offering to discuss in principle what Moscow would yield in return for removal of the recently deployed Pershing II and cruise missiles in Europe. Reagan, says the author, apparently had pushed ahead with deployment to administer a "psychological jolt" to Soviet leaders. The new US offer "in principle" switched the talks from posturing to a businesslike approach. But still it took "well over a year of hard bargaining before an agreement was hammered out." That accord included phased withdrawal of US missiles, accompanied by similar withdrawal of Soviet SS-20s from Eastern Europe. Continued negotiations after that depended on a revival of "linkage"—a tacit understanding that Soviet leaders would not, as they had in the 1970s, attempt to "take advantage of improved relations to follow adventurous policies in various parts of the Third World."

President Reagan's conservative credentials and personal popularity enabled him to blunt the edge of neoconservative Republican criticism and breeze the accord through Congress. The entire episode was reminiscent of Richard Nixon's opening to China a decade earlier.

That success set the pattern for further superpower bargains:

Looking back at the course of the negotiations during the last years of the 1980s and the first half of the 1990s, the pattern which led to the landmark treaties of 1997 and 1998 can be easily sketched out. Building on the agreement of 1986, Soviet and American negotiators began focusing on the command and control systems of nuclear strategic forces. A modest beginning was made when hot-line communications facilities between the Kremlin and the White House were dramatically improved. And, after initial hesitation, the Soviets eventually accepted a standing American proposal for a jointly staffed crisis control center with communication links to the Pentagon and Soviet military headquarters. This in turn served as a blueprint for similar control centers in the capitals of all nuclear powers. In time, the haunting fear of a sudden decapitating strike abated as short-time-of-flight weapons were gradually restricted and ultimately banished altogether. By the mid-1990s, the arms talks had shifted from limitation to the actual reduction of existing nuclear arsenals. The malevolent nuclear genie was being squeezed piecemeal into a secure bottle.

Arms cooperation next leads the big two to regional conflict solutions. Kaylani spells out balanced agreements on Afghanistan and Central America, with the latter leading to a thaw in US-Cuban relations. And that, in turn, leads to inclusion of Cuba in a US Marshall plan for the Caribbean basin.

As Kaylani then reports, "diplomatic success tends to be infectious." And so it does. The scene of action turns to the Mideast and a denouement there that is started by a new Israeli prime minister playing the Sadat role. Specifically, the Israeli leader trades an end to settlements on the West Bank for PLO recognition of Israel's right to exist behind secure borders.

The last shoe to drop in this scenario of tackling regional problems involves the two Germanys and, by extension, Eastern and Western Europe. In shorthand terms, this is accomplished by semi-Finlandization of Moscow's Eastern European allies and gradual "Eurolization" of West Germany.

From 2000 to 2010, "ambitious development schemes" are launched in Africa, the Indian subcontinent, and southeast Asia. Kaylani writes:

A combination of US technology, Saudi capital, and local manpower is slowly turning the Sudan into a breadbasket for Africa. The encroachment of the Sahara on arable land has been arrested, and the specter of famine no longer haunts the African states of the Sahel.

In the Far East, the Japanese have taken the lead in the development of China and the ASEAN countries. . . . It is now clear that the population explosion in less-developed countries was closely tied to underdevelopment. When literacy levels improve, infant mortality declines, and life expectancy expands, the rate of population growth begins to slow down. The world population today has not yet stabilized, but the outlook for the future is bright.

American technical writer *Paul Basile,* now working in Geneva, tackled the improvement of the Soviet-American relationship in several novel ways. He postulated a gradual warming of the climate in which a NATO–Warsaw Pact Standing Committee is created. Its task is to carry on continual talks about the level of forces, European stability, and new weapons technologies. The telecommunications revolution penetrates East bloc isolation and gradually brings about more open societies. Then the Swiss, on their 700th anniversary as a confederation (in 1991), propose a melding of East-West and North-South negotiations. In essence, the idea involves setting the superpowers the task of cooperatively trying to do something to help narrow the rich-poor gap. Among the results: universal service programs in many nations, modeled on the American Peace Corps, and a joint space mission.

A congressional defense specialist once said, "The Soviet Union has a military-industrial complex that would have curled Eisenhower's hair—if he had any." That was a reference to the increasingly famous farewell address in which President Eisenhower first called attention to the dangerous conflict of interest of the military hardware sellers and their Pentagon buyers. Sovietologists are in general agreement with the congressional aide's assessment: that the central planning system of the Soviet Union is even more dominated by that nation's military-industrial complex.

Using this theme, *James Werner*, of San Diego, centered his peace scenario on a dramatic shift in the US budget. A newly inaugurated American president shunts a sizable percentage of the Department of Defense budget in 1989 to civilian needs. "Defense contracts" are let for building public transport systems, repairing national roads, aiding the war on crime, constructing antipollution systems, and serving other public needs.

And what about the Soviet Union? Does it take advantage of a new window of vulnerability when the Pentagon diverts much of its budget to putting subways as well as missiles underground? Werner makes a convincing case that for a nation whose physical plant is "worse off than that of the Americans" and whose people are hungering for consumer goods and better housing, there is only one thing to do: follow suit.

Military attachés are an accepted part of embassy staffs around the world. Their task is to observe military tactics, weapons advances, and preparedness levels in the host country. When they ask questions at a defense ministry reception or take notes at a May Day parade, no one blinks.

Despite such precedent, an idea put forward by *Randy Fritz*, of Smithville, Texas, would almost certainly set realists' heads to shaking in disbelief. He proposed that "high-ranking defense officials" from the United States and the Soviet Union be placed at "the highest levels of the opposing country's military structure." This, Fritz asserts, "would achieve an immediate verification capability for any disarmament agreement" and help to ensure cooperation in calming any international military crisis.

Whether or not Fritz is correct in his assumptions, his scenario is stimulating. And why should an exchange of military observers at high levels be that much more unthinkable than exchanges of military attachés? It is obviously a matter of degree and trust. And also a matter of definition as to how much access the high officers would have to the councils and plans of their opposite numbers.

Fritz arrived at his startling proposal by way of a scenario that emphasizes lessons from game theory, as taught in business schools. He envisioned new, younger leadership in both superpowers coming to the conclusion that cooperation is "ultimately more successful" than competition—and acting accordingly.

Looking at the 1300-plus scenarios submitted to the *Monitor* peace contest, it is clear that a majority of entrants felt any realistic plan for peace in the next quarter century would have to deal with the Soviet-American rivalry first. For them, that was the key to unlocking other problems—bitter regional quarrels, North-South inequities, world economic growth, world pollution control, and exploration of the universe. Other essayists, as we shall see in the next chapter, reverse that priority.

February, 2010
Geneva, Switzerland

Dearest Marie,

You are right. You are right to insist on peace for the future in which you will raise Annie and young Zach. You are right, too, and have a right, to be hopeful and expectant that the peace we cherish will live on, healthy, vigorous, and strong. Your mom and I shared these hopes twenty-five years ago when you and Mark were very small. For that matter, we still do.

It is up to us, of course, to keep peace alive. Peace, you know, is not the effect of some cause, is not a finished product, some widget to be created or fabricated, or even something to be achieved like a high score on a college entrance test or an Olympic medal. Nor is peace a kind of dimly outlined passiveness, an absence of war. Peace is the negative of nothing, it is positive action. Lived, it lives; unexpressed, peace withers, decays, and is lost.

I believe peace lives now, because I have watched, during the last two and a half decades, despair, fear, xenophobia, self-righteousness, and greed give ground, cautiously and grudgingly (but surely), to hope, cooperation, trust, and compassion in the minds and hearts of many, many individuals from all corners of the globe. I have witnessed the making of peacemakers.

Your questions carry my thoughts to the ideas and events which in the last quarter century have cleared away the brambles of tension and hostility, and have nourished a tentative, budding peace. Yet reflection on the past has value only as it guides the present and future. I reflect here in that spirit.

Armaments Control

. . . Several factors contributed to success in armaments control. Technology was one. The early 1980s witnessed the development of extreme precision in the guidance and delivery of weapons (including guided submunitions and techniques for real-time surveillance), technologies which enabled conventional weapons to meet the same objectives as had been intended for tactical nuclear weapons. (I find it grates, like fingernails scraping slate, to write the words "tactical nuclear weapons." Yet there was a time, less than thirty years ago, when serious consideration was given to the use of nuclear weapons for other than ultimate deterrence.)

The new technologies enabled NATO to strengthen its conventional (nonnuclear) defensive forces and thereby, and this is the important outcome, to "raise the nuclear threshold": raise to a very high level of conflict (hopefully an unimaginably high level) the point at which nuclear weapons might have to be used. And thus was started the long, slow process of NATO weaning itself from its long-standing doctrine of "flexible response"—a morally dubious policy, I felt, in which NATO granted to itself the right and willingness to use nuclear weapons when and if it pleased.

With a little help from technology, then, arms control came out of adolescence; I would fix the date in 1986, the year in which NATO issued its courageous "no first use" (of nuclear weapons) declaration. The declaration gave, particularly to its critics, surprisingly strong reinforcement to the credibility of NATO's defense-only objective. The NATO declaration also contributed to the environment in which the NATO/Warsaw Pact Standing Committee could be created. This was a tremendous breakthrough, providing an ongoing mechanism for the two sides to talk about forces, defensive weapons, new technologies, and so on and thereby to encourage, promote, and eventually ensure stability in the East-West relationship. The Standing Committee won quick, broad acceptance and largely silenced its critics by swiftly agreeing to ban chemical weapons.

These events, and (not insignificantly) the new, younger regime of leaders in the Soviet Union (and, I might add, in the United States) in the late 1980s enabled the now famous and Nobel Peace Prize–winning "new negotiators" to achieve major breakthroughs in arms talks. Attitudes gravitated away from "fortress America" (and comparable sentiment on the other side) to a realization that negotiation is not battle: One must give ground, not take it. Negotiators must *want* to reach agreement to be successful; they must see that the best self-interest is agreed mutual interest. Without such realizations, the new negotiators would never have been able to secure eventually agreements prohibiting all military applications (except surveillance) in space, banning all nuclear tests, and severely limiting arms trade. . . .

Each side, too, accepted *balance* as the key to controlling military buildup, recognizing that if either were too strong, it would be tempted to initiate hostilities, which could frustrate the other (weaker) side to use nuclear weapons first. This was destabilizing, as were of course the continued efforts by each side to be stronger than the other. Those times are, I think, consigned to history.

Technological Advances

The telecommunications revolution crumbled, to a degree at least, the iron and bamboo curtains and what has been called the ignorance curtain: the lack in Third World countries of easy access to technological and political information. Information breeds understanding, understanding breeds trust, and trust breeds peace. I remember being impressed with the superb peacemaking work of the International Telecommunications Union in fostering agreements on the widespread and free telecommunication of information via satellites.

Telecommunications satellites also enabled better weather forecasting and disaster control and improved techniques for mineral and fuel prospecting, thereby easing a few of the periodic economic pressures on peace in developing countries.

Improvement of grains requiring very low amounts of water, new fertilizers and crop rotation techniques, and other developments have relieved, to a great extent, warmongering famine.

Technology of a very different kind has made its peace contribution, too. I vividly remember answering your thoughtful and imaginative questions about the "message" from another star system (apparently) that had been picked up by a SETI (Search for Extraterrestrial Intelligence) receiver. Detection of intelligent life in the universe—easily, in my estimation, the greatest event of the last century if not of the last 2000 years of mankind's history—seemed to galvanize the public mood to a greater brotherhood, a comradeship and closeness that comes from knowing "we're not alone." (We should be receiving their answer to our response later this year, given the 21-light-year round-trip distance.) Would the spirit of unity have come to pass absent the SETI discovery? I think so (I like to hope so), given the persistence and effectiveness of the Swiss.

The Swiss Initiative of 1991

Think of the tremendous imagination and great energy exhibited by the involved officials and businessmen in neutral Switzerland to initiate, successfully negotiate, and bring into being, nearly all of it very quietly, the so-called Compass Commitment announced in 1991, the 700th anniversary of the Conference Helvetica! I remember how pleased we all were to be there, living in Geneva, feeling the palpable excitement.

The initiative was, even at the beginning, impressively comprehensive (hence the appropriate term "compass"). The two agreements—the East-West Accord (originally between the United States and the Soviet Union) and the North-South Accord (involving several industrialized countries of the North and a number of developing countries of the South)—sought to encourage peace by bringing earth's social, political, and economic poles closer together. (I enjoy recalling the Compass Commitment in this year 2010, which was the title of an Arthur C. Clarke novel and movie in the mid-1980s involving a particularly important US/ Soviet cooperative mission, a trip to Jupiter. Who knows, maybe this helped inspire the Swiss to develop their initiative by 1991.)

The East-West Accord covered a whopping list of areas, including cooperation in engineering and science, particularly space flights, telecommunications, defense technologies, high-energy physics, astrophysics, and biochemistry, as well as joint ventures in sociology, anthropology, mathematics, business, and economics, and in the arts. . . . The Accord provided a mechanism for a tremendous flood of exchanges of scientists, managers, artists, teachers, students, engineers, and more. (I tend to believe— prejudicially, I suppose—that the joint space exploration efforts were and are among the most useful. They create such a positive feeling of shared heroism, shared discovery, are so much more efficient than the old duplication of effort, and have reaped such a harvest of commercially viable ventures.)

Among the results of the East-West Accord: a durability provided to peace through the enmeshed interdependency of the Soviet Union and the United States.

The success of the North-South Accord has proven to be equally gratifying. The original Accord included agreements on *refugees,* with internationally organized and staffed centers in participating countries; *transfer of agricultural technologies,* concentrating on development of local capabilities and applications; *trade,* which proved to be a slow process of opening channels and of developing local, competitive specialities; and *population control,* building on the highly successful programs already implemented in a few east Asian nations.

Accordingly (as the TV announcers used to enjoy saying), many of the common hostility-inducing tensions among nations were eased.

A surprisingly large proportion of the initial funds for the Compass Commitment, you will recall, came from private businesses and from foundations and institutions in support of research and the arts. Government contributions of course added a degree of public legitimacy and accountability; their rather small share in the overall funding made the program relatively acceptable.

Nonetheless, there was initially plenty of opposition among the suspicious and fearful, especially in the superpower countries. The Compass Commitment's successes have, now, largely quieted those voices which shouted the world into "us versus them" corners. People are, I think, no longer afraid of each other. Although peoples disagree on many important topics, even value systems, they have learned, with substantial acknowledgment to the Compass Commitment, to live in peace.

Universal Service

It was very nearly fifty years ago when President John Kennedy of the United States in his inaugural address told Americans to "ask not what your country can do for you, ask what you can do for your country." Twenty-five years later, a courageous and foresighted few in America started to assemble what would turn out to be one of the most successful, popular, and effective armies of hope the world has ever seen.

Most good ideas are not entirely new but built upon the accumulated wisdom of those who have gone before. The idea of "universal service"—every citizen participating in some form of national service—was to my knowledge first proposed precisely 100 years ago by William James in his essay "The Moral Equivalent of War."

Most of the universal service programs around the world today retain many of the original elements of the United States model: minimum age, 17 years; high school graduates only (with a initially modest but eventually very substantial program for helping nongraduates receive their diploma); a minimum nine months and maximum (usually) twenty-four months service; a wide variety of choice of service (including military); and very low pay but generally with housing and some meals provided (frequently using housing renovated and food raised by the participants).

The program's great popularity among the initial volunteers led to its being made compulsory in America nine years after it started and for the program's being quickly copied by several countries in Europe and Asia. The program's popularity should not be surprising, in retrospect: It was a natural consequence of the searching by young people for a higher purpose, for more lasting and worthwhile expressions of their capabilities. They were, and are, a tremendous resource, deserving of fulfilling and challenging activities.

One of the most dramatic benefits of the program was the almost precipitous drop in unemployment throughout Europe and in the United States. It had been, largely, the young who were without jobs and without prospects. In a universal service program, they cleaned streets, renovated buildings, improved the environment, worked in schools and hospitals, helped the needy. They loved it.

The program met some pretty stiff opposition, especially in the first years in the United States, for a long list of (in retrospect, silly) reasons. I think the opposition was dissipated not only by the immediate and undeniable popularity of the program but also by the program's creative funding mechanisms and evident economic benefits.

About $30 billion a year was the estimated cost for the universal service program for roughly one million participants, or about a third of all eighteen year olds in the United States. The federal government would pay half the cost by matching funds paid by participating employers—who could have access to federal loans for this purpose. Furthermore, the government contributed 10 percent of each participant's wages to a special pension fund, which rapidly grew to enormous size and which made investments in (that's right) the employer firms, organizations, and local governments involved in the Universal Service Program. Savings in unemployment benefits and, often, welfare payments, reduced even further the net cost to the taxpayer.

And the program was, even in its early years, a bargain. Dramatic increases in labor productivity in virtually all sectors produced an enviable robustness and continuity in the economies of countries with an effective Universal Service Program. People simply work better when their city is cleaner, safer; when bridges are repaired, and buildings renovated; when social services are effective and efficient.

Critics claimed that it "could not be done," that the program would be too big to manage. But they had not reckoned with the hundreds of thousands of unemployed professionals eager to manage and participate, nor with the enthusiasm of city governments, firms, schools, and hospitals to take on, train, and use participants in the Universal Service Program. People like to serve; and do it well, given the chance.

Other Thoughts

I welcome the ever clearer separation of religion and politics in many countries today and believe this division encourages peace. It is important, of course, that religious principles and concepts guide the good judgment and sound leadership required in governments, yet religious states, or even states with one dominant religion, have been tempted, all too often, to ascribe to their institutions (and political parties) the same divine authority attached to their faith—with disastrous, unpeaceful results. The apparent conflict between spiritual ideals and earthly realities is not new and should not tempt us to confuse divinity and humanity.

Of course, people of vision have often faced the challenges and occasional hostility of so-called hard-boiled realists; but true visionaries are not impractical. I still love a wonderful remark by the late diplomat Charles Yost: "Show me a man with both feet planted firmly on the ground and I will show you a man who can't get his pants on."

We have the elements of a permanent peace today, I feel. We have a degree of mutual understanding. We have mechanisms for sharing each other's hopes, resources, and skills. We have a high degree of interdependency, we have fewer armaments and stronger agreements to control them, and we have, and I think this is most important of all, peace in the hearts and minds of millions and millions of individuals, peacemakers, who are committed to and are in the process of living at peace. This gives me confidence that our world peace is permanent, evergreen.

You are, I know, among the peacemakers. Continue in your good work of demanding, and cherishing, peace.

Love,

Dad

(Paul S. Basile)

By the time the new American president was sworn in on a frosty January day in 1989, his peace plan was ready to be launched. The election results were a clear mandate: The public agreed that if peace was to become *normal,* the economic basis of the arms race had to be changed. Throughout the election campaign the president had said that profits made on the arms race must be converted to profits based on peaceful production. The big corporations and many smaller companies that had thrived by producing weapons for the Department of Defense would have to be lured into producing other things that were clearly needed in America. The economic side of the American dream needed to be realized: the opportunity for everyone to find a job, a decent place in which to live, and the chance to develop his or her native talents.

During the election campaign the opinion polls indicated that 85 percent of the eligible voters believed the nation's security could be maintained without spending an ever increasing proportions of the national budget on defense. They were ready to devote 10 to 20 percent of the defense budget to strengthen the economic system by means of "defense contracts" to build public transportation systems, repair deteriorated roads and public buildings, and to do other socially useful tasks that were being neglected.

In January 1989 the president boldly created the Public Works Division of the Department of Defense and directed it to begin soliciting bids from defense contractors to build modern transit systems in Los Angeles and other cities and to upgrade the existing systems in New York, Chicago, Philadelphia, Boston, and other large cities. As expected, people were happy to see the defense money being spent on things they could *use* instead of on armaments that no one really wanted to use.

Some critics said that defense funds should not be used for peacetime projects, but new opinion polls showed that voters felt that comprehensive defense of the United States included a strong economy that produced what society needed. So the second step the president took was the creation in the Department of Defense of the Environmental Defense Division, which was given the job of awarding contracts to "defense contractors" who would build antipollution systems. The systems were to be given without charge to businesses or government agencies that were causing acid rain, air pollution, and contamination of water and earth. At first, nonpolluting companies complained that the government should not be giving equipment to polluting companies, but when it was pointed out that, based on past experience, their own companies might in time be found to be producing some type of pollutant, they began muting their complaints. Besides, they had never received any of the rockets, planes, missiles, and other weapons that the defense money had been spent on in the past. The general beneficial effect of cleaner air, safer water and earth became obvious to all, and if it could be paid for out of the defense budget, so much the better.

The third division the president created in the Department of Defense met with warm approval by the public, though some grumbling was heard at the Department of Justice. The new division was the Anticrime Division, set up to wage unrelenting "war" on the underworld in the United States, using armies of specially trained detectives, accountants, lawyers, and military personnel to track down and convict in court the organized criminals whose operations were undermining the life of the country.

The public was delighted to see defense funds spent to catch criminals who preyed on the young by encouraging drug addiction, prostitution, and pornography. It was no longer accepted that criminals who claimed to be "anticommunist" might be used as partners in foreign intrigue. The emphasis on making America the kind of country that everyone wanted resulted in a gradual de-emphasis on propping up foreign governments threatened by native revolutions spawned by poverty and inequality. . . .

What about the threat from the Soviet Union? By the late 1980s the economic burden of Soviet defense policy had left that nation's physical plant worse off than that of the Americans. The Soviet people were hungering for consumer goods and a freer life; their roads were dilapidated and their public buildings, including housing, were deteriorating. When Soviet leaders saw that the United States was using part of its defense budget to strengthen the American economy and physical plant, they heaved a sigh of relief and began planning to follow suit. Their past feelings of paranoia abated as they saw the United States turn its efforts to civilian production rather than trying to get one up militarily on

the Soviets. The prospect of spending less on weapons and divert-
ing defense money to socially useful products was not immediately accepted by the Soviet *military,* but the party leaders
saw the advantages of upgrading the domestic economy and nonmilitary advisers gained more positions of influence. Fear of
American military attack was replaced by a new party line that
peaceful nonmilitary competition was an activity in which communists could successfully compete with capitalists. Competition,
or even compromise with the capitalists (as the Chinese had
shown), was clearly better than an endless arms race and the
possibility of catastrophic nuclear conflict. . . .

As American society was strengthened by using an increasing
portion of the defense budget for nonweapon production, the increasing cultural and scientific exchanges with the Soviet Union
made Soviet citizens envious of the good life that Americans were
enjoying. They came to believe that Americans were not trying to
do them in and on the other hand that Americans did not fear
them. American armaments were more than sufficient to devastate
Russia, as were Russian armaments vis-à-vis America, but the
Americans were not wasting their production on pointless overkill; they were building the American dream that still needed com-
pleting. A nonthreatening America was an America with which
the Soviets felt comfortable negotiating. The old, impossible position of negotiating only from superior military strength had become irrelevant to both sides. Overkill was not strength; it
represented wasted resources that weakened the rest of an economy and left a country shortchanged in many areas. . . .

Former defense contractors became adept at using their personnel and facilities to produce the new products solicited by the
public works and antipollution divisions of the Department of
Defense. The great variety of products needed provided plenty of
work, and the improvement in living conditions was appreciated
by all, greatly relieving the guilt some defense workers had felt
about producing instruments of destruction while some Americans
lived in poverty.

. . . Once the defense contractors realized they could do very
well as producers of nonweapon products, their patriotism (and

their lobbying) began to support peaceful activities instead of armaments, and peace gradually became as institutionalized as had the old arms race on which they had previously thrived.

. . . With the lessening of old Soviet fears came a relaxing of relations with the United States and a relaxing of the rigid rules governing Soviet citizens. Russians were allowed to travel more freely abroad because their own standard of living had increased as Soviet defense spending was diverted to areas that improved life for the ordinary citizen. Both the Soviets and the Americans were able to provide more economic aid to Third World countries because their defense spending was kept within reasonable levels. Peace did not *immediately* descend on the entire world, but as America and the Soviet Union industriously tended their own national gardens, the peace they enjoyed gave hope to the rest of the world.

(James Werner)

The peace that has come to the world in the year 2010 is a lasting peace because it is anchored in a simple but profound human truth: Cooperation is ultimately the most successful form of competitive human behavior. Religious tension still exists; nuclear technology still exists; economic suffering still exists. The one thing that no longer exists is hostile and violent conflict between nations.

Before the events that led to this unparalleled state can be described, it is necessary to develop the basic assumptions that led to peace. In the late 1980s, game theory led international thinkers and world leaders to a remarkable conclusion: Cooperation is the most successful tactic to advance the interests of any nation.

Game theory consists of concepts that originally were taught in business and public affairs schools. Its primary application is to develop decision-making strategies in an environment of uncertain opposing behavior. Game theory situations arise when the consequences of cooperation or noncooperation are known but the behavior of opposing parties cannot be anticipated with certainty.

The most famous example of this type of decision making is the

Prisoner's Dilemma. It is a classic dilemma with obvious parallels to the problems that beset the world in the mid-1980s (nuclear arms buildup, terrorism, East-West tension, and increasing militarism in the developing world). Here is the problem: Two thieves, A and B, have been caught and await trial. They are locked in isolated cells and are unable to communicate. The prosecutor explains their options: "Confess and implicate your partner, or maintain your silence. If you confess, and he stays silent, he gets 10 years while you go free for turning state's evidence. If you both stay silent, you'll each serve two years for lack of stronger evidence. But if you both confess, you'll get 8 years each."

Thief A reasons like this: "If B doesn't confess and I do, I get off scot-free. But if he confesses, and I don't, I have to serve 10 years and end up looking like a sucker. So no matter what B does, I'm better off confessing." Thief B reasons identically. Both confess and each gets 8 long years. The lesson is that in situations of uncertainty and high risk, logic can often lead one to act against one's own best interests.

Many years ago, the philosopher Kant advanced this theory of superior human conduct: Follow only those rules that you can sincerely wish everyone else to follow. The Prisoner's Dilemma supports this notion and goes further by postulating that cooperation often is the most effective means of protecting one's own interests. . . .

Late in 1987, a thoughtful group of Democratic leaders realized they were being given a significant opportunity. The political disaster of 1984 had been softened by their slim recapture of the Senate in 1986. But now the country's attitude seemed hostile to political leadership of any sort. An annual budget deficit of $300 billion and the unprecedented growth of the arms race made the public's mood bitter, cynical, and unresponsive. Four years earlier, the Democrats were faced with the task of rebuilding their party into something more modern and centrist. Now they were faced with an apparent public hostility to any political ideas.

As the Democrats were wrestling with their dilemma, the Russian leadership was undergoing a similar struggle of rebirth. Following Chernenko's death in 1987, the Communist party had turned to their younger membership for new guidance. The days of the old, stodgy, glowering leadership seemed to be over. Repeated agricultural failures, lagging technology, and the interminable waste of manpower and resources in Afghanistan had finally convinced the leadership that the time was ripe for new ideas and a less dogmatic approach to their worsening problems. Objective observers of the international scene compared this struggle of identity to the changes that came over China following Mao's death in the mid-1970s.

With the leadership of the Communist party in Russia and the Democratic party in America simultaneously groping for new solutions to their intractable problems, an opportunity of the rarest kind arose: an opportunity for two hostile and suspicious nations to mutually attempt true revolutionary strategies for survival. These strategies would do much more than eliminate the immediate threat of annihilation. They would promise economic recovery by allowing resources to be diverted from the costly arms race. They would promise a united front against terrorism and the sale of arms to support conflicts in developing countries. They would promise cooperative endeavors in the development of high technology, medicine, and space exploration. And they would promise cultural exchanges leading to a higher quality of life.

Prior to 1988, a cooperative effort between Russia and America on such a radical scale would have been unimaginable. What brought about the success of this revolutionary endeavor was the growing realization on both sides of the Atlantic that idealogy, rhetoric, and posturing had to become relics of the past if the world was to survive. A daring search for new and pragmatic ideas had to be initiated. The combination of economic suffering at home, escalating tension abroad, and this realization launched the idea that would bring peace to our world. . . .

It is not possible within the scope of this report to describe every event that occurred after 1988. What is important to understand is the basic idea that informed these events. . . .

Shortly after the inauguration, the new secretary of state sent a message to the new Russian foreign minister. The highly classified message advised the Russians that a new set of offers would be forthcoming from the American government, and a significant good faith gesture would precede these offers. The message also asked for a pledge of complete secrecy in the coming negotiations. The secrecy was granted. Shortly after transmission of these messages, the American space shuttle *Discovery* retrieved several newly deployed laser satellites that formed the backbone of the Star Wars defense system. Following this operation, the American government asked for immediate disarmament negotiations with the promise that the satellites would stay grounded as long as the talks were proceeding in good faith. The talks began in a secret neutral location.

The American negotiators proposed a deceptively simple strategy designed to eliminate the uncertainty inherent in any situation similar to the Prisoner's Dilemma. The Americans reasoned that if the Prisoner's Dilemma were altered so that the prisoners could communicate, they would undoubtedly cooperate every time to ensure their mutual benefits. The proposal was for each country to place a group of high-ranking defense officials into the highest levels of the opposing country's military structure. This would achieve an immediate verification capability for any disarmament agreement as well as virtually ensure cooperative behavior in any volatile international situation.

Reciprocity would be guaranteed because the quid pro quo nature of the arrangement would easily betray any breakdown in cooperation or trust between the two countries. The particulars of the arrangement were hammered out over the course of several months. Following these successful negotiations, the negotiators turned to comprehensive arms control. While these talks bogged down late in 1989, the sense of urgency and continuing good faith that initiated the talks finally brought the two countries to agreement on a wide-ranging arms control pact in the summer of 1990. The agreement sought complete disarmament by the year 2010 through a gradual elimination of existing nuclear weaponry.

The breakdown of nuclear arms proceeded with only minor difficulties, largely because of the integration of opposing officers in each country's military. The military integration was finally achieved in 1993 after stiff resistance from the American right-wing was overcome. The idea that was given eloquent support ten years earlier was finally proving its worth and efficacy. Cooperation was leading to prosperity and a dramatic reduction in world tension.

Peace between the two superpowers would not necessarily bring peace to the rest of the world, however. The struggles in the Middle East and Northern Ireland as well as the numerous conflagrations throughout the developing world continued. It took almost fifteen years for the success of the Russian and American tactics to spill over to these places.

As opposing armies in the developing world began to realize that they could no longer count on the conflict between East and West to sustain their wars with the necessary military hardware, the conflicts began to diminish. Central American conflicts subsided four years after the original agreements took hold. African struggles began to die soon after that. By the year 2000, only the Middle East and Northern Ireland continued to sustain armed conflict.

Change came to these troubled regions in the same form as the Russia-America pacts. Catholic and Protestant factions integrated in 2004 after an impassioned plea from the Pope. In 2003 an unprecedented number of women and children were innocently slaughtered, and the outrage of the Pope brought peace through military integration. A change in leadership in Israel led to establishment of a Palestinian homeland in 2006 in the occupied lands. This was made possible through a complicated military integration agreement worked out among Israel, Jordan, Egypt, and Syria, designed to guarantee Israel's complete security in exchange for the autonomous Palestinian homeland. For their part, the Palestinians established a representative form of government modeled on Israel's Knesset, and the first act of this new body was passage of a resolution outlawing the PLO or any similar terrorist organization.

The peace that has come to the world in 2010 has brought some wonderful related benefits. Cooperative endeavors in space between Russia and America have resulted in revolutionary breakthroughs in medicine and horticulture because of the possibilities of gravity-free research. Diversion of scarce resources from defense needs to manufacturing have resulted in a 3 percent unemployment rate in the United States. Cooperative relief efforts between the two superpowers have greatly reduced world suffering caused by famine, drought, and flood. And possibly best of all, the children of the world are growing up in an environment of cooperation and support. These children have no reason to expect hostility, aggression, and violence. As they take the leadership positions of 2020 and 2030, the world will be in the hands of young adults who have always known peace, have come to revere it, and will likely protect it for many years to come. The cycle of aggressive armed conflict has finally been broken.

(Randy Fritz)

4

How Others Can Influence the Superpowers

As we saw in chapter 3, late twentieth-century recipes for preventing war or ensuring peace usually start with Soviet-American relations. According to the orthodox view, the biggest threat to peace is mutual suspicion in the two superpower capitals—because their excess nuclear warhead capacity potentially endangers everyone else on the planet. So building peace must start with Hatfields and McCoys, not with the rest of the neighbors.

But orthodoxy breeds contrarians. War and peace analysis is no exception. Among the essays submitted to the *Monitor* peace contest, a substantial minority chose scenarios that emphasized acts by nonsuperpower states. In many of these, US/USSR confrontation was either softened or outflanked by actions of other nations, actions which effected worldwide change. Among the agents of change thus cited are:

1. China influencing its Asian neighbors and, with Japan and the two Koreas, helping to found a Pacific Common Market.

2. China's competitive market economy influencing the Soviet Union.

3. China's agricultural success influencing overpopulated, food-poor lands of the Third World.

4. Arab-American and Jewish-American business leaders holding talks that lead to joint ventures in the West Bank and Gaza Strip—new schools, libraries, hospitals, cultural and athletic centers, light industries—and eventually a Palestine settlement.

5. The two Germanys chaperoning a settlement in the Mideast in order to defuse East-West tensions and then applying the same principles to a Central European settlement.

6. Success of neutral Austria and Finland spreading to Hungary and beyond to create a Central European buffer zone and defuse East-West tension.

7. Talks between retired NATO and Warsaw Pact generals—followed by similar East-West encounters of retired diplomats, editors, scientists, and businessmen—leading to a Union of Europe, which in turn buffers the superpower struggle and increases development aid to the Third World.

8. A simple act by the prime minister of Canada—inviting the Soviet ambassador's family to holiday dinner—starting a chain of behavioral changes in East-West relations.

9. Multinational corporations (increasingly serving global markets) developing a vigorous interest in reducing tensions, preventing war, and creating widespread prosperity.

One of the more intriguing scenarios provoked by the 2010 competition was submitted by Fung Waiman, a Geneva resident of Hong Kong origin. His approach builds on several major new factors in today's world. One is the extraordinary reversal of China's Marxist revolution, with the Mao-Stalinist approach to central industrial planning turned on its head by Deng Xiaoping and his handpicked followers. A second factor is the ingenuity and trade success of the Japanese economy—and its neighbors, the so-called Asian minidragons of Korea, Taiwan, Hong Kong, and Singapore.

Fung's scenario goes into high gear with the reintegration of Hong Kong into the Chinese mainland in 1997. The great economic surge that China had experienced in the late 1980s had "become fitful" in the early 1990s. But the remarriage of the ebullient Hong Kong economy into the most populous nation in the world serves to increase the momentum of Deng Xiaoping's free market counterrevolution. The economic upsurge is especially notable "in thirty-two special economic regions in eight inland provinces . . . which were among the least developed [and which] were opened up to direct partnership development with Hong Kong." Wages are up in all sectors. Profits rise in many. Entrepreneurship helps to modernize the world's most ancient still-existing civilization. Hong Kong surpasses Singapore in gross national product for the first time.

Then the prime ministers of China and Japan help to seal an improved relationship between North and South Korea that leads to a Korean nonaggression pact—and eventually a nonaggression treaty among all four nations. That accomplished, the China-Japan-Korea entente sponsors round-table negotiations toward the formation of a Pacific Common Market, with the United States participating as an official observer.

Harmony between the two halves of Korea has not gone unnoticed in Europe. In his scenario, Fung next discusses the lengthy vicissitudes of attempts to write a nonaggression pact for the two Germanys that could lead to the normalization of relations between Eastern and Western Europe.

Other essayists see the great Chinese experiment as having a different impact—directly on the Soviet Union. *Barbara K. Rossiter* of New York paints a future history in which Soviet leaders do not openly admit being influenced by the Deng tack toward a market economy in China but nevertheless move in that direction. The Kremlin turns inward, toward raising the Soviet standard of living. As it does so, it edges away from its dream of world revolution. The United States in response, is less prone to react to every Third World reform or rebellion as a case of Soviet expansionism. The resulting more tranquil world then becomes a more fertile ground in which China's experiment can serve as a model for nations with too much population and an inhospitable environment for food production.

Anyone who has followed the writings of the so-called Siberian school economists in the Soviet Union will realize that the impact of China's enormous economic switch has been felt in the Soviet Union. Although there has been some restrained criticism of Deng's departure from Communist orthodoxy, much evidence points to an anxious fascination with the Deng experiment. Some ideological glee is expressed when signs of inflation appear as China shifts to competitive market pricing and reduces subsidies for food, housing, and transport. But the more reform-minded Soviet economists have argued for some Soviet version of market pricing and local profit and investment to stimulate the stagnant, overcentralized Stalinist system.

The problem, faced first by Yuri Andropov and then by his protégé, Mikhail Gorbachev, is how to stimulate productivity without upsetting (1) workers, when phasing out basic subsidies and (2) the great middle bureaucracy, by taking away their control over economic planning.

Several essayists tackle these difficulties standing in the way of Soviet mimicry of the Chinese experiment. As noted above, Rossiter postulated only that the Chinese moves inspired "second thoughts" in the Politburo about the Stalinist economic system. Those thoughts led to economic reforms that turn Moscow's attention inward. But other essayists pictured Moscow's Eastern European allies as influenced by the Deng switch to free market economics and the East bloc example, in turn, as influencing Moscow.

China, of course, is not the only engine of change in the world in addition to the superpowers. Edmonde A. Haddad, president of the Los Angeles World Affairs Council, presents a comprehensive global scenario whose most creative component is perhaps its method of problem-solving for the Middle East.

The impetus toward resolution of the differences between Arabs and Israelis did not emanate solely from Washington and Moscow, nor did it come only from governments in the region. Ultimately, the combined and unrelenting efforts of both the Jewish-American and Arab-American communities resulted in surmounting the tortuous emotional roadblocks that heretofore had made it impossible for the long-feuding governments and peoples to accomplish peace entirely on their own. . . .

Important Arab-American and Jewish leaders, initially from the business community, began a dialogue. What resulted consisted of a series of major joint ventures primarily located in the West Bank and Gaza Strip. Highly visible cooperative efforts, including new school wings, hospital extensions, libraries, cultural and athletic centers, recreational parks, and light industry for the troubled area, were first negotiated and then implemented.

This joint effort bears fruit in a Palestinian settlement when Haddad next tackles the Gordian knot of Jerusalem:

Israel's withdrawal from Lebanon, helped by the tacit cooperation of Syria, gave renewed impetus to the search for peace. In exchange for the creation of a Palestinian state in what previously was the occupied West Bank and Gaza Strip, King Hussein, President Mubarak, and other thoughful Arab leaders agreed to a substantially enlarged Jerusalem which would remain the capital of Israel and continue under Israeli administrative and military control.

The larger Jerusalem was designed to encompass those Jewish settlements now located closest to the walls of the Old City. East Jerusalem was designated the capital of the new Palestinian state, with full administrative autonomy, including a local police force. Also set in the final treaties were specific guarantees by the Americans for both Israeli and Palestinian security, plus appropriate and enforceable protocols for the preservation and enhancement of religious holy places.

The author notes tersely that such a solution could do much to neutralize extremism in the name of religion that had grown so ominously in the region. He also notes that "many on both sides found compromise painfully difficult"—a sentiment that skeptics may echo in raising questions about the realism of the Haddad plan. But then skeptics have questioned the realism of every architect's vision for that area—Theodor Herzl's Zionism, Otto Lilienthal's water-sharing scheme, Anwar Sadat's peace venture, Jimmy Carter's Camp David, and Ronald Reagan's Palestinian-based comprehensive settlement.

One of the three contest winners, *Steven H. Horowitz,* links Mideast peace to European peace. Horowitz, who once worked on a sheep-raising kibbutz in Israel, describes a situation in which economic difficulties increasingly occupy the attention of the United States and the Soviet Union. Because of West Germany's expanding *Ostpolitik* (opening to the East), the two halves of Germany have steadily developed common aims. But there is still widespread fear of German unification in both the Eastern and Western camps: "After a series of limited mutual diplomatic initiatives," writes Horowitz "the two German states decided to test the waters for further advances."

First they seek to calm fears that they intend to withdraw from their respective alliance systems. They emphasize that European unity must come first, with German reunification "only a very distant political possibility." This attitude wins wide support. Then, continues Horowitz:

bolstered by diplomatic success, the two Germanys sought, through consultation with their respective allies, to determine

the next step in the direction of a European peace initiative. . . .
The consensus was that for any hope of a practical Pan-
European security system to develop, some mechanism for
peace exclusive of superpower bipolarity must be worked out
on Europe's southeastern periphery, namely Turkey and the
Arab-Israeli Near East.

The intricate Mideast solution that emerges starts with
general Eastern European recognition of Israel. It moves
on to creation of a Palestinian-Jordanian sovereignty encompassing the west and east banks of the Jordan River.
When a democratically elected government is formed
there, it exchanges mutual recognition with Israel. The
next step in the two Germanys' plan is a Mideast conference between Israel and the new Palestine-Jordan entity
"to negotiate the basis for equally shared rule in the disputed territories." And, finally, the German plan "called
for Jerusalem to be an open city—and the capital of the
two nations living in peace." (It's at least mildly inter-
esting to observe that the Arab-American Haddad is
generous toward Israel in his plan for Jerusalem,
whereas the former kibbutz worker, Horowitz, is equally
generous in the opposite direction, having Israel yield its
present hold on the ancient city to joint status.)

The rest of the essay describes how this paper plan is
translated into reality and how the bread cast on the waters by the Germanys returns to help bring about a European peace settlement benefiting them.

Erazim Kohák, writing from Vienna, also starts his essay
with the superpowers threatened by serious economic
crises. But his scenario arrives at a European peace settlement without recourse to the Middle East and without
beginning in Germany. His schema envisions a spread of
the process that began with the creation of neutral Austria and Finland.

Western strategists have long feared the "Finlandization" of Western Europe. That fear rose to a peak in

the period when "Eurocommunism" was a catchword that had migrated from scholars to popular press headline writers. The worry was that Western Europe would be neutralized, American forces sent home, and all of Europe would effectively come under the sway of Soviet military power.

In Kohák's scenario, the Finlandization (or more properly, in this case, Austrianization) begins in the East, rather than in the West. Hungarian trade with Austria has exceeded levels reached in the old Austro-Hungarian empire. Eventually Moscow, recognizing the success of the postwar Austrian experiment entered into by Nikita Khrushchev, agrees to a neutral Hungarian-Austrian confederation. Kohák outlines several strategic reasons for this Moscow decision. He then postulates an American cut in forces in Italy—and a gradually spreading buffer zone between the two superpowers in Europe. The process culminates with the inclusion of the two Germanys.

Brigadier Michael Harbottle's essay likewise envisions a broad East-West European settlement. Harbottle is a veteran British army officer who served in Africa, Cyprus, Europe, India, the Middle East, and the Near East. He was also chief of staff of the UN peacekeeping force on Cyprus and is currently director of the Centre for International Peacebuilding in London, as well as a member of the organization Generals for Peace and Disarmament.

The chain of events set forth by Brigadier Harbottle is detailed and complex, beginning with world economic difficulties and a Soviet-American search for rapprochement. Its European chapter commences with a group of retired NATO and Warsaw Pact generals meeting in Vienna—echoing a 1981 meeting of international physicians to discuss nuclear war dangers. The generals seek to devise confidence-building measures in both military and political areas. They also discuss alternative strategies of European defense, with an eye to increasing stability and security. They promote the "idea of Europe as a Continent of Peace for which all European countries would be responsible."

Following the "dialogue of the generals," other East-West professional dialogues are opened: former diplomats, editors and broadcasters, educators, scientists, churchmen, businessmen, and industrialists. These exchanges become a regular arrangement in the last fifteen years of the twentieth century and lay the foundation for a peaceful, undivided Europe. Harbottle writes:

It might seem that the emergence of a "Union of Europe" would have isolated the United States from a major theater of world influence. This was not the case, largely because the ties with the United States were not severed to any degree by the European development, but rather were strengthened. The processes of disarmament had been proceeding in a desultory fashion during the second half of the 1980s and the first part of the 1990s. Some concessions had been made by both sides, but nothing substantial. . . . When the Union [of Europe] was created, the European arsenal of nuclear weapons became obsolete and so, over a period, the tactical intermediate weapons of NATO and the Warsaw Pact, and the independent nuclear deterrents of Britain and France, were withdrawn and dismantled. . . . Europe was once more in charge of its own destiny, with the United States and Soviet Union retaining their leadership role in international affairs, tempered by a more rational approach to global issues.

But, continues Harbottle, small wars, malnutrition, and poverty still threatened much of the world.

It took the North [northern industrialized world] a long time to realize that stability could never be achieved so long as the imbalance between the rich and poor nations remained, but finally, in 2000, governments accepted that it was up to them to tackle the root of the problem—the fight for survival in the poor countries which depended greatly on the need for population control.

Harbottle goes on to describe an effort in which "the independent UN specialized agencies were brought together in a single civilian relief operation for each designated disaster area. Surplus commodity 'mountains' in Europe and North America were leveled and distributed. . . ." (Harbottle's description of how East-West professional dialogues worked is found in chapter 7.)

A far less sweeping technique by which an outside agent affects East-West relations is described by Morley Whillans, of Galiano, British Columbia. He describes the technique as "aggressive friendliness." As a precedent he cites Anwar Sadat's "bold and friendly aggression for peace" in Jerusalem. He then describes an example of how similar behavior influenced East-West relations. He does so through the eyes of a Soviet author:

Late in 1985 a long message came from our embassy in Ottawa. It described a striking change in the behavior of Canadians toward the members of our embassy staff. For example, our ambassador and his wife received an informal invitation to a family dinner at the prime minister's home during the Christmas season. He accepted and reported that he and his wife had thoroughly enjoyed themselves. Other members of his staff . . . received similar invitations from Canadians, always informal, always to a home. . . . The ambassador suggested in his report that he required a policy directive. It was important, he thought, that the hospitality should be returned in full measure and in kind. . . .

About this time, similar reports arrived from Washington and from our embassies in many other countries. We in Moscow could see a pattern of international coordination in this outbreak of informal hospitality. No political motives were apparent, no quid pro quo had been hinted at. Our ambassador in Ottawa, now on friendly terms with the prime minister, asked him to explain it all over lunch one day. He relayed the prime minister's reply:

"We thought it was a great mistake to have you people here in Canada without trying much harder to make you feel welcome. We should have a great deal in common, and it pays us, we find, to deal with friends who understand us and our difficulties. You have been foreigners; now we hope you will be friends as well. For some time we have been quietly consulting with our friends south of the border and in many countries, and we all agreed that a change in our attitude and behavior was overdue."

(In a footnote, Whillans explains that his son Ian, who teaches geology at Ohio State University, was host at an international glaciology symposium at that university. For the weekend, Ian planned for various national groups attending the seminar to make pleasant visits outside the city. Ian himself took the Russians to a village on the shore of Lake Erie. "The friendly inhabitants were naturally inquisitive about the Russians," reports Whillans. "Language barriers were not so much a problem as knowing what was expected. The Russians were too often wooden and reticent. Finally Ian said, 'Look, guys, you've got to be friendly. Do something Russian!' The prescription acted like magic," the senior Whillans notes. "The Russians now knew what to do. Every time hands came forward to be shaken, the Russians responded with Russian bear hugs. The natives loved it, and so did the Russians.")

In contrast to this prescription for changed behavior among individual diplomats, several essayists mentioned changed attitudes among international corporations. Both J. Tayloe Washburn, a partner in a Seattle law firm, and Laura Bernice Barker, of Wichita Falls, Texas, commented on the potential influence of multinational firms on world peace.

Barker summarized her approach bluntly at the start of a tightly reasoned analysis of world economics

Over the past twenty-five years so much international investment has taken place that nobody would be fool enough to bomb their own holdings in somebody else's country—nor would they need to; conquest is unnecessary if you can participate in the coveted country's prosperity without it.

Washburn's scenario takes us from a world of nuclear tension, starvation, and protectionism to a world sufficiently cooperative by the year 2010 to launch a UN Mars mission with 400 pioneers from seventy-six nations aboard:

Looking back over the last quarter century, modern historians have been struck by the fact that partial credit for the dramatic progress made in elevating global prosperity and reducing global tension must be given to groups which earlier had been labeled most responsible for producing world tension, namely large multinational corporations and ruling governmental elites in the United States and the Soviet Union. Only now do we recognize that it was the dramatic change in attitude by business and governmental leaders in the 1980s and 1990s that served as the catalyst for the era of global peace and prosperity now within reach. . . .

Perhaps the greatest threat to world peace came through the inexorable strains on the global economy in the late 1970s and early 1980s. This period was characterized by the increasing number of energy and natural resource cartels, a skyrocketing Third World debt to international banks and Western governments, growing diversion of limited national resources to military expenditures, and, most important, the resurgence of protectionist policies in the industrialized nations. This protectionism was the core of an attempt by developed nations to reverse their decreasing production of industrial products, such as steel, ships, cars, textiles, shoes, and other commodities, which increasingly were being produced in less-developed nations. . . .

While many observers dwelt on these disturbing trends, others came to recognize and support certain positive trends which were developing at the same time, for along with the displacement of many industrial workers in advanced nations in the 1980s, a new form of product, a "global" product, gradually was emerging in Third World nations, such as Brazil and Korea. This new product first became apparent in the auto industry, where parts were made in over a dozen nations. Multinational corporations, which produced a range of products all over the globe, replaced large national corporations as the dominant force in the global economy.

High quality and increasing efficiency of these global products and the steady increase in both heavy and light industries in developing nations were to make consumers and businessmen in industrialized nations much more dependent on Third World economies. This recognition manifested itself in political pressure in the industrialized nations, from both consumer groups and businessmen, to lower protective barriers. . . .

Government subsidies in the form of tax credits to depressed industries, which had served only to prolong their survival artificially, were removed. This permitted more resources to be devoted to retraining and reinvestment in new growth industries.

A second trend which came to play a positive influence in the world's economy was the expansion of regional trading markets, . . . lowering trade barriers within the groups, . . . and creating a strong and lasting incentive [to work] toward economic interdependence and away from the hostility and suspicion which had earlier characterized relations among many of these nations.

In the industrialized nations, the new worldwide interdependence was best exemplified in the rapid commercialization of space. . . . The 1990s ushered in an international effort to develop a network of four space stations orbiting the earth. The Soviet Union and Japan actively participated along with Europe and the United States in the production of the component parts of these massive stations. This effort ultimately led to partnerships between the participant nations in an ever-increasing number of commercial ventures, which included space factories, solar energy collectors, research laboratories, and, in recent years, even burgeoning [space] tourist trade.

They may very well have begun in China—these twenty-five years of comparative global peace which we have been enjoying and for which we have all paid so much in changed perceptions, priorities, and actions. It was just about a quarter of a century ago that the People's Republic of China began to experiment with a form of communism which rewarded individual incentive and moved away from collectivism—first agriculturally and later industrially. . . . It no longer fit the old Marxist-Leninist mold, which had atrophied the Soviet Union. . . .

For the United States it meant that we could accept with more equanimity the overthrow of existing political structures throughout the world without feeling that each case necessarily had to fall into "our" camp or "their" camp. . . .

Russia itself, viewing the long-run gains of the Chinese experiment, must have had second thoughts about its own economic system. While we have no evidence that it ever recanted original Marxism, it certainly became much more difficult to export that system to every troubled nation when clearly there were more attractive political and economic alternatives emerging all the time. The last several years it appears that the Soviet Union is devoting itself more to raising its own standard of well-being and less to its original dreams of world domination.

We, too, as viewed from the perspective of a quarter century, have greatly depolarized, probably due to others' persuasion as much as our perception of changed circumstances. Too much praise cannot be due West Germany and Japan—which is not to minimize the contributions of Canada, Australia, and the Scandinavians—for their initiative and subsequent untiring efforts in sitting down with us and with the Soviet Union to help us to alter our views of each other. . . .

Today we talk to the Russians and, above all, we *listen* to them. We talk at every level at which dialogue can be established—economic, cultural. . . . We have not let intransigence in the arena of arms control discourage us from weaving a net of supportive agreement in other areas. . . . Their paranoia about America is being given no opportunity to grow.

Administration was the point our allies constantly emphasized when they talked to the Russians about us. "Suppose you could leave the entire United States in smoking ruin and somehow escape retaliation," they patiently asked. "What then? How would you propose to govern the rest of the globe without the resources of what you consider your arch enemy?"

To us they kept making proposals about aiding the East bloc nations and also Cuba to achieve a higher standard of living, something which Mother Russia was never able to do for those nations. . . . We have not seen any of the iron curtain satellites break away. . . . But there has been no additional expansion of the Soviet Union either. . . .

Now in 2010 we are more convinced than we were in the last century that peace is not an absence of war, a passive hiatus. It is an active experience of well-being and a focused pursuit of human betterment. It cannot be said to exist unless it is felt, and it cannot be claimed to be felt for long where the most fundamental human requirements are lacking. While misery and despair do not, by themselves, foment belligerence, they can be exploited to that end. For this reason, it has been so vital that our planet's burgeoning population be fed and housed.

Here again China has stood in the forefront. The sheer urgency of feeding a quarter of the globe's population, without the great level grain basket which Europe and North America enjoy, has spurred that nation into bending every imaginative effort toward finding ways to force food production from many kinds of inhospitable environment. Often this had to be done without great capital expenditure, and in that sense it has served as a model for poor and overpopulated countries throughout the Third World.

The Western nations, for their part, have researched and experimented with many plans for food distribution to the world's hungering people. . . . The earth's surfaces and the rich harvests of the seas are sufficient to sustain an even denser crowding of mankind than we are now experiencing.

However, the technical and bureaucratic problems associated with getting that food to the most remote areas of need continue to plague us and require a tireless unselfishness on the part of the world's favored nations. . . .

The most significant contribution the United States has made to the peacekeeping effort of the last quarter century is Operation Peace-Think. This is a program to define the terms of peaceful coexistence in many strata of society. . . .

Undoubtedly the most far-reaching program of Peace-Think is the "overseas year," which has become a widely accepted part of the college curriculum. Initiated by the Ivy League colleges and quickly followed by the state universities, it provides that a year shall be spent in one of the Third World countries, making some specific contribution for college credit. . . .

Nowadays no résumé looks complete without this hybrid of the junior year abroad and the Peace Corps. Certainly no graduate program is acceptable without it.

With more history, geography, and languages being taught at the secondary level, young people are taking more interest in their world and are making some remarkably fine contributions. Premed students teach sanitation, as would be expected. Architecture majors busy themselves with setting up simple schoolhouses and infirmaries; future engineers lend a hand with road-building and drainage projects; business majors set up model cottage industries, tussling with problems of markets, raw materials, and transportation; the biologists develop seed strains; and *everyone* teaches reading. . . . We are, of course, by no means the only country engaged in such a program. The practice is widespread. The interchange is enormous. It makes warfare even more untenable. Would one want to detonate nuclear warheads if one were striking at some of one's own youth?

There was a high price tag on Operation Peace-Think, not in dollars but in terms of every citizen's pride. We have all had to admit, in these twenty-five years, that our country is taking its place *among* the nations of our world. No longer can we boast of being *the* richest, *the* most powerful, in every way *the* best. (Our staggering national debt prevents that.) It's been sobering and humbling to recognize that we have to substitute imagination, creativity, initiative, and sweaty effort for shear wealth if we are to exercise leadership among nations. With typical American innovation and grit, we seem to be doing it. . . .

Could hardware for the peaceful exploration and utilization of outer space be the alternative to the manufacture of armaments? . . .

It's human nature to fight, we've always been told. Now, with the shadow of annihilation hovering over all of us for more than a quarter of a century, we have taken a sober look at the dangers of permitting the bellicose to go unbridled. . . . Brutality is less condoned on television than it was in the 1980s. Perhaps it is a sign that we are maturing to a realization that manliness is more cerebral and subtle than a quick punch in the jaw. . . .

It is possible that the greater presence of women in every sphere of influence has had its mark on the diminution of "national anger.". . .

We have kept peace for a quarter century, gradually retreating from that point twenty-five years ago at which nuclear holocaust seemed least preventable. All of us on earth are showing a willingness to alter our perceptions and to keep them flexible. Our econopolitical perceptions about ways in which nations can govern themselves have been expanded. . . . Our changed—in many ways improved—perceptions have taken form in useful actions. There will never come a day when we shall not have to win peace anew, to earn it again and again. We shall be able to do it. We *are doing* it.

(Barbara K. Rossiter)

By the end of the 1980s the historical momentum for the division of Europe and global bipolarity had waned. Economic growth, the military and industrial engine of both superpowers, had become stagnant. In the West, the contradictory role of the US dollar as a source of stability and expansion had gridlocked the international monetary system. The deterioration of NATO's economic institutional framework undermined the political and military foundation on which the historic partnership had been built.

In the East, economic dislocation severely strained the Warsaw Pact alliance system as well. After nearly two decades of expanding financial and trade linkages, the ensuing recessionary freeze placed untold hardship on communist and capitalist economies alike. The Soviet Union's ability to attain crucial hard currency shrank as European economic conditions worsened. With mounting subsidies to its Eastern European allies, Moscow was forced to make difficult decisions regarding domestic economic reform, bloc liberalization, geomilitary strategy, and ideological alterations in the face of pressures for new political initiatives. The fiscal crises of the state, long a symptom of Third World political economy, had become the norm in the first and second worlds as well.

In Europe, the impact of this new economic environment was to increase the importance of *Ostpolitik* (the diplomatic stance taken by West Germany to the countries of Eastern Europe, most especially East Germany). In an era of severe fiscal restraint, the political difficulties within the separate alliance systems had lowered the threshold for military miscalculation. Hence the two Germanys had become the focus of increasing international attention as fear mounted that the economic crises could produce an accidental European war. Pan-Europeanism and economic integration became the buzzwords of the 1990s as intellectual opinion coalesced around the idea that a political solution to the division of Europe was a solution to the economic crises as well.

Ostpolitik had never been easy. Any perceived movement by the two German states even hinting at reunification was always quickly repudiated across the entire spectrum of European politics. Yet with the emergence of the peace movement of the 1980s and the economic crises nearly a decade later, the pressure intensified for a resolution to the division of Europe—and with it, the space for inter-German maneuverability.

After a series of limited mutual diplomatic initiatives, the two German states decided to test the waters for further advances. In consultation, they decided to calm traditional European and Soviet fears by discrediting the popular domestic idea of a neutral reunified Germany. In a joint resolution, the two governments stated unequivocally that unilateral or bilateral withdrawal from the present alliance systems was out of the question. Instead, they emphasized European unity first—and German reunification as only a very distant political possibility.

Because it sought to resolve the German problem through a broader continental context, the joint declaration engendered a wide range of support from all European states including the Soviet Union. In a government statement, Moscow astonished the European and world political community by affirming its support for further inter-German initiatives. Concretely, this meant that Moscow too sought relief from its burdensome financial responsibilities by allowing the Pan-European economic integration movement to proceed unimpeded by military and political diversion. But even more important, it signaled a more dramatic shift in

Soviet policy, holding the promise of even greater breakthroughs in the years ahead.

The East Germans speculated that Moscow appeared to be following a more moderate line of European socialist détente. By repositioning themselves to the conforming European view, the new young leadership in the Kremlin was squarely facing the geomilitary disadvantages that the age of monetary restraints had placed on them. Unlike the United States, which faced no conventional military threat, the Soviets were surrounded by a wall of containment stretching from the European Arctic Circle through the Continent to their southern border in Turkey, into Asia and at times including Iran and Afghanistan but most certainly Pakistan and China, and linked to the American Arctic Circle in Alaska through important bases in Japan and the Philippines. The economic luxury of a global checking action against this arc of fire had worn thin in the face of diminished world demand for oil, gas, and precious metals. With foreign reserves dwindling and unprecedented political and financial burdens from its East-bloc partners, confidence across Europe spread that policy had changed and more European-oriented wisdom held court in the Soviet capital.

Bolstered by diplomatic success, the two Germanys sought, through consultation with their respective allies, to determine the next step in the direction of the European peace initiative. After a flurry of diplomatic activity, the consensus was that for any hope of a practical Pan-European security system to develop, some mechanism for peace exclusive of superpower bipolarity must be worked out on Europe's southeastern periphery, namely Turkey and the Arab-Israeli Near East.

After over two centuries of major power penetration and intrigue, the Middle East—doggedly and almost unbelievably—still held the key to Europe's future. With the exception of Germany, where American and Soviet forces squared off in nuclear stalemate, no other area on earth reflected the clash of the superpowers more than this ancient region. With a population base much smaller than Africa or Asia, and with natural resources (other than oil) nearly minimal, the Middle East nation-states had the highest per capita expenditure for arms in the world. The vast majority were purchased from the superpowers. Why?

After World War II, the Marshall Plan, the Truman Doctrine, and the Baghdad Pact had institutionalized the "wall of containment" as US geomilitary strategy vis-à-vis the Soviet Union. Not content to accept military encirclement, the Kremlin adopted a leapfrog policy to challenge Western power in the Arab East. Curiously, the Soviets achieved in the next three decades—first by their support of the establishment of the State of Israel and then by dramatically switching sides in the 1950s to the newly emerging Arab Nationalist camp—a certain amount of success. However, neither superpower came close to achieving a hegemonic position, while the region unfortunately became a testing ground for military equipment and preparedness. Since 1973, with the emergence of the energy crisis, the strategic importance of the region had intensified. With the Carter Doctrine of 1979 and the second cold war of the next decade, fears mounted that Europe could be drawn into a nuclear conflagration that had its trigger in the Arab-Israeli Near East.

By the 1990s, Western European strategic thinking had begun to crystallize. If European détente was to continue, some new security arrangement outside the superpower confrontation and the wall of containment needed to be found to ensure the peaceful flow of oil from the Persian Gulf. The Western European states argued that genuine European peace could never be achieved while leaving the Middle East either "Finlandized" or in a heightened state of bipolar confrontation. For the two Germanys, this meant their peace and the peace of Europe had ironically become the peace of Israel and its immediate neighbors as well.

Surprisingly, and with more independence than many thought possible, the East Germans moved first. In a series of stunning diplomatic dispatches, East Berlin sought not only to establish relations with Israel but also to suggest strongly that all communist nations do the same. Next, East Germany accused both superpowers of undue manipulation and control of Middle East affairs. In a high-level pronouncement, the government stated unequivocally that this kind of penetration was only possible "given the unrealistic and maximalist aims of all parties to the conflict." They suggested that continued Israeli occupation of the West Bank or annexation of the same would foreclose any hope of a negotiated settlement. However, East Berlin then reversed directions dramatically, stating that any return of the disputed territories either to Hashemite (the present ruling family of Jordan) control or for the creation of a West Bank Palestinian state would be antithetical to Israeli security.

In an electrifying dual initiative, both East and West Germany (independent of their superpower patrons) announced that they had conceived, in mutual cooperation, a four-point outline for what they called the Inter-German Plan for Mideast Peace. They claimed that this plan had the active support of nearly every government in Europe on both sides of the Elbe.

First, the plan called for a Palestinian-Jordanian sovereignty to be based on free and open elections, on the principle of one man, one vote, to be held jointly in the occupied territories and the East Bank of the Jordan River (currently Jordan). Second, the plan called for mutual recognition between the duly-elected government in these elections and the State of Israel. Third, it called for a Mideast conference between these two governments alone to negotiate the basis for equally shared rule in the disputed territories. And finally, the plan called for Jerusalem to be an open city—and the capital to two nations living in peace.

The Israeli government had been truly surprised by the strength of the Inter-German Plan. For the first time since the founding of the state, the Israeli-Arab conflict had been placed outside the bipolar nexus. The plan's Pan-European urgency and its underlying challenge to Soviet intentions in Europe and the Mideast, vis-à-vis its coordinated East-West authorship and support, gave it weight that could not easily be dismissed. After nearly half a century of conflict and isolation—and with the prospect of deepening strains over finance with their Washington backers—hard-pressed Israeli leaders could not easily disregard the diplomatic and economic advantages the plan portended.

Furthermore, Third World and nonaligned states alike had seen in the Inter-German Plan the distant hope that the potential reworkings of the political maps of Europe and the Mideast could be used as an important bridge for the North-South issue to outflank and weaken the East-West one. China and many African states began urging both Arabs and Israelis to see the wisdom of the plan. These states argued that a Mideast alliance inclusive of Israel offered not only the hope of peace with security for all but also a leadership role for the "two Jerusalems" among the family of nations. In early June of 1996 the Chinese government recognized the State of Israel, calling the Inter-German Plan a historic compromise and its principle of joint sovereignty a revolutionary development fulfilling the biblical prophecy that "Jerusalem shall be like a light unto nations."

Even with the prospect of strong international support, domestic considerations provided the plan strong political popularity. For Israeli Laborites, the old idea of bringing the Hashemites into a West Bank partition plan had worn thin. Jordan's King Hussein was either too smart or too weak to deliver, or both. Without partition, the only logical political choice for Labor was the shared-rule concept.

For Likud, the Inter-German Plan offered a kind of international recognition for the idea that Jordan represented part of historic Palestine and that its territorial inclusion was integral to any settlement. Likud feared a West Bank Palestinian state for its potential security threat; the prospect that regional balkanization would only intensify East-West rivalries was also feared. However, the Israeli right had not been opposed to the idea of Palestinian nationhood. By placing absolute sovereignty outside the West Bank and by circumventing the sticky issue of Palestine Liberation Organization recognition through democratic processes, Likud seemed satisfied that shared rule in Judea, Samaria, and Jerusalem was the appropriate historic compromise needed for a just and secure peace.

From the Palestinian perspective, the Inter-German Plan represented a unique blending of opportunity and challenge. In particular, it meant a dramatic break with the past by unlocking the stalemated Palestinian-Jordanian-Israeli triangle through rapprochement with Israel. The PLO could potentially achieve sovereignty and simultaneously challenge the political domination of their movement by both the Hashemites and the Syrians. After nearly thirty years of Israeli occupation—and the constant intrigues and setbacks of Arab politics—this bold German plan held open the possibility of an entire reworking of the political map of the Arab East. By placing their authority east of the Jordan River, linked to a capital in Jerusalem and connected to joint rule with separate citizenship for both Arabs and Jews on the West Bank, a resurrected Palestine could fulfill the dream of a regional alliance stretching from the Tigris to the Nile.

While the PLO and Israel carefully weighed their responses, the Mideastern political game heated up. Both King Hussein and the Syrian government rejected the plan outright. But surprisingly, Egyptian-Israeli and Egyptian-Iraqi diplomatic relations improved as international pressure mounted for the compromise solution. Cairo officially called the plan "eminently fair" and urged the PLO to accept the "international strategic implications of peace." Meanwhile, Baghdad, still embroiled in a strangling war with Shiite Islamic Iran, called the plan "the beginning of a historic partnership among fellow Semites" and concluded that it "promised an era of genuine equality between the Near East and Europe."

With West Bank Palestinians strongly supportive of the plan and with their traditional Arab patrons appearing to line up against the Jordanian King, the moderate Fatah leadership (the PLO faction) was forced to choose between Israeli détente or the possible crumbling of all international and domestic support. With both superpowers strangely quiet, yet duly impressed by the potential new constellation of forces, all the international factors in the Mideast politics had converged into the moment of truth for Israelis and Palestinians.

Then it happened. With the international stakes mounting, both the PLO and Israel—entranced by the political possibilities of affirmation—accepted the general outline of the Inter-German Plan for Mideast Peace.

Conclusion

With a stunned world watching, the dramatic events of the Middle East in the year 2000 heralded what was popularly called "the decade of Europe and Jerusalem." Palestinian elections were indeed finally held, and moderate Fatah candidates had won a clear majority. But more important, the Middle Eastern conference following these elections had institutionalized a startling new military concept which would alter the course of European and world history.

Since sovereignty in Jerusalem and the West Bank was to be shared, the Israeli and Palestinian governments created a joint elite corps of military forces integrated into a single defensive unit. The relevance of this idea of a military condominium for the purpose of a monitored defense of the territories took the two Germanys and all of Europe by storm. Across the Continent, expectation ran feverishly high that what had been accomplished in the Holy Land by Pan-European and interbloc initiative could be accomplished across the division of Germany and Europe as well.

Within a short ten years, the budding supranational economic institutions of Europe were complemented in the military sphere by the new Jerusalem concept. Central Europe was declared a "defensive military zone," and NATO and Warsaw Pact forces retreated from German soil. A joint East German-West German military command was created, and the two states instituted defensive integration procedures. Negotiations were begun for similar structures involving France and Poland, the Netherlands and Czechoslovakia, and Belgium and Hungary.

By the year 2010, the Mideast Peace had held strongly for a decade, while Pan-European détente and bloc integration leading to potential bloc dissolution had become a raging force. Likewise, a formal Near East Security Alliance involving Egypt, Israel, Palestine, Iraq, and Turkey had formed. Under the bylaws of this alliance, neither US nor Soviet equipment or personnel were allowed in the military operations of the respective countries. Only European material (not including Soviet) was allowed to be bought. Furthermore, the Near East Alliance formally backed the idea of a military-free zone in the Indian Ocean. Meanwhile, finance and industry ministers from Near East Alliance countries had also begun negotiation on a supranational framework for economic cooperation. Intellectual speculation suggested that formal economic linkages between Europe, the Near East, and Africa would become the next step in the quest for economic recovery. Many nations north and south supported this concept.

In hindsight, the economic crises of the 1990s had changed the nature of the nation-state in many international spheres. The superpowers were faced with great restraints on their power by a combination of the multilateral actions of smaller states working cooperatively and the domestic fiscal and political pressures caused by economic dislocation. In the process, the East-West military conflict diminished in perceived international importance. North-South issues more vital for economic recovery became paramount. What began slowly as a European economic initiative had advanced to include a structure for Mideast and European peace and a twenty-first century supranational agenda for an African-Mideastern-European economic community.

In the Soviet Union, the political perceptions involving the concept of a unified Europe as an important bridge between North and South had moved foreign policy toward European détente. The tremendous response by the nonaligned and communist countries to the Inter-German Mideast Peace Initiative had strongly reinforced Moscow's thinking.

Meanwhile, in the United States, the severity of the economic recession had moved the political center of gravity to a more social-democratic position. Both political parties realigned on foreign policy issues to a more isolationist position. The Republicans had become more libertarian, while the Democrats became more socialist. Both parties emphasized a more cooperative approach to North-South problems in the Americas.

The year 2010 was in no way a utopia. However, it was a realistic beginning for the establishment of international institutions to plan more equitably the world economy and secure the peace. If these structures for peace can hold, the twenty-first century promises even greater progress in eliminating once and for all the deadly nuclear menace. We can then usher into place the swords-into-plowshares Messianic era.

(Steven Horowitz)

We have come to take peace so much for granted that we find it hard to imagine the world of just a quarter century ago, reluctantly preparing for a war it thought it could not prevent and knew it could not survive.

Yet those of us who, as young reporters, rode the president's campaign special through Ohio in the fall of 1984 can recall the sense of the end of an era. . . . For over a generation the country had been devoting nearly a tenth of its national product to armaments. . . . The long-neglected rail system had sunk to a Third World level. Pollution-spewing automobiles, the only practical means of transport, created monumental traffic jams at each of the president's campaign stops. The ramshackle stations and the decaying inner cities around them testified that the country could not afford another huge arms budget. . . .

A wholly new approach was needed.

We might well have ridden on to disaster. It seems doubtful that the president's historic "New Peace" proposal would have had any hope of success—or would have been made at all—had it not been for the Great Depression of 1986 and the series of disastrous harvests in the Soviet Union. Not that the depression came as a surprise. For years, the United States had financed heavy deficit spending by borrowing overseas. A combination of vast military expenditures and individual entitlement payments far exceeded available revenues. Artificially high interest rates kept overseas capital flowing in, but at the same time increasingly eroded America's ability to export and to service its debt. When the spectacular failure of the ———— Bank in the fall of 1985 reversed the flow of capital, the depression became inevitable, shattering the illusion of guns-and-butter-on-credit. . . .

The agricultural disaster in the Soviet Union should have been no more of a surprise. The rigidly centralized agricultural system had been ailing for years. In 1984 the Soviet grain harvest fell below 175 million metric tons, far short of the minimum of 225 million tons needed. Some leading experts, Mikhail Gorbachev among them, saw the handwriting on the wall already in the early 1980s and diagnosed the cause. The need to maintain a strict control over a disaffected empire, however, precluded the obvious solution, a loosening of the controls that were strangling Soviet agriculture. . . .

The president proposed to let peace grow by encouraging the growth of neutral buffer zones between the great powers instead of seeking to impose it on a divided world. . . .

The division of Europe was hopelessly artificial and fundamentally nonviable. No amount of rhetoric about "Eastern" Europe could transform Berlin or Prague into "Eastern" cities—or half of Germany into the 51st American state. The armies poised along the Elbe were not stationed along the boundaries of an "Eastern" Europe or of "the West." They were stationed in the heart of Europe, far beyond the borders of their respective homelands. . . . Only a massive Soviet armed presence—as the Polish events of 1980 had clearly shown—could preserve the illusion that Poland, Czechoslovakia, half of Germany are not an integral part of Europe but of a mythical entity labeled "the Eastern bloc." . . .

The president's proposal was, in effect, a call for Soviet-American cooperation in letting Europe be Europe, a neutral buffer zone between the two great powers rather than the theater of their confrontation, and to extend the pattern of buffer zones throughout the world.

Today, success of the buffer zone approach has become so obvious it is difficult for us to realize how utterly unacceptable it appeared a quarter of a century ago. . . .

If the impossible yet came to pass, it was, in part, because, between depression and famine, neither of the two great powers had the strength to continue the confrontation. In part, though, it was also because, unnoted, seeds of the new peace were already present in the divided world. There was Finland, neutral through the years of confrontation, providing the Soviets with by far their most secure border. Then there was Austria, the sole remnant of Nikita Khrushchev's fleeting flirtation with the idea of buffer zones. In its neutrality, Austria, too, provided the Soviets with a carefree border and a valuable bridge to the West. By the 1980s, trade between Austria and neighboring Soviet-occupied Hungary had exceeded the levels of old Austro-Hungarian times. Though separated by an iron curtain, the two countries remained linked by centuries of common history. . . .

There was another factor as well. Hungary did not appear nearly as crucial to Soviet European strategy as Poland or Germany. Originally, the purpose of stationing an expeditionary force in Hungary had been to assure the Soviets of effective control of the Balkans. Forty years after the war, though, the Balkans had become a strategic backwater where neutrality offered as good or better hope of stability than a costly occupation.

Perhaps that is why the Soviets in 1988 felt safe enough to make their offer of Hungarian neutralization in confederation with the already neutral Austria. . . . Moscow faced the prospect of confronting, on the other side of the Elbe, no longer a group of disparate states but one solidly integrated West Europe. . . .

Washington's decision to reciprocate with a drastic reduction of American forces in Italy played an important role. Still, the chief reason was deeper: The restored Austro-Hungarian confederation, whose disintegration destabilized central Europe in 1918, represented a powerful stabilizing influence.

In all likelihood it was the success and stability of the new Danube Federation and the important role it acquired as the Soviet Union's major trading partner that influenced Moscow's surprising decision to allow Czechoslovakia to join it at the time of the Czechoslovak upheaval in 1992. At the time, the announcement came as a bombshell, arousing a wave of suspicion. Still, there had been omens. Romania's withdrawal from the Warsaw Pact in 1990, matched by the Norwegian withdrawal from NATO, had passed uneventfully, with no major effect either on Romania's pro-Soviet or Norwegian pro-Western orientation. . . .

The world, too, was changing, even though the headlines continued to stress the opposite. The surprisingly successful neutralization of Afghanistan had set a precedent of Soviet-American cooperation, paving the way for disengagement in Central

America and for cooperation in bringing stability to the Near East. Unable to play off the powers against each other, Third World countries lost much of their destabilizing power.

In that context, even the thorniest problem, that of the division of Germany, began to appear soluble. . . . Over the years, the two German states had built up an effective partnership de facto, though never admitting it de jure. . . .

By the turn of the century, the framework of the new peace that we take for granted today was largely in place: After years of confronting each other at the heart of an arbitrarily divided Europe, the Soviets and the Americans could at last greet each other as partners in peace across the expanse of a neutral Europe, united from Portugal to Poland, strong enough to impose a buffer, not strong enough to pose a threat.

The blossoming of the world in the past ten years has been largely the fruit of that new peace. The Soviet Union, freed of the crushing burden of maintaining a rebellious empire, could at last turn to the urgent task of domestic reform. . . .

We, too have changed. The lifting of the burden of the arms race made so much possible. As the recent election campaign proved, we have not become a race of angels—the campaign rhetoric has been no more benign than a quarter century ago. . . . [But] we have come to recognize conspicuous consumption amid public wretchedness as no more desirable than a luxurious home in the middle of a slum.

So, too, must peace. The most important lesson of the new peace: that peace must be allowed to grow from natural foundations, not be imposed by force. . . . Perhaps it is that recognition that made possible the current talks between the Kurds and the countries that had parceled out their homeland among them, the Soviet Union, Turkey, Iraq, Syria, and Iran. . . .

Whatever the reason, we have much to be grateful for—a peace that can grow as a shade tree, not be balanced by force as a pyramid stood on its peak.

(Erazim Kohák)

5

The Machinery of Peace

Wars are ended by either creative proposals or exhaustion—often both. All·recent major wars (since the Napoleonic era) have also ended with creative ideas for preventing future war. The victors tried to design international political machinery that would create a lasting peace. That machinery, like the states drafting it, became increasingly complex, permanent, and professionally staffed—but not correspondingly successful.

Neither the Congress of Vienna nor the League of Nations nor the United Nations fulfilled the promise each offered at the start: to provide an apparatus short of supranational government that could nevertheless keep the peace.

It is not the purpose of this book to provide an exhaustive examination of any of these multinational peace regimes. How each worked and didn't work is important as we look at where mankind might improve on those regimes' performances in the next quarter century. It suffices to concentrate on the latest and most elaborate—the United Nations—before viewing the ideas for world machinery put forward by Peace 2010 essayists.

What went before—whether alliance systems of ancient Mesopotamia, commercial arrangements like the Hanseatic League, or attempts at a clockwork regional balance of power, such as Prince Metternich's Vienna congress—was simply prelude to the truly global United Nations.

So let us look at where the United Nations has faltered and then turn to the essayists' ideas for repairing (or moving beyond) it and its related organs, such as the World Court.

Most analysts of the United Nations' decline recognize that the fault, dear Brutus, is in ourselves (the nation-states who use, abuse, or disuse the machinery), not in the ideals or ideas of the sober but hopeful political architects in 1945. One can be sure that, if the UN Security Council regularly used the teeth the UN Charter theoretically gives it, nations would be slower to make border incursions, shoot down planes, or practice apartheid or genocide. But members of the club are loathe to let the teeth bite for fear that they (or their friends or clients) might themselves be bitten on some future occasion—or, for fear that some group of great powers (or self-righteous majority of lesser powers) might try to make the council into a proto–world government and trample the rights of other states.

So strident rhetoric and vetoes are substituted for joint sanctions against offenders. And any leader who has ever recited "sticks and stones can break my bones, but words can never hurt me" knows how little heed he or she can get away with paying to the council's resolutions. The world body that Roosevelt, Churchill, and Stalin thought would keep the nations in line has some deterrent effect, but its manipulators usually see to it that the Security Council accomplishes little because little is attempted. As a result, the general formula for leaders intent on power politics is: make your raid, then send in your foreign minister to claim it was a case of self-defense. It is easier to blame the world body than its members. So the general perception is that the United Nations—like the League of Nations—has dwindled, not that its members have failed to make it work.

Of course the institution itself has not been without fault. International civil services are assembled on roughly a national quota basis. Newer nations are often loathe to give up their best sons and daughters to serve some international good. As a result, many departments of the United Nations and its sister agencies are either inefficiently staffed or overstaffed. And any political institution that is not, by definition, subject to a two-party system of ins and outs has no easy way of refreshing its bureaucracy on a periodic basis.

Remarkably, though, the UN office charged with peacekeeping has been consistently dedicated and efficient. Lean and hardworking, it has been skillfully led during the four decades since the end of the most widespread war in history, coinciding with the beginning of the nuclear age and the founding of the United Nations. Under a black American Nobel Peace Prize–winner, Ralph Bunche, and a Scots former paratrooper, Brian Urquhart, the policing side of the peacekeeping effort has been carried on by a thin rank of polyglot troops volunteered by more than a score of nations.

Given the dedication on the 38th floor of the UN building, has the peace been kept during this four-decade span of modern history? The wider peace, yes. No nuclear war has broken out—even though the world has had close scrapes during the Cuban missile crisis and Vietnam and at that shrouded point when the Soviet Politburo reportedly considered a preemptive strike at China. But nuclear peace—the prevention of major missile warfare—is largely a matter of nuclear stalemate, not UN peacekeeping.

Meanwhile, smaller scale peace has not fared so well. One defense scholar has recorded 130 wars around the globe during the four decades since World War II. Most were small. But some (Korea, the Arab-Israeli wars after 1956, the Congo, and Vietnam) risked pulling the nuclear superpowers into collision. Why, then, did these 130 conflicts elude the skills of the UN negotiators and peacekeepers?

There are several answers to the question. The first, and simplest, has to do with what streets the world policemen are allowed to patrol. In general, disputes, insurrections, raids, or wars involving the two superpowers are considered off-bounds for UN peacekeeping. That was not always so. UN forces played a major role in the Korean and Congo wars, both of which pitted American and Soviet interests against each other. But both were aberrations.

Since then, superpower interests or lesser-power vetoes have kept UN policing (and sometimes even fact-finding and mediation) out of such significant global crisis points as Vietnam, Cambodia, Central America, the Persian Gulf, Angola, Ethiopia/Eritrea, and Afghanistan. It should be noted that the UN's secretary-general has been given some quiet leeway to probe for solutions of cases like those of Cambodia and Afghanistan. But, in general, the reality is: it's all right to stop lesser conflicts or out-of-the-way ones, but remember who's got the veto, the bomb, and the checkbook.

A second answer to the question of why a generally efficient UN peacekeeping team has not pacified the globe lies in the team's limited purview. It is not empowered to rush about stopping crises before they can grow. Nor is it often asked to supply mediators for confrontations in progress. Fact-finding is sometimes called for by the members of the Security Council. But even that step is approached with wariness and sometimes tardiness.

If "peacekeeping" is the word that describes peace refereeing—keeping the brawlers apart—"peacemaking" is the coverall term for creative conflict prevention. It includes sighting potential crises before they happen and—as just mentioned—ordering objective fact-finding. It also includes mediating, arbitrating, lending good offices, or creating incentives for the parties to resolve their disputes at less cost than they would face if they went ahead with ultimatums, brinkmanship, military buildups, or actual warfare.

Society may be getting used to the currently popular idea that preventive health care is more sensible than remedial care. But UN officials have not been granted a similar mandate for prevention. On an ad hoc basis, the UN secretary-general and his political team are occasionally allowed, or even asked, to move into a potential trouble spot while it is still a small cloud on the horizon. But, generally, the same rules of thumb apply as in peacekeeping: (1) Don't disturb the great powers without their assent. (2) Don't expect to get far with even smaller powers unless they are anxiously seeking outside help.

Much has been written about the changed composition and outlook of the United Nations in its first four decades. It is certainly true that the organization has become both more universal (159 current members versus the original 51) and in the process more diluted in terms of power. What was once a reasonably controllable, Western-dominated club has become a large body with many power centers. Even the crucial Security Council has been enlarged to accommodate more Third World presence. Any other course would have been blind to changing reality.

But the ultimate power—the veto in the hands of the original victorious allies of World War II—prevents all the aforementioned change from going much beyond a shift in the rhetorical balance of power. The outcry by some American officials and pundits about a United Nations run by Third World zealots is hard to credit. Without veto power or the power of the purse strings, the supposedly powerful Afro-Asian-Latin American majority can rely on little more than the power of oratory and the power of lopsided votes in the General Assembly, votes that are not binding.

Furthermore, many of the supposed Third World zealots are quite reasonable in outlook, although it must be said that all sides would profit if the envoys of the first, second, and third worlds (that is, Western, communist, and developing countries) would orate less and consult more.

Adlai Stevenson said that if the United Nations didn't exist, we would have to invent it. That's ear-catching. And probably true. But it misstates the current problem of world organization. The United Nations already exists. But the world also needs to reinvent it if it is not to stagnate and become only a what-might-have-been footnote to twentieth-century history. The ancillary operations of the United Nations and its family of organizations are practical and help the globe to run better: weather information exchange, civil aviation governance, feeding of starving children, collection of world census information, clearinghouse work on all kinds of practical knowledge—to name just a few functions. But without consistent success in the peacekeeping and peacemaking fields, the organization loses its core reason for being.

Not surprisingly, then, most Peace 2010 essayists whose scenarios foresee a world made better through international political machinery use UN improvement as their main theme. Some see the United Nations being transmuted into a more vigorous organization. Some have it concentrate on disarmament. A few move it toward world government. A few substitute a totally different global organization.

Overall, a relatively small percentage of the 1300-plus entries made strengthening of the United Nations, the World Court, or other international organizations a central theme. Many made passing references to such strengthening. But those were often vague. There was a tendency to wave a semantic wand and insert a sentence reading something like, "Then they made the United Nations more effective." Often there was no substantiating detail. The few who did use UN strengthening as a backbone for their concepts were, by contrast, elaborately detailed.

Unquestionably the most thoroughly detailed was a year-by-year scenario submitted by *Robert Muller,* assistant secretary-general for the commemoration of the fortieth anniversary of the United Nations. His schema begins with a General Assembly request to the secretary-general to prepare a fifteen-year plan for world peace (by the year 2000) and total disarmament (by the year 2010). The UN leader is to consult with "governments and the best brains of this planet." Member governments are also asked to submit their own proposals. Their plans are expected to cover food, health, literacy, industry, employment, population, environment, and telecommunications.

Then, envisioning what these government plans would produce, Muller wrote about a series of concrete actions:

The UN Security Council is to meet at least once a year at the head-of-state level. The role of those sessions is to "settle disputes, finalize agreements, and give instructions for further action." The council is to meet in different parts of the world, "including trouble spots." What is not described is how the heads of state would deal with disagreement among themselves as they seek to settle disputes.

Heads of state are encouraged to schedule bilateral visits and to report on such visits to the General Assembly.

A world conference is to be called to "hammer out a world security system." Again, no details are given of how to overcome disputes among the great powers.

Planning is to begin for creation of a World Disarmament Agency.

A Marshall Plan for massive help to poorer countries is to be launched, funded with savings from arms reduction.

A teleconference system is to be set up linking the heads of state of Security Council member states and the secretary-general.

Steps are to be taken to strengthen the secretary-general's hand in conflict prevention.

With this launching pad in place, the Muller scenario moves into an extremely detailed series of steps for what can only be called managing the earth.

Dietrich Fischer, assistant professor of economics at New York University and author of *Preventing War in the Nuclear Age* (Rowman and Allanheld, 1984), arrived at a strengthened United Nations by means of another route. Where Muller's script sees apparently spontaneous big power moves to yield sovereignty to the world organization, Fischer envisions a US/USSR missile crisis frightening other major powers into mapping a UN solution.

Fischer's crisis erupts over Guatemala. His script combines elements of the Nicaraguan tension of 1985 and the earlier Cuban missile crisis. Each of the superpowers takes steps it believes will enforce its will without danger of major war. But the steps escalate gradually to the brink of catastrophe.

First, a Guatemalan dictator is overthrown by a Marxist-led revolution. Moscow turns down a request for missiles but does send advanced jets. Neighboring Honduras, feeling threatened, asks the United States to destroy the planes and their bases. The United States demurs but provides a naval quarantine. Remembering Khrushchev's humiliation over the blockade of Cuba, the Soviet leadership, made bold by nuclear weapons parity, dispatches an ultimatum to Washington. The American president's response: sinking of a Soviet ship. Moscow replies by moving in missile submarines and downing a US surveillance satellite. To prevent Soviet laser attacks on US laser stations in space, Washington decides to move first.

At this point, writes Fischer, an alarmed UN secretary-general

hastily called a teleconference with the leaders of Brazil, China, the European Community (which had achieved political integration in 1994 and chosen an Italian as president), India, Japan, and Nigeria. After ninety minutes of intense debate, a peace proposal began to crystallize.

The proposal called for an immediate cease-fire in the Caribbean; banning of weapons from space; creation of an international satellite agency to monitor military movements around the world and to make the information available to all countries, thus reducing fear of surprise attack; and free elections within six months in Guatemala and Honduras, both to be observed by UN teams.

Fischer then describes steps toward strengthening world order. His main vehicle is a special conference called by the UN leader to which "100 of the world's leading thinkers, humanists, scientists, writers, including some current and former military and civilian leaders" are invited. They are to "remain in session until they come up with a series of proposals that [are] bold enough effectively to prevent future wars and at the same time realistic enough to win overwhelming acceptance."

What is not stated is how the 100 leading thinkers would be selected, what system would prevent such a gathering from becoming a modern tower of Babel, how overwhelming acceptance would be measured, or how the United Nations would enforce the recommendations of the conference. Nevertheless, Fischer's essay contains a stimulating discussion of how the conference debated and analyzed the problem of making the world work more peacefully.

An essay by *S. Edward Eaton,* of Hingham, Massachusetts, applies conflict-resolving techniques to improve superpower relations. Eaton argued that the resulting improved international atmosphere will allow a flowering of UN activity in the area of international economic, environmental, agricultural, population, health, and education problems. To resolve conflicts, Eaton uses the "principled negotiation" methods developed by the Harvard Negotiation Project. In his essay Eaton proposes a US Institute of Peace and Conflict Resolution, whose research on peaceful negotiation of international disputes leads to the formation of an official National Peace Council. The council helps design long-range strategies for reducing the "root causes of wars and global discontent." The council's staff is drawn not only from scholars in the field, but also from representatives of all branches of government dealing with war and peace. In that way, its impact is felt throughout the government. Eventually a parallel peace council is set up in the Soviet Union. Regular informal meetings are held between the two organizations.

Other 2010 entrants use conflict-resolution techniques as a central ingredient in their peace strengthening concepts. James W. Eaton, of Orem, Utah, transposes labor/management negotiating methods into the diplomatic sphere. In his essay the American secretary of state has previous experience in labor/management relations and persuades the president to adapt the concept to foreign relations. Among the tenets set forth by James Eaton are:

1. Parties consult on identifying and describing problems.

2. Each party recognizes the right of the other to exist and pursue its interest.

3. Agreed "rules" require negotiation, frequent contact.

4. Parties agree that they will keep such contacts going over the long haul, not letting the relationship be broken.

A thoughtful and comprehensive entry from *James H. Andrews*, of St. Louis, coins a phrase in the conflict-solving area that deserves to become widely used. He wrote about an international system of "circuit breakers" that would be triggered by events that might threaten war. He does not explain his system in detail but simply indicates that it would use "increased involvement of international mediation organizations and peacekeeping forces."

Two essayists—Richard K. Wagner, of Los Gatos, California, and Lieutenant Commander Torkel L. Paterson, US Navy, Newport, Rhode Island—propose revisions of the United Nations that, among other facets, emphasize regional organization.

Wagner's thesis is that in 1990 a new UN organizational meeting is held in San Francisco. The meeting, led by the original five veto powers, conducts a search for ways to reinvigorate the world organization. The result is the creation of a new body, the Regional Council, which

was ultimately to replace the General Assembly as the major governing body over the next fifteen years. The Regional Council was composed of representatives from all geographical areas of the world and more effectively focused on interests of these areas.

Wagner does not describe how his new regional body would operate or how its actions would meld with the acts of such existing regional organizations as the Organization of American States, the Organization of African Unity, etc. He does, however, go on to prescribe strengthening the World Court by seeing that newly written international laws call for adjudication by the court. And he proposes a "permanent UN peacekeeping force . . . with rotating and shared command, plus periodic service requirements for all countries."

Commander Patterson takes a different approach to

regionalism. His essay posits a Chinese proposal for revising the UN Security Council. This shift would allow any of the UN member states "to join any one of eleven substantially regional nominating caucesses." What Patterson designates by "core states" are automatically members of their respective caucuses. (Core states include such great powers as the United States, the Soviet Union, China, Japan, and India, as well as such agglomerations as COMECON minus the Soviet Union, ASEAN, and the European Community). The caucuses meet once every three years to nominate one of their members to serve on the Security Council. Nominees must then run a gauntlet. They must be approved by a committee comprised of the old veto powers. One international organization veteran who looked at this plan said that its added emphasis on regional interests is novel, but he wondered if the emphasis on the veto states' power over the nominating process, would not in effect mean that the veto wielders would never approve any candidate except themselves or their most faithful clients—in order to preserve veto privileges.

Douglas H. Young, of Ft. Lauderdale, Florida, takes a different tack on UN reorganization. He envisions creation of several new international organizations that would either supplant, regroup, or reinforce existing UN and World Court functions. A primary new creation is the World Disarmament Organization (WDO), headquartered in Switzerland. Its job would be to verify arms reduction stages and to monitor world military forces. To resolve different American and Soviet views of how the WDO could enforce its decisions, an elaborate system of voting is designed. Basically this system would provide no veto but would require a vote of three-quarters of the ratifying states to permit enforcement.

Young's scenario calls for considerable reinforcement of existing machinery for settling international disputes. To a strengthened World Court it would add both a

World Equity Tribunal (for nonlegal disputes that threaten peace) and a World Conciliation Board to help with mediation of disputes that parties voluntarily refer to it. Major nations also consider adding an International Court of Human Rights to hear complaints from states or individuals.

The most striking—and in today's terms, controversial—of Young's proposals is for "a large tax-collecting bureaucracy" established under the WDO to collect a levy from each nation based on "its ability to pay." A maximum of 4 percent of gross national product could be collected. Any calculation of the revenue from even 1 percent of world GNP would indicate that funds at the disposal of the new world organ would be enormous. In today's world none of the major nations—superpowers or medium powers—have shown a willingness to put such sums in the hands of an international bureaucracy. That is one area in which the United States and the Soviet Union are ideological twins.

Altogether, the essayists tackling the subject of world organization as a way of preserving peace have opted for bold steps beyond national sovereignty. Fine tuning of existing machinery was not favored. If these essayists are to see their prescriptions realized, it seems likely that major changes in either superpower relations or grass roots thinking would first have to come about. Possibly both. The second of these themes, changes of individual or citizen group thinking, is taken up in succeeding chapters. Meanwhile, the question students of this subject must ask themselves is a simple one: If superpower relations improve and the average citizen's thinking about war and peace changes, to what extent is a world organization with vastly enlarged sovereign power needed?

In the long history of war followed by new inventions to prevent further war, the subject of sovereignty has always been the sticking point. The symbolic descendants of Athens and Sparta remain wary of yielding what each considers to be its superior way of life and government to international control, which might undermine it. Hence the tacit Soviet and American agreement favors a weak United Nations and a circumscribed secretary-general, civil service, and Security Council. The service these realism-busting essays perform is one of forcing people to think about what might be accomplished if the superpower formula were to change.

...

1986

On the basis of governmental proposals and the Fifteen-Year Peace Plan of the secretary-general, the following ten world steps were set into motion during 1986 (International Year of Peace):

1. Security Council to meet at least once a year at the head-of-state level to make decisions, settle disputes, finalize agreements, and give instructions for further action. Council to meet in various parts of the world, including trouble spots.

2. Summit meetings of Eastern, Western, and nonaligned countries, capped by a yearly summit meeting of all nations during the General Assembly.

3. Bilateral visits of heads of state, especially of the United States and the Soviet Union fostered. Yearly reports on such visits to General Assembly.

4. A world conference on security is decided for 1988, to remain in session, like the Law of the Sea Conference, until it has hammered out a world security system.

5. Revival and considerable strengthening of the Military Staff Committee of the Charter, with the tasks of (a) planning the creation of the World Disarmament Agency foreseen in the McCloy-Zorin agreement, (b) reviewing and adopting measures to prevent a nuclear war by accident, (c) planning military cooperation in multiple fields, including the creation of a UN fleet to control the

seas and oceans and of a UN satellite system to control disarmament as proposed by France.

6. Preparation of a Marshall or Manhattan Plan for massive help to poor countries, hand in hand with savings from disarmament in rich and poor countries. Implementation of a series of major world engineering and power projects to increase dramatically the overall productivity of the world economy.

7. Fostering of nuclear free zones and neutral nonarmed countries guaranteed by UN forces.

8. Setting up of high-technology direct communication, video, and teleconferencing systems between the heads of states of the members of the Security Council, especially the permanent members and the secretary-general.

9. Bold strengthening of the secretary-general's office for conflict prevention. Establishment of a high-technology peace room for the secretary-general and the Security Council to forestall, track, contain, and solve conflicts.

10. All UN agencies and world programs requested to revive major plans and projects for world cooperation that had been shelved as a result of the East-West rift. Concept of risk capital to be applied to world cooperation, which requires bold, new approaches commensurate with the magnitude of the world's global problems and growing interdependence.

All the above steps to be implemented at the latest by the year 1995, fiftieth anniversary of the United Nations.

1986–2000

By 1988, the Economic and Social Council of the United Nations had drafted a Marshall Plan for the dramatic improvement of the standards of living of the poor countries.

By 1995, the UN Conference on World Security had completed its work and adopted a treaty for ratification by member governments within a year.

The Military Staff Committee completed its work on the prevention of nuclear accidents by 1988, a UN satellite system for disarmament control, a UN fleet by 1990, and the detailed blueprints for a World Disarmament Agency by 1995.

All other ten world steps were implemented by 1995, creating a good deal of enthusiasm, emulation, and stimulation among governments who were now convinced that world peace was possible, if taken seriously, with all necessary precaution and without undue haste.

The entire period 1986–2000 was characterized by an unprecedented flourishing of ideas, activities, and achievements, including by the advent in 2000 of a new planetary age. Here are a few examples:

In 1986, the centennial year of the US Constitution, the United States appointed a group of eminent jurists to draft a World Constitution, which was proposed to all nations in 1992 on the occasion of the 500th anniversary of the discovery of the New World. It contained provisions for world democracy, world elections, and world public opinion polls, all rendered possible by the computer age.

Costa Rica had its borders and unarmed neutrality guaranteed by UN forces from neutral countries. Several other countries followed its example and received premium international economic assistance as a result of their disarmament.

The United States and the Soviet Union agreed to tone down their claims of total righteousness and to allow the respective achievements of their systems to be studied and evaluated objectively in the United Nations and in a joint US/USSR institute for the study of socialism and of the free enterprise system.

The United States and the Soviet Union similarly agreed that the concept and practice of freedom be studied and evaluated throughout the UN system and in the joint US/USSR institute for the study of socialism and the free enterprise system.

A world cadastre of property was established in order to determine what exactly the legal status of ownership was in the present world: world commons, national and state property, municipal properties, corporate properties, religious and private associations ownership, and invidual ownership.

Following the example of the world navigation satellite of the UN International Maritime Organization, several other common satellite systems were created and joint US/USSR space ventures organized.

New world conferences were convened on soil erosion, mountain areas, the world's cold zones, and the family. Repeat world conferences to review achievements became a common practice.

A World Institute for the Study of National and World Management was established.

Several new world agencies were created: the UN Outer-space Agency, the World Organization for the Handicapped, the World Organization of National Parks. The International Bureau of Informaties in Rome and the International Standardization Organization in Geneva became specialized agencies of the United Nations. A United Nations International Fund for the Elderly (UN-IFELD) was created on the pattern of UNICEF: a world office for the study of prevention was created by the United Nations; the UN Institute for Training and Research (UNITAR) was transformed into a world academy, and UN statistical services became the World Statistical Office.

Several countries had their delegates to the United Nations elected by popular votes.

Several countries changed the names of their ministries of foreign affairs into ministries of world affairs and cooperation.

A Commission on Subversion was created in the United Nations to which governments can submit complaints against foreign subversion.

A World Foundation was created to allow private citizens to contribute to world cooperation and peace through the United Nations and its specialized agencies and world programs.

The United Nations flag and emblem gained considerable ground as a one world symbol. The UN emblem was displayed on all international civilian aircraft to discourage terrorism and military interference.

A World Court of Media Ethics was created to receive complaints against unethical treatment by the media.

Several nations replaced national holidays by world days, such as World Environment Day (5 June), International Day of Peace (third Tuesday in September), United Nations Day (24 October), and Human Rights Day (10 December).

Multinational sovereign political arrangements, such as the European Common Market, the European Assembly, and the European Court of Human Rights, were adopted in other regions.

Several countries followed the example of the United States and Canada and created National Peace Academies. The University for Peace in Costa Rica developed a comprehensive peace strategy and training program concerned with every layer of our planet's reality (outer space, the atmosphere, the seas and oceans, the continents, the atom, and the human condition (world peace, peace among nations, races, religions, sexes, generations, cultures, political systems, minorities, corporations, etc.)).

More world ministerial councils were established along the pattern of the UN World Food Council.

A World Ethics Chamber was created to determine what was ethical from the world's and humanity's point of view rather than that of nations, other subgroups, and special interest groups.

The United Nations created a body for world ecumenism and religious cooperation to diminish religious fanaticism and dogmatism.

As a result of renewed willingness of the big powers to cooperate internationally within the United Nations, the normal rule of decision making became consensus rather than voting.

A meeting of former presidents of the General Assembly held

during the fortieth anniversary year of the United Nations stream-
lined and energized the procedures and decision-making processes of the General Assembly.

A minute of world silence for prayer or meditation together with
the delegations to the General Assembly on its yearly opening on
the third Tuesday of September (International Peace Day) was
widely implemented in the world.

A World Core Curriculum was developed to serve as a common
guide for global education in all schools of the earth.

Following the creation of the United Nations University in Tokyo,
the University for Peace in Costa Rica, the International Maritime
University in Malmö, and the International Institute for Training in
Nuclear Physics in Trieste, several new world universities were
created under the auspices of the United Nations and its specialized agencies.

A World Peace Service was created, allowing young people to
do world service in poor countries instead of national military
service.

World standardization made considerable strides, for example,
the UN convention on road signals and traffic rules was applied
worldwide, as was the World Health Organization's standard
nomenclature of pharmaceutical products.

International consumer protection was promoted through
worldwide cooperation of national consumer protection agencies.

Strong revival of work on international taxation in order to combat
international fiscal evasion. The United States formalized its proposal for the establishment of a UN World Bureau on Income
Information.

(Robert Muller)

Looking back from the year 2010 it seems hard to understand that
only one generation ago the leaders of the two most powerful
nations on earth relied on the threat to destroy each other's coun-

tries with nuclear weapons, risking human survival itself, in the vain but deeply rooted belief that this would bring them security.

Change, in fact, did not come easily. Many thoughtful proposals for a safer world order were dismissed as "utopian" or simply ignored. Those who raised warning voices were ridiculed as prophets of "doom and despair." A stark look into the face of nuclear extinction finally shook the world sufficiently to abolish the war system, at the last possible moment. . . .

The security policies pursued during the late twentieth century resembled the economic policies of the Hoover administration during the Great Depression, by worsening the problem that they were supposed to cure. . . . Only after the Great Depression was the world ready for Keynes's seemingly counterintuitive proposals that a temporary government deficit could bring a stagnating economy back to life.

Similarly, only after the carnage of the Second World War was the world ready to create the United Nations. Many began to fear that only after a nuclear war would the world be ready to abolish nuclear weapons. But that might well have been too late. . . .

We narrowly escaped that fate and got away with a near-catastrophe. . . .

Despite the warning of the vast majority of the independent scientific community that the proposed Star Wars system would be destabilizing, the United States began in 1992 to deploy some initial space stations equipped with hundreds of powerful x-ray lasers, designed to shoot down enemy missiles in flight. The Soviet Union caught up with a similar system three years later.

The two superpowers continued to compete for positions of influence in the Third World, through economic assistance, military interventions, and proxy wars, while seeking to avoid a direct military confrontation. Many crises that could have escalated into a nuclear war erupted, but in all cases one or the other side discreetly backed down in time—except once.

In 1996, the government of Guatemala, a repressive dictatorship, was overthrown in a violent revolution backed by Indian peasants and guided by a group of Marxist intellectuals. Fearful of possible US intervention, they asked the Soviet government to deploy nuclear missiles on their soil as a deterrent. The Soviet Union declined, having no desire to provoke the United States excessively. But it agreed to modernize the Guatemalan armed forces and, in particular, to supply Guatemala with advanced fighter planes to match the Honduran air force deployed on Guatemala's borders.

The Honduran government, a staunch ally of the United States, felt threatened and was infuriated by the Soviet move. It asked the US government to destroy the recently delivered Soviet fighters with air strikes against their bases. The US government refused, seeking to avoid a war, but promised instead to set up a quarantine to prevent the introduction of further weapons into Guatemala.

The Soviet leader vividly remembered Khrushchev's downfall as a result of his humiliating defeat in the Cuban missile crisis when the United States possessed an overwhelming nuclear superiority. He had no desire to repeat the mistake. Emboldened by the rough nuclear parity the Soviet Union had since achieved, he addressed a strongly worded ultimatum to the US government, borrowing language from Kennedy's pronouncements on Cuba and Carter's warning about US interests in the Persian Gulf. He said that any interference into the fraternal relations between Guatemala and the Soviet Union would be considered a direct attack on the vital interests of the Soviet Union and would be resisted by any means necessary.

The US president took this as a thinly veiled threat of nuclear blackmail. He was not about to fall to his knees and sue for peace, particularly not with elections coming up. As a clear warning, he ordered the sinking of a Soviet vessel that tried to break the blockade.

The Soviet leader placed the Soviet armed forces on a worldwide alert. Soviet submarines carrying nuclear cruise missiles were moved closer to the shores of the United States. The greatest Soviet armada in history converged on the shores of Guatemala. The Soviet Union destroyed a US satellite that had been used to observe naval movements in the Caribbean.

The US president realized that he faced a critical situation. At any moment, Soviet space lasers, which were designed to destroy US missiles, could just as well destroy the US laser stations in space. Unless he acted quickly and decisively, it could be too late. He saw no other choice but to destroy the Soviet space stations before they could destroy the United States' own.

Would the Soviet Union back down now or go one step further?

Until now the whole world had stood by, deeply concerned, hoping that somehow the crisis would be resolved, as in similar cases before. But suddenly it appeared as if the end was near.

The UN secretary-general hastily called a teleconference with the leaders of Brazil, China, the European Community (which had achieved political integration in 1994 and chosen an Italian as president), India, Japan, and Nigeria. After ninety minutes of intense debate, a peace proposal began to crystallize and included the following elements:

An immediate cease-fire in place in the Caribbean.

All weapons to be banned from space. Remaining battle stations to be destroyed.

An international satellite agency to be created, which will monitor military movements around the world and make this information available to all countries, to reduce the fear of surprise attacks.

Free elections, observed by the United Nations, to be held in Guatemala and Honduras within six months.

Great care was taken to offer both sides a face-saving way out of the crisis. The proposal was presented to the leaders of the United States and the Soviet Union. Both pretended that this was what they had always stood for, that they had no desire to impose their own political system, and wanted only to prevent interference from the other side. Faced with the alternative of mutual annihilation, they accepted the proposals, each side claiming victory. It was far easier for each of them to accept the verdict of an impartial body than to yield to pressure and threats from their opponent. . . .

The world was relieved that the immediate crisis was defused but was too apprehensive to celebrate. People realized that without some fundamental changes in the world system, similar crises were bound to recur and could well lead to human extinction. Living in an anarchic world full of tension and hostility and packed with thousands of nuclear weapons was like walking along the edge of a cliff on a dark night.

Now the world was suddenly willing, even eager to listen to proposals for alternative world orders. . . .

The UN secretary-general called a special conference to develop realistic proposals for a viable new world order. One hundred of the world's leading thinkers, humanists, scientists, and writers, including some current and former military and civilian leaders, were invited, under the condition that they remain in session until they had come up with a series of proposals that were bold enough to prevent effectively future wars and at the same time realistic enough to win overwhelming acceptance, given prevailing habits of thought and behavior. They solicited and received thousands of ideas and suggestions from around the world.

Many of the participants had worked on such ideas all their lives but had been persistently ignored. Now their chance to be heard and taken seriously had come.

Those who thought deeply about the human predicament following the invention of nuclear weapons came to realize more and more that no matter how difficult nuclear disarmament seemed, it was not even sufficient. War itself as a human institution had to be abolished. For as long as conflicts among the major powers continued to be settled through war, each side would be under strong temptation to reintroduce nuclear weapons, out of fear that the other side might do so first.

They were convinced that, contrary to widespread popular belief, war was not at all part of human "nature," but was a learned cultural aberration. Despite the numerous wars fought throughout history, peace was in fact the normal state of human affairs. Most people had lived in peace most of the time.

The conference undertook a systematic investigation into the conditions leading to lasting peace. Opinions were divided into two groupings. Some were convinced that only world government could guarantee survival in the nuclear age. Others stressed that the major powers were not prepared to hand over responsibility for their security to someone else. Yet on further reflection it was found that there was no contradiction between the two views. An improved global order was needed to resolve conflicts without war. At the same time it was necessary for countries not to become totally defenseless and therefore a tempting target for aggression but to maintain a capacity to protect themselves if necessary.

A survey was made to see which countries had been able to avoid war for the longest period and how they had done it. The two countries with the longest record of uninterrupted peace were Sweden and Switzerland. What was their secret? The answer was at first surprising but in retrospect quite obvious: They did not seek victory in war! They had no plans to disarm an aggressor by carrying the fighting into his home territory. They restricted themselves to defending themselves only inside their own borders. They maintained a strong defense, but deliberately avoided acquiring any threatening offensive arms that could have created fear among their neighbors. . . .

The conference finally proposed a combination of the following four methods to the prevention of war.

First of all, greater efforts were to be made to eliminate the causes of war. Too much effort in the past had been expended merely to deal with the symptoms of problems while ignoring their causes. Governments reacted to crises, rather than anticipating and averting them. They limited themselves to firefighting, instead of building fireproof structures. It was realized, for example, that the best way to deal with the danger of war in Central America, which had almost sparked a nuclear world war, was to eliminate the problems of economic and social injustice that created political instability.

To protect themselves against outside intervention, all countries were encouraged to resolve internal disputes peacefully and to grant adequate protection to minorities. An international civil court was created in which individuals could seek protection against persecution by their own governments.

If the first barrier broke down and an international conflict erupted nevertheless, it was to be resolved through negotiations. If negotiations failed, countries were to accept mandatory jurisdiction by the World Court. The World Court was instructed to seek imaginative judgments that held out something attractive for both parties to a conflict. If one side was the clear loser, it might prefer to go to war rather than give in. The court was given substantial resources to make its decisions attractive to both sides and was also supplemented with an international police force to stop offenders.

If the World Court should fail, a third protection against war was dissuasion of aggression by making peace more attractive to a potential opponent than war, through mutually beneficial trade, through scientific and cultural exchange, etc.

As a last resort, if all other methods should fail, there was defense against aggression. A new UN Agency for Transarmament was to be created, which would assist countries in better protecting themselves against potential aggression without becoming a threat to their neighbors. Whereas disarmament means abandoning defense, transarmament means a shift to a different form of defense, suitable only to prevent aggression but not to carry out aggression.

. . . This multilayered approach was able to maintain peace for a sufficiently long period that ultimately mutual fear diminished. The whole world became a community similar to the Organization for Economic Cooperation and Development in the 1980s, where countries dealt with each other in a businesslike manner, resolving conflicts through negotiations. They did not agree on everything but did not go to war with each other over disagreements, in the same way as competing business firms do not kill each other's employees.

In 2006, an agreement was reached to destroy all nuclear weapons and to set up an international inspection system that could prevent their reintroduction. That step turned out to be feasible only after the threat of war had been banned. Johan Galtung, founder of the International Peace Research Institute in Norway, had once predicted that "disarmament does not appear to be the road to peace, but peace may be the road to disarmament."

With the fear of war banned, the world has begun to concentrate its efforts toward the solution of the old problems of hunger, disease, and ignorance. People today find it incredible that in 1985 US farmers were paid billions of dollars not to plant crops while millions of people in other parts of the world were starving to death. The enormous resources of nature and of human labor and ingenuity have been harnessed to eliminate poverty.

Today it seems incredible that until less than two decades ago people murdered each other on a large scale for the alleged purpose of national security. Until quite recently, the abolition of war seemed to many a utopian goal. But the abolition of colonialism, slavery, or cannibalism must have appeared as equally utopian to people brought up with these institutions. Humanity has finally evolved from barbarism.

(Dietrich Fischer)

January 1, 2010

Dear Grandchildren,

When we were all together last Christmas you asked me what it was like to live through all the wars and other crises of my day and why the world seems able to live more peacefully now in 2010. Well frankly it was pretty discouraging and frustrating, not only for us adults but also for young people like you. The problems seemed so immense and our efforts to deal with them so ineffectual that the future looked pretty grim.

After the Second World War ended with the dropping of the first atomic bomb on Japan, one of the worst prospects was that our whole civilization might be wiped out if even a fraction of the nuclear bombs built up by the major nations were to be launched intentionally or by mistake. Other problems included the heartbreaking plight of the hungry and poor, especially in developing countries; the degradation and pollution of the planet's environment and depletion of its resources, made worse by runaway population growth and consumerism; the inertia and self-centered interests of individuals and of our massive military, industrial, and other institutions, which produced injustices, corruption and inflexibility. It seemed as if we were always reacting to one crisis after another with Band-Aid cures that didn't stick, rather than developing a lasting remedy that dealt with *all* the contributing *causes* of the problems.

It's easier to look back now though and to see how things began to change in the mid-1980s. We started to analyze seriously our global situation and our own values, motives, and behavior. We came to recognize a number of basic truths and principles that allowed us to develop gradually a more appropriate pattern of living with our fellow creatures and our fragile earth. A number of ways of viewing the human situation on earth became generally recognized. To mention a few:

The remarkable growth in communication and understanding through satellite TV, airplane travel, and computerized information processing led to a growing awareness that all nations of the world have similar basic needs, that we are all dependent on each other and on the continuing ability of our common earth to sustain us. For instance, a nation's well-being is affected by its agricultural land, water, forests and climate, and natural resources, which are in turn affected by global consumption and increases in pollution. These in turn affect the world's economic health and tensions between nations. US and Soviet relations are dependent on the nature of their power structures, values, goals, and technological capabilities, which are in turn dependent on their economic resources and human strengths. The problems and needs in developing countries affect relations between the superpowers, and so forth.

We began to realize how our own self-interests and shortsightedness had led to patterns of living which were threatening not only to each other but to the earth's environment on which we all depend. Yet for a while we all clung to the accustomed patterns of behavior, pressing even harder for *more* economic "growth," *more* consumption of resources, *more* arms for security, and *more* striving to win, even at the expense of other people.

A basic solution to each problem must be integrated with long-range solutions to the others for satisfying and lasting results.

All nations need the basic necessities of life and the opportunity to earn a fair share of its human benefits, for example, security, social betterment, dignity, and freedom.

While self-interest is a fundamental drive of the human race and necessary for its survival, personal freedom must be tempered by responsibility to others and the common good in order to serve our long-term self-interests.

To be lastingly effective, institutional goals must be guarded by and for the people served.

Scientific developments, while intended for the benefit of humankind, must receive continuing attention to guard against misuse.

Scholarship, research and development on the causes and potential cures of problems are vital tools for maintaining a just and sustainable future.

Our educational systems must encourage continuing open-minded reappraisal of our priorities, attitudes, and values in order to achieve a humane perspective on such issues as the logic of wars as an easy way to settle disputes; the relative importance of survival, freedoms, a sustainable environment, etc.; the wisdom of short-term gains at the expense of long-range costs; the validity of economic growth and materialism as measures of important human values.

Reliance on mutual military deterrence promotes arms escalation because parity is difficult to define. Another approach to peacemaking is necessary.

Pictures of the earth from outer space not only startled us by their unique beauty but reminded us of the earth's fragility and the necessity for us to respect its finite capabilities.

New Concepts and Tools

So it was that in the mid-1980s the world had developed a growing consciousness of its global interdependence and the need for peace to be sought on many broad fronts. We realized our awesome responsibility for survival of the human race in the face of potentially calamitous disaster from nuclear and environmental threats. Fortunately, our human wisdom was also stimulated to develop the understanding and skills to deal with the problems. These new concepts and tools offered a refreshing new approach to living together on this unique planet. Although we now consider the ultimate solutions to be consistent with ancient teachings, the means by which such teachings could be applied in a practical way had not somehow dawned on us before. Examples include: . . .

Conflict Resolution

The technology of conflict resolution (how to reach agreements) was advancing strongly. It applied many of the teachings of psychology in human relations such as role playing, "active feedback" listening, use of trained arbiters, agreement on principles before specifics, and maintaining a friendly atmosphere. . . .

Principled Negotiation

Application of the "principled negotiation" methods developed at the Harvard Negotiation Project proved to be a key factor in reaching agreement with the Russians on arms control. It focused on deciding issues on their merits rather than through an adroit bargaining process often involving threats and recriminations. The method separated "people" from the "problem" so that participants came to see themselves working together in a civil, noncombative manner to attack the problem, not each other. It focused on underlying interests and common grounds, not stated positions. It invented a wide range of possible options for mutual gains that could advance shared interests and reconcile differing interests. It insisted on previously agreed on principles and criteria (such as equitability and verifiability) for reaching agreement on specifics.

Such negotiating took a good deal of preparation, fact-finding, analysis, and creative problem solving. During the actual negotiating it also took much patience, diplomatic and communicative skill, and perception and sensitivity to the other party's feelings and reactions.

US Institute for Peace and Conflict Resolution

In 1984, Congress established the US Institute for Peace and Conflict Resolution to conduct research on the causes of conflicts, to develop techniques for the resolution of international conflicts, and to develop education and training programs. Though initiated and at least partially funded by the US government, the Peace Institute was an independent, nonprofit institution. Thus it could attract qualified scholars of high professional ability, regardless of their political inclinations. It could also support nongovernmental efforts, such as the development of the theory and practice of conflict resolution mentioned above. It did not, however, signify a definite US commitment to achieve peace, nor did it assign a focal point of action for carrying out its own teachings.

National Peace Council

In order to achieve those objectives, therefore, in 1986, Congress set up a *governmental* agency, the *US National Peace Council* with clear responsibility and accountability to achieve a sustainable peace with other nations and with the earth itself. The Peace Council paralleled the National Security Council in rank and stature. It reported directly to the president, advised and assisted him on all policies relating to a peaceful and sustainable future, and was his principal forum for national peace-securing issues. It assisted the president in coordinating foreign policy decisions relating to the development and maintenance of peace in a sustainable international community. It also facilitated the placement of the US and foreign governmental Peace Institute "graduates" in key peacemaking posts.

The Council's head was highly motivated to world statesmanship and had an understanding of the long-range global nature of the challenge facing the United States and the world. The Council's working body consisted of a small staff, plus representatives from all the branches of government whose functions related to international peace. . . .

Because of this representation the recommendations made to the president could be implemented and coordinated efficiently as a united national effort, even though various, sometimes overlapping agencies were involved in the activity.

The Council's long-range strategies were derived from the analysis of the root causes of wars and global discontent. These causes were seen to range at the visible level from international disputes over land ownership or ruling power to internal revolutions over leadership, poverty, oppression, ideological or tribal differences, etc. At a deeper level, the cause may lie in the need for security or freedom; access to resources or ports, preservation of principles, etc. At a still deeper level, causes may be found in destructive human motives stemming from the need to demonstrate the worth of the nation and or its leaders. Almost all the causes of conflict boil down to the need for at least one of the parties to achieve some basic ingredient for a satisfying human existence—ranging from feelings of self-worth, identity, and respect to the material necessities for survival. . . .

Because the Peace Council was set up to give full consideration to the *long*-range needs for lasting peace, it was not intended as a means of crisis management. It was, however, effective in greatly reducing the occurrence of international crises by providing *direction* for short-range tactical decisions.

The Council did not call for any unilateral reduction in military strength preparedness but relied on the improved skill available in conflict resolution to achieve mutual, verifiable arms reduction agreements.

Because the Council itself and its programs represented only a consolidation of personnel and a modification of existing responsibilities and programs, no major addition to the nation's cost was necessary. As major arms reductions were achieved, the savings could be applied to increased international economic aid.

Recognizing the interrelationship of the planet's environmental problems with its human activities, the Council was able to incorporate its recommendations for peace in practical terms that preserved the ecology for sustainable and fair utilization by not only all present nations but also by future generations, of which you children are members.

As a result of all these developments on all the major problems, a gradual but persistently dramatic advance toward sustainable peace began to take place. The watershed change in world affairs came about as a result not of any one thing but of the contribution of the many factors I have mentioned. Although the progress seemed agonizingly slow at times and had many setbacks and doubters, by historical standards the changes were remarkably fast because they were right for the times and conditions. People knew something was badly wrong and in need of change. ("There is a tide in the affairs of men which taken at the flood leads on to fortune"—Shakespeare.)

Our invitation to set up a parallel Peace Council in the Soviet Union was accepted and regular informal meetings were held between the two countries. This produced mutual understanding and acknowledgment of their respective basic interests and needs, perceptions, expectations, customs, priorities, values, and underlying motives. It resulted in an agreement by which arms controls and gradual military reductions could be brought about.

After the breakthrough in arms reduction to the level of nuclear stockpiles which could no longer threaten the extinction of the human race, the momentum and trust thus developed carried through to joint cooperation on methods of preventing proliferation of nuclear arms to other nations, and other constructive projects. . . .

United Nations Strengthened

The improved atmosphere between the superpowers then became reflected in the deliberations of the United Nations. With the example of greatly reduced rivalry and tension and by the concrete evidence of cooperation, other countries found it in their best interests to get into the spirit of collaboration in the common interest of world survival and social betterment. The United Nations was then able to flower and greatly expand its effectiveness in dealing with most of the other problems facing the world, such as poverty, injustice, health, resource conservation and development, environmental and climate protection, reclamation of agricultural land and forest, protection of a diversity of biological species, and population stabilization and reduction through education, economic development, employment, health, and women's rights.

As trained conflict-resolution specialists had helped the United States and the Soviet Union reach the crucially important arms reduction agreement, similar UN negotiators could help to mediate impartially other national disputes and further stabilize the civilized world. Security risks were reduced and unproductive military consumption of scarce resources curtailed.

It became possible to reduce self-centered nationalistic postures in the United Nations. It also resulted in the willingness of more countries to provide the necessary peacekeeping forces to carry out UN decisions.

Gradually the pros and cons of different forms of government became evident in the forum of public opinion, and the most successful features in each society tended to be adoped by others.

Obviously, we have not achieved utopia because there are always new problems to challenge us, but, at least some basic processes for globally cooperative problem solving toward a sustainable future for all the world's people seem to have been established.

And that, my dear children, is the way it was back in my day and why you are enjoying what I believe to be the better world we sought to bring about for you. May God help you continue to make improvements in the process of global survival and development so that you and your children and grandchildren can continue to enjoy the great gift and privilege of life as much as we have.

Your grateful Grampa

(S. Edward Eaton)

Notwithstanding the great advances humankind had made down through the ages, to most people in 1985 a stable, worldwide peace still seemed a remote utopian fancy. The developments of the ensuing twenty-five years that caused fancy to become reality entitled that period to recognition as one of the truly seminal eras in human history.

Ironically, the single most important event of the period began with what was widely denounced as a near-act of war.

The worrisome act was the irrevocable commitment by the United States in the late 1980s to proceed with the development of a space-based ballistic missile defense system (BMD) capable of shielding the nation from strategic nuclear missiles launched from anywhere on the globe. Despite the BMD's manifest attractiveness, many people in the United States and elsewhere feared that it would so destabilize the superpower balance of terror that the Soviet Union might be provoked into a preemptive nuclear strike.

What finally won the skeptics over was the second step in the BMD adventure, a step that was, if anything, even bolder and more controversial than the first.

This was the decision by the United States to share the BMD technology with the rest of the world, including the Soviet Union. This was an act of geopolitical "generosity" (actually of enlightened self-interest) almost without parallel in history.

The consequences of this decision were twofold. The first one, obviously, was that it ended the danger of a nuclear holocaust. Whatever other ills men might visit on each other in the future, they no longer were capable of blowing up the planet.

But the symbolic effects of the great BMD episode far outweighed the literal consequences. In addition to lifting the mushroom cloud that had hung over mankind for half a century, the episode lifted an even blacker, more ominous cloud that had settled onto the collective spirit of the world's inhabitants.

Courage and moral perspective were being leached from human thought as sheer survival started to become paramount over mankind's nobler values and aspirations. The growing perception that events were in the saddle and mankind no longer was in control of its destiny gave rise to fatalistic stoicism and, even worse, despair.

The lifting of the nuclear threat had a profoundly cathartic effect on human consciousness. Humans were seen as having retaken the reins of history into their own hands, and the resulting confidence quickly bore fruit in other areas of endeavor. It was also significant for world morale that science and technology—which had started to be viewed by some people as "evil genies" whose release ultimately would bring more ill than good—had been harnessed for the common security.

The nuclear threat was not the last, nor perhaps even the most difficult, of the problems mankind had to solve to end war, but because of the far-reaching effects the elimination of that threat had on mankind's vision of itself, the accomplishment has to be regarded as the linchpin event of the era.

The second major challenge facing world leaders in the area of defense was how to lessen the chances that nations would—or successfully could—resort to nonstrategic weaons to settle international disputes.

The populations of the industrialized nations were gradually aging, with the result that these nations had a diminishing pool of manpower available for military purposes. Also, nations were finding it increasingly difficult to sustain the relentlessly rising costs of maintaining large standing armies.

During this period, world diplomats made some important breakthroughs in reducing the danger of military conflict among nations. Through imaginative new rules of engagement and the increased involvement of international mediation organizations and peacekeeping forces, the world community managed to create a system of "circuit breakers" that could be triggered when countries seemed near the brink of war.

As an outgrowth of the cooperative effort to reduce international confrontations, the major powers also made great strides in curbing both the proliferation of nuclear technology and the world-wide traffic in conventional arms.

Major shifts in the climate of world thinking and several notable developments in international trade and economics were advanced. The four key intellectual developments were a banking of the fires of nationalism, the demise of Malthusianism in its latter-day incarnations, a subsiding of religious fanaticism, and the passing away of communism as a serious paradigm for the ordering of human societies.

A closing word: As important as the foregoing developments

have been to bringing about the peaceful conditions the world now enjoys, people should not be misled into thinking that peace is simply the product of impersonal forces or clever international arrangements. Nor should they believe that peace is static and immutable. Mankind has not attained a millennial state. The age-old enemies of peace—fear, ignorance, want, bigotry, and hatred—remain in one form or another. The price of peace, like that of freedom, is eternal vigilance.

In the last analysis, peace is not a condition but rather, like love or virtue, an attribute of character. It is a creation of human heads and hearts attuned to the deeper meanings and purposes of life. Though building on the legacy handed down to it, each generation must create peace anew for itself. The great lesson of history is that those majestic words of Scripture, "on earth peace, goodwill toward men," are not so much a promise of what shall be as of what can be. They are not a pledge, but an injunction.

(James H. Andrews)

_____

6

Change of Consciousness

Few of the entries in *The Christian Science Monitor*'s Peace 2010 contest suggested a religious solution to the current mistrust among nations that manifests itself as a worldwide arms race. On one level, the lack of this approach among the entries illustrates the status of organized religion in the world today. There may also have been a reluctance or even bashfulness about showing how an approach dealing with the ethical and possibly even the spiritual dimensions of our existence could be significant to a large enough segment of mankind to be advanced as the way to worldwide peace. There may also have been a feeling not too far below the surface of thought that linked the institutions that promote morality with the institutional wars fought in their name over the centuries.

In looking at Christianity in the West, one need only recall the Thirty Years War, fought intermittently from 1618 to 1648 and occupying most of central Europe at one time or another during that generation. At the end of the war, Catholics and Protestants more or less agreed to let the religious status quo be. But a more decisive result of the war was a weakening of organized religion among the leading classes of the countries that had been involved.

Will and Ariel Durant, in *The Age of Reason* (Simon and Schuster, 1961), write that ˉ

> though the Reformation had been saved, it suffered, along with Catholicism, from a skepticism encouraged by the coarseness of religious polemics, the brutality of the war, and the cruelties of belief . . . . Men began to doubt creeds that preached Christ and practiced wholesale fratricide . . . . Even in this darkest of modern ages an increasing number of men turned to science and philosophy for answers less incarnadined than those which the faiths had so violently sought to enforce. . . . The Peace of Westphalia ended the reign of theology over the European mind, and left the road obstructed but passable for the tentatives of reason. (pp. 571–572)

If our essayists did not see the organized institutions, called churches, as the main agents of change in the next twenty-five years and if individual charismatic religious figures were also lacking in the scenarios for peace, there was nonetheless a strong idealistic content in the essays. Some of the writers saw the peace process being advanced by a more metaphysical, or spiritual, outlook, whereas others took off from an enlightened sense of humanity—of a humanity merely looking outward and enlarging its borders of concern. Whatever the source of this new outlook, these essays saw peace being advanced by a kind of change of consciousness that religious leaders would call a religious awakening. Thus the organizations of religion may have played a small role in the writers' scenarios, but the ethical and moral dimension present in all major religions is still functioning and functioning strongly at the level of individual thought.

In these essays we found an approach to peace different from those in the other chapters presented so far. In many essays, of course, there is some intermingling of geopolitics with ethical concerns. But the chapters of the book to this point have advanced solutions that came out of geopolitical strategies, nuclear disasters or other kinds of disasters, or economic urgency. From this point forward in the essays, the agency of change is a fundamental shift in perspective. The solution lies in seeing the problem in a new light. But it is more than a simple redefinition of the problem. The problem is seen in a new light because of a change in outlook by the seers themselves. The solution obviously has a politically practical application that may not be altogether different from some of the scenarios already advanced.

Geoffrey Grimes, international director of Hands around the World, DeSoto, Texas, wrote in his cover letter, "The factor that this essay addresses is the emergence of the world citizen as a critical new center of power and the definition of positive world peace with the capacity to check the failure of negative world peace traditionally defined as the goal of sovereign states." In his essay, it is the redirection of the individual that eventually changes the state of the world.

This redirection has resulted in the emergence of a social role completely new in the evolution of Western culture. Not since Benjamin Franklin, as the "self-made man," strolled into the court of Louis XVI in 1776, dissolving the meaning of European aristocracy, has a new social role developed to impact world order so significantly. This role is the figure of a world citizen whose touchstone is a conviction of personal responsibility for the well-being of the global community.

The joint essay of *Craig Schindler* and *Toby Herzlich,* of Santa Cruz, California, also emphasized the role the individual can take in making peace. The effectiveness of individual action may seem difficult to envision in terms of large countries' governments' eventually coming to have a new attitude toward each other. Yet it was present in many different versions. In the Schindler-Herzlich essay, many people across the United States came to the conclusion that, because of the strength and freedom enjoyed by the United States, it was up to this country to take the lead in finding peace. They wrote about meetings across the nation in which hawkish and dovish positions on foreign policy were gradually resolved—as the first step.

You could see when the tide was beginning to change. Though it manifested itself ultimately in an expression of national unity, the pivotal turning, the fulcrum, was the individual. I don't remember what the first pledge of personal responsibility said or where it came from. It was translated into so many different languages in so many different places. Everybody had his or her own version. My pledge goes as follows:

I pledge to take personal responsibility for preventing nuclear war and renewing the quality of life on earth. I will make it a priority in my life to reach other people so that they will take responsibility, starting with my circle of friends and associates. I will work for a world which acknowledges the reality that in the nuclear age the only victory possible is a victory for everyone.

Michael Nagler, of Tomales, California, named his essay "Strength through Peace," turning around a catchy political phrase of 1984. Nagler is a student of nonviolence, and his essay portrays the changed world that resulted from an associate of Gandhi's winning the Nobel Peace Prize. This brought nonviolence into the public consciousness with a new vigor. In Nicaragua the contras ran into a new kind of resistance, and the Soviets found the same phenomenon some years later when in 1994 they invaded Poland. What happened? Discussing previous peace scenarios, Nagler claims they

could not happen until the consciousness of enough people—the famous "paradigm shift" popular in peace movement literature of the 1980s and 1990s—accepted their reality. If the international changes bought time by obstructing war and the intrasocial changes bought a stable economic regime in which fewer causes of war arose, ultimate peace came through a change of vision. . . . Most of the peace institutions we enjoy today—legal, educational, research—began as impromptu work undertaken without official sanction by absolutely ordinary people.

Nagler also has the pattern of media violence, which contributed to warlike solutions in society, being broken—again, by ordinary people.

It is clear that the breakthrough which occurred in the closing decades of man's second Christian millennium—the breakthrough which saved our planet from extinction as a home for life—had a quality that resists analysis. Some historians still regard it as unaccountable: why, for example, large numbers of people began to break the bubble of media violence. Yet it was simply the result of thousands of decisions, each one made and remade and made again by perfectly ordinary people—decisions which in retrospect could have been made long ago by every one of us.

Douglas D. Alder, a professor at Utah State University, Logan, Utah, wrote an essay in which a potential nuclear disaster evolved into a change of consciousness on the part of the world's leaders. Attention was focused too much, he said, on the mistakes of the past. Starting with the Geneva talks now in process, he wrote:

As has so often been the case in history, the negotiators of 1985 did not realize that both sides were focusing on the wrong enemy. Just like the diplomats at the 1815 Congress of Vienna who did not realize that France would no longer be dangerous or those at Potsdam in 1945 who worried needlessly about renewed German fascism, so in 1985 negotiators were focusing too much on a possible East-West conflict.

What happened instead was another Middle East war in 1999, in which conspirators in the Middle East tried to trick the big powers into responding. "What we learned from that first blast in the Mediterranean was that the West and the East needed each other." Negotiators for the major powers met in emergency sessions in an underwater laboratory to draw up a plan that would not allow war to happen again. Their close confinement helped them to come to terms with the basic fact of their common humanity. From the short Middle Eastern war, they had learned, Alder said, their mutual vulnerability.

This peace is firm today only because no country can ever again be invulnerable. . . . We know we cannot endure an East-West split. We know we need each other, not out of idealism but the reality of saving each other from the abyss. We know now that the Russians and Americans and Chinese actually saved each other. No one can mount a defense technology that is secure. To believe the contrary is simply an illusion, one that has been popped.

Taking personal responsibility for peace, nonviolence as one form of personal involvement in the process, and the lesson of mutual vulnerability—these are all forms of a change of consciousness in the sense that, if one looks at their opposites, it is obvious how much our present approach to peace is still influenced by the opposite concepts: thinking peace is the job only of our elected leaders, the acceptance of the arms race as absolutely necessary to establish our commitment to peace, and the belief that one nation or group of nations alone can establish peace. The shared humanity theme of many essays can have a deeply spiritual base to it, or it can come out of failed past human experience that teaches the danger of thinking one group or nation can advance without respect for the legitimate interests of others.

Kenneth Boulding, professor emeritus at the University of Colorado (best known for his work as an environmentalist), wrote about a document that caused a widespread change of consciousness. Issued in 1985 by some people connected with the United Nations University, it was entitled "A Call to Human Maturity in a New Region of Time." The manifesto argued that the world had crossed a threshold (of both nuclear weapons and population growth) and that the lessons from the immediate past were no longer entirely relevant. There was nothing that prevented either the Soviet Union or the United States from having national policies to create security through a stable peace.

The simple idea that we are entering a new region of time somehow caught the imagination of people all over the world. The religious organizations picked it up, a wave of mass celebrations spread through the world, even into the communist countries, and the idea that something new was happening gradually penetrated to the political leaders.

A lasting peace will depend not on treaties between the superpowers but on an understanding and acceptance of the human situation. That situation can be described negatively as the acceptance of our mutual vulnerability, which transcends both the Soviet expansionism carried out under the umbrella of the shopworn and incorrect theories of Marx and Lenin *and* the American urge to bring Western-style personal freedoms to all the world. That same situation can be expressed more positively as a deep-seated human need to expand the bounds of family and tribe to a community that, at least in thought, although perhaps impossible of attainment in practice for many generations yet, includes mankind. That is the community based if not on actual love, then on the acceptance of a mutual responsibility for one another.

Something akin to this thought was expressed by J. Edward Barrett, a professor of religion and philosophy at Muskingum College, New Concord, Ohio. His essay (already mentioned in chapter 2) took an approach to peace that began with the United States and the Soviet Union finally taking the first tentative steps toward arms control and building from that confidence-building measure. Although not specifically constructed around the concept of a change of consciousness, such a change did occur as the peace process took shape. In this sense Barrett's essay presents a realistic scenario, since the architecture of "thinking peace" is somewhat easier to envision if the foundation stones of peace can at least be seen as having been laid. At the end of the peace process, Barrett writes:

Why believe that we in 2010 have come to a "lasting peace"? Perhaps it is the conviction that there comes a time when the time has come, when what we human beings could not previously do we now can do, should do, must do. Paul Tillich called such historical moments a *kairos,* from the Greek meaning when the time is ripe. Such a *kairos* came during the nineteenth century with the abolition of slavery. Since then the world has not looked back. Ten years ago, in the year 2000, the joint resolution on world peace, signed by every member of the General Assembly of the United Nations, noted that "disagreement is inevitable but war is unacceptable." Today, no one is interested in looking back.

———————————

. . . For the first time in the evolution of nationalism, something fundamental has taken shape during the last twenty-five years that is finally beginning to alter the relationships among sovereign powers. . . This fundamental change among nations has been effected not so much by the threat of more accurate targeting of still greater engines of destruction . . . as much as it has been a most remarkable redirection of affairs at the local level. . . . Because of this redirection by key people in the community at the base of the mountains, those massive guns above are beginning to rust in their silos.

This redirection has resulted in the emergence of a social role completely new in the evolution of Western culture. Not since Benjamin Franklin, as the "self-made man," strolled into the court of Louis XVI in 1776, dissolving the meaning of European aristocracy, has a new social role developed to impact world order so significantly. This role is the figure of a world citizen whose touchstone is a conviction of personal responsibility for the well-being of the global community. . . .

The slow dissolution of "official" tensions in the last two decades between major powers reflects the failure of sovereign states to set aside the outdated attitudes that originated in the political realignments following World War II and in the years of the cold war during the 1950s. . . .

Against this backdrop of a seemingly unresponsive, unsympathetic government, a fundamental, grass roots movement began to surface among small groups of Americans. Disenfranchised from the traditional centers of power, many of these people gave voice publicly—some for the first time—to a new sense of self-worth and basic human dignity. This new voice was a vital self-assertion that in a few short years was to blossom throughout the world. To many, it appeared to be the only voice capable of countering the carefully manicured rationalizations of the US military establishment that would have had them accept the threat of the earth's conflagration as the only authoritative source of a lasting world peace.

The popular reaction in America was echoed in countries the world over. This ground swell for peace was, in part, a reaction against the futility of national governments to find acceptable alternatives to terrorism and war as solutions to international crises. Additionally—and unmistakably—it was a demand for an end to the incessantly spiraling nuclear arms race. On both counts, it reflected the growing suspicion that, in a global setting, national leadership was out of its element and out of control. It questioned myopic foreign policies that, hopelessly atrophied, had effected the final dilemma from which there was to be no recourse—at least no recourse to be found from within the systems that had fostered that dilemma. . . .

Nurturing this protest was a new faith in mankind's ability to participate meaningfully in circles of responsibility beyond the traditional arenas of family or career. In fact, the fundamental element in sustaining peace during the past twenty-five years has been this general, global consciousness-lifting: a discovery of and a commitment to the realization that the individual can contribute in valuable ways to the development and maintenance of positive world peace. This realization and commitment rests at the heart of a new internationalism. It is this realization and commitment that effects a positive rather than a negative world peace. . . .

Positive peace is the only answer to the ultimate failure of negative peace, an atomic holocaust fomented by the distended foreign policies of nuclear-tipped sovereign states. The absence of hostilities, the absence of open war, and fundamentally, the absence of annihilation and death of its citizens—the criteria of negative peace—are the most hopeful objectives for nations that have accepted mutually assured destruction as a key to military deterrence of global conflict. To these ends, nations must commit themselves; to ensure these ends, they must at every moment and forever maintain a balance of nuclear power. However, such a stalemate among adversaries anticipates far less security among nations than do the promises of a positive world peace.

Positive peace grows from contexts that embrace rather than fend against what are perceived to be adversarial bodies. Positive peace stems from the contexts of community and an interpretation of the self that finds identity in the community of others. Such patterns assume a comfortable sense of self and stability and are characteristic of both the individual and institutions, even at the national level. Out of such contexts positive peace answers its negative alternatives. . . .

Thinking Globally: The Seed of Transcendent Life

Twenty-five years ago the concept of world citizenship was metamorphosing in a ground swell of personal initiatives. Throughout the world and in every social, economic, and professional circle, individuals began feeling their way into the global arena, following no shepherd, tracing the steps of no high priest who could illuminate and interpret the way. That their impulse was at once both universal and self-sustaining is a sign that a new paradigm had emerged. This new paradigm of the world citizen with global responsibilities was self-authenticated by the creation of each new network among people who agreed to serve, as both time and circumstances might permit, greater issues beyond the topical and domestic in their lives.

The concept of a citizen whose commitments ranged beyond local affairs was a startling new but uplifting perception of life in the trenches. In the 1980s, Dr. Willis Harman, senior social scientist for the Strategic Environment Center at Stanford University, challenged each local citizen of the world to "think globally, act locally, and perceive newly." To each person, like himself, already at work in the world, this formulation of transcendent living needed little explication, as its practitioners were too busy implementing their brave, new world in a myriad of cultural, educational, and economic exchanges. . . .

Thinking globally, acting locally, and perceiving newly—the principles of a new internationalism—became a paradigm for key individuals throughout the world who, in the last two decades, have accepted personal responsibility for world peace. Probably no other factor has been more important, in retrospect, in neutralizing the dilemmas of stalemated national governments—at loggerheads in the global arena—than has been this new consciousness-lifting worldwide. . . .

(Geoffrey Allan Grimes)

. . . There was a time when it looked pretty grim. I remember when my son was a small boy, wondering if he would be killed in a nuclear war before he grew up. We were closer to the edge than most of us were willing to admit to ourselves. By the mid-1980s we had accumulated more than 50,000 nuclear warheads worldwide . . .

By 1985, we Americans were spending more money on national defense than any nation in history. We were siphoning our money away from our own needs. Schools for our children, social services for the disadvantaged, research and development, even our space program—all had begun to suffer severely. The economic stress of arming ourselves was beginning to tear apart the fabric of our national life. Our national debt rose higher than ever before; for the first time the United States owed the world more than we were owed.

We were on the edge. Little did we know that we were also on the edge of a breakthrough toward world peace. . . .

Just like any major step, at the time it seemed so far out of reach. But now, historians of the twenty-first century refer to this period from 1980 to 2000 as the time of "the great turning." They generally agree on four stages of development. . . .

Stage one began in the early 1980s as thousands of people began to voice an unprecedented level of concern about the increasing threat of nuclear war. There were movies, television programs, public school curricula, and the active participation of professional and community groups—all with the purpose of informing ourselves about the factual consequences of nuclear war. The public became increasingly involved in the debate over arms control, particularly the nuclear freeze movement. There was a massive shift in public sentiment: A large percentage of the American public expressed the view that a nuclear war was not winnable, likely to destroy most life on earth, and hence must not be fought. . . .

Stage two began as more and more people recognized that it was up to the United States to take the leadership toward world peace. We were the only nation with both the strength and the freedom to take the initiative. Only by healing the divisions in the United States could we sustain a steady course toward lasting peace. Warily at first, we began to step across our narrow partisan boundaries—to listen to each other and to understand each other's point of view. Soon there were discussion groups and house meetings across the country, bringing together hawks and doves in a common search for the way out of our predicament. . . .

It was a kind of national reconciliation. People of different viewpoints—hawks and doves—responded to the call to participate actively in the search for a common solution. The message spread from person to person, through friendship circles, neighborhoods, and professional associations. There was no stopping it and no telling who was doing it. And what was the message? The essence was that each of us was taking personal responsibility to contribute our piece of the puzzle. . . .

There were neighborhood gatherings and town meetings which focused on discovering the elements of a new national consensus.

Television and media played a critical role, enabling us to conduct national discussions via satellite and to communicate with each other in creative new ways. Satellite television, coupled with personal computer systems, became a vehicle for a new level of electronically based interactive democracy.

You could see when the tide was beginning to change. Though it manifested itself ultimately in an expression of national unity, the pivotal turning, the fulcrum, was the individual. I don't remember what the first pledge of personal responsibility said or where it came from. It was translated into so many different languages in so many different places. Everybody had his or her own version. My pledge goes as follows:

I pledge to take personal responsibility for preventing nuclear war and renewing the quality of life on earth. I will make it a priority in my life to reach other people so that they will take responsibility, starting with my circle of friends and associates. I will work for a world which acknowledges the reality that in the nuclear age the only victory possible is a victory for everyone.

The efforts of committed individuals and groups began to be expressed in our national life. In the fall of 1986, there was a National Day of Listening, which involved people from all walks of life as well as prominent Americans in the process of expanding our perspective to include the relative truth of different perspectives. By facilitating better listening and understanding, we discovered new options for national action and began to define a shared strategy for preventing nuclear war. . . .

(Craig F. Schindler and Toby Herzlich)

His disciples said to him, "When will the Kingdom come?" [Jesus said,] "It will not come by waiting for it. It will not be a matter of saying 'Here it is' or 'There it is.' Rather, the Kingdom of the Father is spread out upon the earth, and men do not see it." (*Gospel of Thomas* (Gnostic text of the third century A.D.))

Something spooked the cats and Mrs. Degranfenried was making one of her early morning phone calls, so Grandpa went out to investigate. He came right back, stabbing his eyes over his shoulder to the young man standing behind him with a sawed-off shotgun: Riley Arzeneau, 23, on the run from the Fort Pillow State Penitentiary. Riley had spent the night under a rug in the Degranfenried garage and hadn't figured on being discovered so soon. Gesturing with the gun, he demanded money and the keys to the Degranfenried's truck. But he hadn't reckoned on "Grandma." Calmly telling her friend she would call back later, Mrs. D., a 73-year-old black lady who had lived in Tennessee all her life, hung up the phone and said the words that are now famous: "Put that gun down young man; we don't allow no violence around here."

Almost to the hour that Grandma Degranfenried was fixing Riley Arzeneau breakfast and eggs, getting him to pray and turn himself in to the Tennessee correctional authorities, his cohorts from the same break were confronting another couple, and things were not going so well; for here the man of the house produced a .45 (almost half of all American homes had handguns for "protection" at that time) and was, of course, instantly killed. His terrified wife was released a day later, physically unharmed, clear across the state.

The papers duly "covered" both events, without attempting to make the slightest sense of them. That was 1984.

We have, most of us, personally lived through a breathtaking revolution in human history. Many are alive who thought their eyes would close on a searing holocaust, who perhaps had long abandoned hope of a future for their children—alive, wondrously, in a fragile but temporarily secured peace. How did we get here? The dark side of the curtain still looms so close behind us that the precise steps by which we have arrived blinking in the welcome light is hidden by its still waving folds. How can we retrace those steps? How can we pull back the curtain, forever, so the darkness of war does not close in on us again?

The historian's job is complicated by a paradox: People on the other side of the curtain could not, almost by definition, understand what to record. Today any high school student in a beginning nonviolence class could explain how the Degranfenried story ended as it did, in simple but scientific terms. When it happened, virtually no one who read it would have understood its significance: How "lucky" of Mrs. Degranfenried not to get shot.

We have to document, then, not just the big political events that made world peace but the changes in social structure that made it stable and, most difficult and most important, the change in consciousness that made both possible.

Let us begin in 1985—coincidentally the International Year of Peace—when something happened which electrified the Middle East: Abdul Ghaffar Khan, a close associate of Gandhi during the Mahatma's nonviolent struggles in India and now nearly a hundred, received the Nobel Peace Prize. This focused world attention on the plight of the Pathans, to dramatize whose condition Khan had gone to live in Kabul in his extreme old age. Now those rugged, enduring people, symbolized by the saintly old man who had served them through such incredible hardships, touched the awareness of the world. "Afghanistan" was no longer an abstraction, a token in the mindless game of East-West power but a living people in their own right. Though the venerable Gromyko's remark to India's foreign minister in 1983 was—as subsequent disclosures showed—perfectly true: "We are seeking a political solution," it was a truth that suddenly had to be acted on.

But the Khan prize was to have a more momentous effect even than undoing the link that bound a Soviet military presence to Afghanistan: By the nature of the award, the publicity surrounding it, and Khan Saheb's great speech when accepting it, he succeeded in raising consciousness about nonviolence at a critical juncture of history.

The first effect was felt in Nicaragua late in the same year, when stepped-up counterrevolutionary raids were foiled by volunteer international, nonviolent resistors who had been operating in Central America without a trace of world media attention since 1983.

The appearance of doggedly nonviolent, partly spontaneous, cheering, incredibly courageous men, women, and children, who would neither yield to the US-backed "contras" nor hate them made a stunning impact on news screens around the world. Dimly, the sense arose that a completely new factor had appeared on the scene of global power.

It was, of course, far from new, but it was so unkown that the world had failed to understand its potential.

So it was, at first, in Nicaragua. Seeing contra forces rush unobstructed through the border towns, "take" roads, bridges, radio stations, rounding up unresisting civilians and shooting some, how could reporters realize that the roads would still be walked on, the bridges crossed; the radio stations would refuse to broadcast premature contra victory announcements but instead, at the risk and in some cases the loss of life, encouraged the population to not cooperate at all with the invaders—in short, courage was calling the bluff of aggressive warfare.

It began to dawn on the contra leadership, the media, and the world at large that a social, not a territorial, struggle was going on, that for the first time in history (as it seemed) people who had renounced weapons but whose will to prevail was unbreakable were frustrating a superpower; as this happened, correspondents began to seek out resistance leaders who could make sense of it all. The Associated Press dispatch of *Monitor* correspondent Joseph Galvez (fresh from Khan's great acceptance speech in Stockholm), interviewing Norwegian Peace Brigader Marta Tjorberg, became a classic:

I am ready to die in the face of this injustice. I have watched little children being murdered; hate has welled up inside me, but I have not given in to it—it has become our resistance, our nonviolence. We are ready, even if the whole world ignores our struggle: We will not hate the invaders, but we will not give in to them.

But this time the world did not ignore them. Instead it began to question somewhere deep inside itself the rooted assumptions that had trapped them in the age-old system of perpetual warfare: that the only force reliably applicable in hostile relationships—and more and more relationships were becoming hostile because of the assumption itself—was destructive power, violence, that the world of 1985, as usual throughout history, was necessarily divided into East and West.

So the events of that decade began to shake the definition of power itself. It became harder to believe that "peace" would come from a decisive victory of one side over the other. When unofficial peace brigades scored further successes over both state and guerrilla terrorism in the 1990s, people began to understand that peace was not a question of victory at all—unless you meant the victory of harmonious forces latent in every individual over conflict and chaos.

From this conceptual shift emerged the hope—vague at first—that peace did not depend on some miraculous bolt from beyond, that resources for peace were "spread out upon the earth" if you but learned to see them, and most importantly that these resources could be scientifically developed. Peace was something you could work on.

Back in the 1970s an organization of American high school teachers had begun to meet with Soviet counterparts so that each could comment on the way their country was presented in the other's textbooks. It was illuminating. Soviet teachers didn't appreciate finding their country lumped together with the Nazi regime as "totalitarian"; lo and behold American teachers didn't enjoy finding themselves classified with the same regime as "imperialist." Many sobering corrections were offered on both sides, and many were implemented. . . .

So by the end of the second millennium a generation of young people in both countries was moving into careers of responsibility who had not been too severely indoctrinated with polarizing propaganda about the other state. "Evil empire" mythologies could not be sustained in this atmosphere of relative sanity, and most scholars agreed that this, too, had an inestimable effect on allowing the world to take advantage of small advances toward global peace.

That all but unknown teachers' project became, of course, the Committee of Understanding, which is now mandated by the State Department and has counterparts in every nation on the globe. I do not mean to imply the teachers' project made the difference by itself: Guest exchanges between the superpowers continued unabated even through the narrowly averted global economic chaos of the 1990s; so did official ventures like the joint crisis-control center (the "living hot line") established in that era and only recently converted to the Cultural Exchange Commission; even more so the Soviet-American famine relief teams operating first in northwest Africa, became a global volunteer force in our own decade.

But the teachers' project illustrates two important things: First, most of the peace institutions we enjoy today—legal, educational, research—began as impromptu work undertaken without official sanction by absolutely ordinary people. The same men and women volunteers who turned back the contras in Central America organized (such as they were) by Peace Brigades International or Witness for Peace found themselves in smart uniforms drawing a salary on the first unarmed peacekeeping venture of the United Nations, the Abdul Ghaffar Khan Brigade in Lebanon, whose role in bringing peace to the Mideast has been called by historian Masruwale "the first demonstration of the organizable power of nonviolence to a world prepared to understand its significance."

Second, the eventual effectiveness of any peace enterprise lies not only in what it does but also in what it symbolizes—what it teaches about possibility. Before the 105th Congress of the United States ratified GRIT, 300 disarmament scenarios had been duly published in the *Journal of Peace Research*—and duly ignored. These scenarios simply could not happen until the consciousness of enough people—the famous "paradigm shift" popular in peace movement literature of the 1980s and 1990s—accepted their reality. If the international changes bought time by obstructing war and the intrasocial changes brought a stable economic regime in which fewer causes of war arose, ultimate peace came through a change of vision.

All this work and education, then, set the stage for the so-called "miracle" of 1994. As if it were toppling unsteadily toward legitimacy, the West European (at first only West German) Green Coalition had begun actively building civilian defense networks about four years earlier—in retrospect a creative, if not brilliant response to the failure of their demonstrations against NATO military exercises in the late 1980s. Hesse, Baden-Württemberg, and West

Berlin among other regions of the Federal Republic of Germany slowly got used to the sight of green-armbanded "marshalls" of all ages scattering through the towns and countryside checking food supplies, flexing communication networks, and giving workshops on the two basic principles of social defense that Gandhi had worked out as early as 1929: total noncooperation with invading armies and uninhibited fraternization with the individual invaders as people.

Before July 1994, these teams were tolerated with amusement by "defense intellectuals" and the general public alike. Then, when it almost seemed the Greens themselves were running out of verve, the Soviets made their ill-fated—or perhaps lucky—sweep into Gdansk.

Almost before the first tank commander, Yuri Stepankov, defected and made his now-famous speech on West German television, the world realized where the invincible Poles with their hastily constructed armbands and bicycle-networks had gotten their inspiration; almost before it became clear that the invasion had not and could not impose control over that nonviolently resistant population, the world was echoing with the Green slogan: We are ready too. The catch was released which would quietly fold the European "nuclear umbrella."

Without the dogged work of ordinary people—getting the media to open its eyes, building institutions, changing habits— even this dramatic event might not have succeeded in puncturing the mythology of the arms race. With that work it meant more than the end of a gigantically destructive and dangerous cold war: It marked the beginning of the end of *war*. It meant that the *way* the cold war ended—and there was no other way—was by cracking up against a world where the dynamic of nonviolence was known.

When one sees how powerfully peace institutions work today, from our thousands of unknown Grandma Degranfenrieds to the International Court of Justice, the inevitable question is, why on earth did they wait so long? How could they skitter away in fear from the name of peace and think that highly organized violence was safe?

We have to answer this question with compassion. They stood

on the other side of a looking glass from us, trapped in a world (the "free world," as half of it ironically called itself) of dark imagery, systematically degrading the concept of the human being. Peeking into that archive of horrors people perpetrated on themselves in the name of "entertainment" and—by the mid-1980s—even of "news," one gets the queer impression of a whole people inflicting on itself a mass hypnosis of horror and negativity, as though doing everything in their power to put peace further beyond the bounds of possibility.

To sit through half an hour of "The A-Team" (a highly popular violent program of the 1980s) is to understand somewhat better why the world would atrociously expect the marine corps of a concerned superpower to bring peace to Lebanon instead of calling in the International Peace Academy (active since the early 1970s) or a Gandhian peace brigade response team.

By 1984, the National Coalition on Television Violence could show you 20,000 books and articles proving the obvious fact that watching violence makes one more violent. Judging by the *effect* of all this knowledge, they could not show you 20,000 people who had read them. Quipped one historian of the period, "Man was poisoning his mind with violence and his environment with acid rain; the only difference was he was slightly aware of the latter." It almost killed us.

It is clear that the breakthrough that occurred in the closing decades of man's second millennium—the breakthrough which saved our planet from extinction as a home for life—had a quality that resists analysis. Some historians still regard it as unaccountable: why, for example, large numbers of people began to break the bubble of media violence. Yet it was simply the result of thousands of decisions, each one made and remade and made again by perfectly ordinary people—decisions which in retrospect could have been made long ago by every one of us.

Much remains to be done. Popular pressure has forced key governments to give the International Court of Justice binding power; conscientious objection is protected by the world courts as a universal human right, but the mystique of the nation-state still remains, impeding the final transition from the old United Nations to a true global parliament based on geocultural representation, and transition to a stable world economic system awaits fulfillment. There are other problems. But the point is that we now have ways to tackle them. With global and national alternative defense in place, with a sane economic order, most of all with widespread knowledge of "the Degranfenried effect," we have turned toward peace.

The president of the United States summed it up perfectly at the inauguration of the Alternative Defense Institute:

One of my predecessors in this great office used to speak of 'Peace Through Strength.' It was a compelling, but a misleading idea. The kind of strength that phrase implies—or allows us to conceal—never brought peace and never could. Let us speak of strength through peace. Peace, that allows us to see clearly; peace, which enables us to harness our resources in the service of life; peace, in learning whose arts we come to enjoy the power of cooperation and build institutions out of love. That is the strength—the only strength—worthy of us and capable of guiding us to greatness.

It was her finest speech.

(Michael N. Nagler)

The 35th annual Jefferson lecture was delivered in the Kennedy Center yesterday by McGarratt Harriman. . . . Introducing the speaker was Dr. C. Crawford Byrd, chairman of the National Endowment for the Humanities, which sponsors the event and selects the lecturer. . . . He noted that, following a brilliant diplomatic career, including positions as ambassador to India and to China, Harriman was appointed Secretary of State in 1995, serving to the end of the century. Since his retirement he has responded to a dozen special assignments in diplomacy, the last consuming four years as US Chief Negotiator in the International Crisis Convention. Because of the impelling urgency of this year, 2010, the NEH chose Dr. Harriman to address the issues of peace. His lecture follows. . . .

This Western civilization, born in the union or reason and faith, has failed to establish a sustainable saintly community. Rather, the West has often been at its worst, dominated by materialism, secularism, and aggression. Prophets of extinction have recently hung about our periphery again like vultures. They predicted that the year 2000 would bring the modern vandals to finish off the already corrupt Western civilization.

The bombings of 1999 seemed to justify their dire doomsaying. All of us had moments between that year and this high mark of 2010 when we felt like the Londoners in World War II facing the buzz bombs. We went in search of another Churchill. . . .

As I look back over my fifty years of adult involvement with peace, I conclude that we Americans had an inheritance problem. We came out of World War II with nuclear arms. That was terrifying at first. Some experts believed we would be into World War III by 1955. There seemed to be little confidence that the so-called cold war could be contained. The polarity of communism and capitalism was fundamental, and the magnitude of the war machines in the East and West cried for exercise.

We surprised ourselves by reaching 1985 without a nuclear war. Some thinkers became convinced that nuclear weapons had created a viable self-restraint. As we went into the famous 1985 Geneva negotiations which marked forty years of East-West conventional confrontation, both the Soviets and the Americans sincerely believed the massive armed strength on each side would convince the other that a nuclear war could not be won. Military might was valued as a deterrent. We believed our own rhetoric about "peace through strength." We inherited that formula and sought no other. . . .

Doesn't this all sound senseless now? But that is how we were thinking. All of us were missing the point—focusing on the wrong issues.

Then on June 4th, 1999—you all know the rest. We just did not believe the extremists in the Third World would deal with outlaws. We could not conceive that outlaws could function like sovereigns. We ignored the crackpot ideas of a Mafia-terrorist-outlaw linkage. But it happened. We were terribly fortunate that they bungled their first drop or there would be no Israel today. An Armageddon war could have consumed the globe.

I am sobered to remember how close we came, how quickly we assumed Soviet complicity. The hot lines were our salvation. The Russian contact stopped us from falling into an old trap. Just as the extreme nationalists in Croatia and Serbia tricked the Germans and Russians into fighting World War I for them and creating Yugoslavia as a by-product, so the wild men of the Middle East intended to trip the Soviet-American trigger and cause a superpower war. Then, amid the chaos, they thought they could redraw the map of the Middle East according to their fanaticism.

You will recall that it took us four whole days to figure out who the so-called Brethren were, weeks longer to unravel the motivations and intrigues, and years to thwart their surprise detonations. Tempers burst, righteous indignation fulminated. But we gambled on supporting the Egyptian-Saudi-Iraqi-Jordanian initiative. The attempt to draw the East and the West into the oil-fueled religious struggle was thwarted, but only after four more senseless explosions.

What we learned from that first blast in the Mediterranean was that the West and the East needed each other, immediately. But it took us ten full years to institutionalize that mutual dependence. The five explosions that punctuated the first decade of this millennium served to intensify fear and promote doom. In actuality the closure of the Mediterranean mobilized us to sensibility. The environmental damage throughout the Middle East was catastrophic, and we do not fully know what the fallout consequences will be elsewhere. The loss of life has been small in contrast to the possibilities, but it serves as a graphic warning. We now no longer question the weakness of our state systems and the fragility of civilization. We know the climate-altering impact of hydrogen bombs is real, not just alarmism. We have seen our own annihilation defy our best preventions.

Now to conclude, I wish to underscore the principles of the peace just completed. If I have learned anything in this fifty years of wandering in peace conferences and on battlefields, it is this: The issues that peace conferences settle are not the real problems. We have just concluded a conference and a decade of deadly incidents. (We don't fight wars anymore, we just face cataclysmic incidents.) We feel the treaty will halt the dangers of international outlaw terrorism. I underscore the point: That is not the real issue. What led to the terrorist blackmail was an indulgence in ideology, self-justification, and crusading for dogma. It took over in the East and the West. It infected Islam. It polarized Latin America. It decimated Asia. Our minds were occupied with dogma. We could not creatively consider alternatives.

Now we have been forced together. . . . What I hope to establish in all minds is what this peace is about. It is about timeless ethical principles.

Those of us who went through the tensions of Camp David II and of the Malta Conference, those who were driven from Geneva by terrorists, those who met under the sea for four weeks of total isolation, know one thing—that the Thermidore now growing in the Kremlin and now firmly revived in Beijing is a solid base but can erode. The humility forced on us in the West is beneficial but can soon be forgotten.

As we talked informally in those close quarters under the sea each night, we made more progress than we did at the formal sessions. The fortunate idea to confine us all on that tiny undersea laboratory was our breakthrough. . . . The undersea confinement served for us as the concentration camps served for Paul-Henri Charles Spaak, Robert Schuman, and Konrad Adenauer. We knew we had to bury old animosities; they were paralyzing us. If those men could create the Common Market and European unity from the ruins of 1945, we could also look for a common life. In those all-night voluntary "happenings," we came to realize that our daytime structures about trade formulas, Third World equalizing formulas, space station sharing, energy banks, and superparliaments were resting on two common principles.

The first is mutual vulnerability. This peace is firm today only because no country can ever again be invulnerable. Like the Maginot line in World War II, no defense system has or can prevent an attack. We know we cannot endure an East-West split. We know we need each other, not out of idealism but the reality of saving each other from the abyss. We now know that the Russians and Americans and Chinese actually saved each other. No one can mount a defense technology that is secure. To believe the contrary is simply an illusion, one that has been popped.

Ironically we are on the same ground that Metternich discovered, also from weakness, in 1815. We are on the ground of mutual vulnerability. We are all mortal, all flawed. There is no disguising ourselves. No ideology will save us. Nothing is absolutely secure.

Secondly, we have done some tough thinking about ethics. We talked for hours about Marcus Aurelius on the Roman battlefields, with whom we felt a grave kinship. He said, "Do not do anything unless you can seriously recommend all men to do it." That seems like the answer to Machiavelli's maxim that the Prince's duty is war and only war. That guided us to move beyond militarism, beyond national self-interest, not against it but beyond it. We are on firm ground, hard won. We are not thinking of utopia. We are not dreaming of a Kellogg-Briand Pact to outlaw war or a Holy Alliance to treat all men as brothers. We know self-interest will survive. We know there will be new outlaws. We know that greed will continue. We know we are all vulnerable. We have no illusions. We have been beyond the brink and have gotten back only by a miracle. The miracle was the bungling of the terrorists. That may not come a second time.

We shall meet regularly in such isolation to keep thinking about classical ethics and Christian ethics and Islamic ethics and Hindu ethics and Buddhist ethics. No negotiator will be allowed in the core council who has not been subjected to hundreds of hours of isolation with other negotiators, informally, beyond contact for instructions. Only as statesmen are forced to go beyond instructions, beyond sovereignty, beyond despair will they keep this peace alive. This is not just an institution, it is a process.

I believe we have laid the foundation for an enduring peace because all our glib answers failed us. The Marxist ones failed and the capitalist ones too, even the Muslim ones. We have all been humbled, we have all failed. We have been forced into teachability. We have hammered out a workable framework of peace, and we know we have no other choice.

2010 has seen mankind grope to something sublime, pragmatically sublime because we know that man is not the measure of all things. We cannot worship science or self or security. But we are determined to survive for a diversity of higher purposes. And we will.

(Douglas D. Alder)

The past twenty-five years have seen one of the greatest changes in human history and one which everyone will agree is enormously for the better. Large-scale war has virtually ceased to be a problem, though there are still minor eruptions in small areas in different parts of the world. A large part of the world war industry has been transformed into the production of civilian goods, particularly those which are significant for raising the productivity and real incomes of the poor of the world. Population control has spread so widely, coupled with an improvement in soil management, so that virtually every country in the world can now feed itself, either through its own food production or by exchanging goods for the food surpluses of others. The specter of famine has largely disappeared. Nobody expected this to happen in 1984. Indeed, the probability of its happening was then quite small, and the probability of almost total catastrophe in nuclear war and nuclear winter and local catastrophes due to population explosion and political incompetence seemed high enough to be very alarming. For our future generations, it is important to record how this extraordinary change happened.

It began, perhaps, in 1985 with a manifesto, the origins of which, strangely enough, are not too well known. It seems to have originated with a small group of people around the world associated with the United Nations University. The title is *A Call to Human Maturity in a New Region of Time,* and it begins with the ringing words, "The human race has now passed into a new region of time." The full text of the manifesto follows.

The human race has now passed into a new region of time. Time has regions, as well as space. When we cross the seashore from the land into the sea, we enter a different biological region, an almost entirely different set of species. There are no elephants in the sea or whales on the land. Similarly, we pass from one region of time into another, across the threshold of birth into life, across the dark river that is death. Families, nations, churches, whole cultures pass from one region of time to another, where the future is very different from the past. The number 2010 is counted from one of these. The year 2000 may have marked the crossing into a new region of time in which the future will be so different from the past that the patterns and regularities of the past will not be much guide to it.

We can trace the origins of these time boundaries in the past to the great transition that marked the beginning of the twenty-first century. Rivers can be traced back to their origin from the seashore, as persons reaching their maturity at twenty-one, a slightly magic number, can trace their origins back to childhood and birth. Yet that maturation, which the twenty-first century represents for the human race, all so often happens quickly. This great transition can be traced back to the rise of science as a human enterprise, perhaps 500 years. This enormous increase in human knowledge led increasingly to the world becoming a single system in communication, trade, and weaponry. Even a thousand years ago the Mayan Empire could collapse without Charlemagne in Europe or the emperor of China ever hearing about it. But today an event anywhere in the world is flashed to every part of it almost instantaneously.

The long childhood of the human race has culminated in two developments which will end that childhood or end the human race. One is the nuclear weapon and the long-range missile; the other is uncontrolled population expansion and the increasing use of exhaustible resources. The first is the most immediate and the most dangerous. National defense has now become the greatest enemy, not only of national security but also of the human race itself. It is true that we have maintained stable nuclear deterrence for nearly forty years, but it is a mathematically certain proposition that deterrence cannot be stable in the long run. If it were stable, if the probability of nuclear weapons going off were zero, they would not deter anybody. The stability of deterrence in the short run necessitates its eventual breakdown, which in this case could well be the end of the human race or even of the whole evolutionary experiment on this planet. Fortunately, there has been another movement in the last 150 years which can give us an alternative to national defense, This is the movement for national security through stable peace. This began, perhaps, after 1815 in Sweden and Denmark and spread to North America after about 1870. Now we have a great triangle of stable peace stretching from Japan to Australia, across North America to Western Europe, with about eighteen countries who have no intention whatever of going to war with each other. The main reason for this is that they have individually decided that their national boundaries are not worth changing except by mutual agreement, which is almost the only necessary condition for stable peace. It also implies, of course, the mutual recognition of national sovereignty within existing boundaries. As yet we do not have stable peace between the Soviet Union and the United States, but there is nothing to prevent either country from having a deliberate and public national policy to create national security through stable peace. Up to now stable peace has been rather accidental, the result of a number of decisions that could easily have gone the other way. Now is the time to make it a deliberate choice of policy. We have to turn enemies into opponents, threats into therapy, armaments into mutual dependence through civilian trade.

The simple idea that we are entering a new region of time somehow caught the imagination of people all over the world. The religious organizations picked it up, a wave of mass celebrations spread through the world, even into the communist countries, and the idea that something new was happening gradually penetrated to the politicians and political leaders. In 1987 the United Nations, as a symbol, held a major conference in Westphalia in Germany on the New Region of Time. It was argued that when one enters a new region of time, one does not learn much from the immediate past but looks over the whole past of human history to find parallels and episodes which correspond in some way to what is happening now. The episode that was seized on as a symbol was the Peace of Westphalia of 1648, which ended the major religious wars in Europe by mutual agreement to set the religious boundaries and not to disturb them. It was argued that this was what we had to do now between the communist world and the capitalist world. A political agreement, in effect, said, "Let us each do our own experiment for a hundred years and see where we are." The superpowers were rather shy about this at first, but constant pressure made the idea seem more and more respectable.

The next step was an agreement between the Soviet Union and the United States, devised at a summit meeting of the new president of the United States with the new leader of the Soviet Union, which produced an agreement to exchange 50,000 children of the military and powerful decision makers of each country in the boarding schools and colleges of the other. This proposal, made by several people in the 1970s, finally caught the attention of the president of the United States as a way, first, to make it much more difficult to push the button that would precipitate nuclear war when one's own children were going to be the first to die, and second, to produce much great knowledge of each culture by the potentially powerful citizens of the other country. . . .

A movement which undoubtedly contributed to the general change in human consciousness which made stable peace possible was the "image exploration" movement, which developed in the mid-1980s as a result of the spread of cheap and portable home computers. A program on image exploration designed to assist two or three people exploring the images in the other minds in a great variety of facets became extraordinarily popular. The idea behind it was that each person's mind is a vast landscape of images—memories, ideas, and so on—which another person could explore almost as a tourist and so add to the delights and complexities of the explorer's mind. This began almost as entertainment, but it spread rapidly among the political elites of the world who had access to computers, coupled with some programs for assistance in negotiation. It had an extraordinary effect in diminishing the misunderstanding of people of different cultures, ideologies, religions, and so on, which had plagued the human race for so long. Understanding, of course, did not always lead to approval, and in some cases conflict was actually intensified by these devices, but so much conflict was a result of misunderstanding that the overall effect was undoubtedly beneficial and particularly changed the whole atmosphere of international negotiation, diplomacy, and so on. . . .

(Kenneth E. Boulding)

7

Action Groups

A change of consciousness can itself lead to new approaches to the peace process. One particular way in which a change of consciousness can be positive is in its igniting actions, sometimes by only one person in the beginning, that engage whole groups in the quest for peace.

One of the three winners in the *Monitor's* peace contest wrote an essay describing a process initiated by an individual that grew to become a kind of action group. The writer of the essay, *Thomas Fehsenfeld,* a businessman in Grand Rapids, Michigan, did not accept the idea that permanent peace was a realistic goal, because he could not envision a time when the various groups of mankind would not have some conflicting goals. Instead, he saw the possibility of successful conflict management through the pursuit of whatever areas of commonality did exist between the two superpowers.

The founder of his eventual computer networking system, a fictional John McConnell, said during a television interview in 2010, "It seemed to me that we were working backward. Our government was working very hard to make agreements with a government we didn't like or trust. . . . I had begun to look at the United States and the

Soviet Union as partners in the survival of the world." When McConnell first aired his views to a Congressional committee, computer networking was tried as the most efficient means of sharing ideas among busy people. But this was soon seen to have one other positive advantage. "It turned out that by using the computer network, ideas were detached from ego . . . . Participants would come and go, adding their perspectives and experience. A kind of natural selection took place until we began to distill an approach to conflict which was unique and which worked."

Fehsenfeld's essay had more than this to it. It was his pragmatic approach to peacemaking that caught the eye of the judges, and because his essay was a winner, it is printed in its entirety here. You will see that the action group had open access to all who had ideas to share, until it had almost 20,000 active members in the 1990s.

Michael Harbottle, of London (already mentioned in chapter 3), described a process that began with interested individuals in similar fields getting together to share their ideas. Harbottle himself was chief of staff of the UN force in Cyprus from 1966 to 1968 and is currently a university lecturer in peace studies. Noting that the peace movement beginning in Europe in the late 1970s had only limited effectiveness, he wrote that "a new dimension was needed if the efficacy and credibility of the peace movement was to be sustained." Small groups of people began to promote what he calls "people's détente." "They were convinced that only by creating communication links covering the whole spectrum of society of both Western and Eastern Europe could there be any possibility of changing attitudes and perceptions."

A very American approach to peace came from *Dan Baker,* president of Eurocal, Inc., a California business. The approach was American in the sense that Baker conceived of a private corporation, Peace, Inc., whose sole goal was to achieve peace. "They were a small group of California businessmen who felt that when the masses dearly want something and that something is not being delivered to them, what you have is a market. In this case the world wanted some relief from the almost inevitable nuclear war." The group began by lobbying Congress and setting up a new organization, the Conflict and Mass Destruction Weapon Elimination Agency, which was funded with 10 percent of all the funds earmarked for weapons spending. Exactly how the private corporation eventually made the money that paid handsome peace dividends (in dollars) is not entirely clear, but the public relations cum business management approach to peace will not be unfamiliar to students of American business. While it is easy to criticize the essay for being naive about the Soviet system and the reasons other approaches to détente have been frustrated thus far, it is not an idea that one can say has been tried or that could be dismissed out of hand if it were tried. Incidentally, Baker wrote in his cover letter, "Thank you for the opportunity to contribute to world survival. Parts for planets are very hard to come by."

There are peace groups already at work, and the contest brought entries from many members of these as well. *Klaus Heinemann,* president of Eloret Corporation in Sunnyvale, California, and his son, *Joerg Heinemann,* wrote a joint essay taking off on the work of the Beyond War movement. From the perspective of 2010, they say:

As recently as twenty-five years ago, statesmen of the two largest nations on earth treated each other as antagonists—one spoke of the other as the enemy, the evil empire to be eradicated; there was not even agreement that the two had to coexist. We look back on this with a sense of disbelief. How far have we come since then, since those awakening appeals to the human intellect and common sense?

In their essay, they show the steps by which the Beyond War thinking began to demilitarize the entire world.

The League of Women voters is not known as a world

peace interest group, but one pair of writers seized on the league as the ideal forum from which to promote peace. *Ellen Meyer*, who worked at the Nuclear Negotiation Project at Harvard Law School, and *Mark Sarkady*, executive director of Spacebridge, Inc., an organizer of teleconferences, used the vehicle of the league to develop a peace dialogue—first, among diverse groups in the United States, and second, between paired cities in the United States and the Soviet Union. Although one may have to cross a line of disbelief or suspend one's belief to envision a Soviet audience teleconferencing with an American one, it is this ability to envision positive change that will in some way have to be made concrete if today's status quo is to change.

Because of an alteration in public mood, the Geneva arms control talks currently going on were changed in 1988 to the Common Security talks. The essay is written in the form of a classroom dialogue, and a student asks:

In 1988, President Reagan was leaving office. Is this when he announced the goal of "peace in the year 2000"?
Lecturer Yes . . . . It was the commitment to peace that he made with the bipartisan group "Peace 2000" that proved to be the true impetus to advancing the talks. Reagan set a tone that matched the mood of the country. Much like Kennedy's commitment to put a person on the moon in ten years, there was now a year by which people expected there would be peace between the two superpowers.

One writer from West Germany, *Bruno Leuschner*, of Schwenningen, envisioned an organization of writers who decided consciously to promote and serve the cause of peace in their published works. They are led by three Latin Americans, who decide that all literature should be R-rated—R, not for restricted, but for responsibility.

The idea caught fire immediately. Naturally, many literary critics set up a hue and cry as to how anyone could postulate such

an unaesthetic writing principle, but to a certain degree they
were swept aside. On the contrary, critics very soon began to
review books according to the presence of the "R" factor, an
entirely unique situation, for it is really an unliterary principle.

From a group of renowned writers we pass to an individual woman in Chicago for the last essay in this group.
Joan Kufrin's essay portrays an anguished American
woman who writes to her Russian "sister." Out of her
poignant letter comes a response that also requires one to
bridge one's disbelief for a moment. Within months, the
letter of this one woman ends up in millions of letters
being delivered to the doorsteps of the White House and
the Kremlin.

One word about these action groups. What each group
does is independent of the other. Unlike political scenarios, we do not have to take our pick and walk down
one fateful road. That fact gives a degree of strength to
these scenarios that none may possess entirely on its own.
It is quite possible to say that none of them work, that the
problem is more intractable than the optimistic or idealistic Americans who write these scenarios are able to conceive. That could be the case. But there is a compelling
quality about these group action approaches. Americans
have been used to solving many other serious problems
through organizing for their solution. And what should
be borne in mind here is that *all* these approaches could
be tried without one of them getting in the way of the
others.

One can conceive of Fehsenfeld's idea of peace networking by means of computers. At the same time the
professional interest groups Harbottle writes about can
have their meetings and their influence—if not in the
Soviet Union, at least in many countries besides the
United States. A group of private citizens could get together, as in Peace, Inc., and through a media blitz create
the climate for setting aside government funds to invest

directly in the cause of peace. At the same time, organizations such as the Beyond War movement could continue to change thinking and engage in experiments to affect thinking in countries other than the United States about the futility of war and, even more important, the futility of the false divisions among mankind that lead to wars. The League of Women Voters could begin holding teleconferences to explore the possibility of greater understanding, first domestically and then with our potential adversary. Writers may never band together to promote peace in all their literary output, but enough of them may decide the times are critical enough for them to devote their energies to writing about the moral dilemmas faced by mankind and suggesting scenarios in which morality leads the world forward. As for the lonely woman in Chicago, the Soviet system may not be waiting for her to start her letter-writing campaign, but what may become a barrage of letters started as the sincere voice of one individual, and it is entirely believable that there is someone alive today who is going to do something as effective as that letter-writer did.

If one takes all these examples of group action, or what eventually became group action, one sees that, unlike political courses of action, all these approaches could be tried simultaneously. Although one can argue that a particular approach is naive or that no approach would fully work, one thing seems unarguable: if all these approaches were going on at the same time, the climate for a resolution of misunderstandings would be so vastly improved that it would take a very hard-headed realist to claim that the equation for peace had not changed.

There was, in these as well as many other fine essays submitted to *The Christian Science Monitor*, a degree of naiveté about the Soviet system. If they were not exactly reminiscent of the feeling Franklin Roosevelt allegedly had at one point in World War II about being able to deal with "Uncle Joe" much as he would with a Tammany ward boss in New York, there was often the unexpressed sentiment that at the base of our difficulties with the Russians there is merely misunderstanding.

What if the United States under Ronald Reagan really does understand the Russians? What if they don't respond to anything but force or threats of force? What if the Soviets really do understand the threat that the freedoms practiced in the West pose to their controlled society and will take any measures to protect their perceived security interests from Western encroachment? What if they see Western, and particularly US, commercial successes around the world in much the same light as the West sees the Soviets' control of their satellites?

The writers of these essays expressed the quintessential American belief that all problems are solvable if people would only try hard enough to solve them. And, in the end, trying hard enough may just not *be* enough. Optimism may fail us. But were the essayists not also expressing a futher belief, summed up in the Beyond War movement's frequent quotation of Albert Einstein that "the splitting of the atom has changed everything—save our modes of thinking." It *is* time, these writers are saying, to make the leap to a larger consciousness of humanity. Someone must try fitting a new lens on the world if that world is ever to come into focus as reality. They are the vanguard.

It is not surprising that this nation of successful immigrants should still have some buoyancy and optimism. What is difficult for the official policymakers is to distinguish good ideas coming from the outside from sheer mushiness. Action groups are certainly not foreign to the American experience. The abolitionists had a long history before they became a major political group. In the 1960s, civil rights groups forced change on the nation's institutions in Washington. Whether action groups can have the same effect in dealing with issues that arise largely from outside a country's borders is another matter. It also must be of concern to policymakers that action groups whose opinions are based on faulty knowledge or on mere sentiment could do more harm than good. Even with all these provisos, however, one wonders how far group actions such as those in this chapter can, and probably are going to, change the environment for peace.

The following is an excerpt from the online conference "Peace in Our Time," which was held on the MacroNet Educational Network, May 17, 2010.

MN There has been a great transformation in international relations during the past twenty-five years. During most of the twentieth century, nations looked on war as a terrible but necessary part of international relations. War and threats of war were their final resort when diplomacy had broken down.

In the short span of twenty-five years, this view has almost disappeared from the world. Military budgets worldwide have dropped to one-tenth their twentieth century levels (figures adjusted for deflation). The incidence of war has dropped to 0.25 wars per year from the twentieth century level of 1.5 per year.

Another measure of this change is that wars, when they do occur, have become less deadly. The last war to claim 100,000 victims was the Iran/Iraq war of the 1980s. Most wars today are settled quickly with the loss of less than 1000 lives.

To help us understand this great change, we have invited Dr. John McConnell to join our conference. Welcome Dr. McConnell.

McC   Thank you.

MN   You played an important part in the changes that helped establish our current "peace system." Could you explain how the McConnell network was established?

McC   First, I have to disagree with your statement that what we now have is a "peace system." We have as many conflicts as ever between nations—it might be more accurate to say that we have a "conflict-management system." Peace, after all, is not something that humanity naturally seeks.

MN It would seem that everyone seeks peace—statesmen are continually talking about it.

McC Of course they talk about it, but peace has very little to do with life, which is full of conflict. Nations seek prestige, wealth, power, and security. They look for peace only when the wolf is at the door and usually find that the wolf is not very interested in peace.

MN Isn't this merely a semantic quibble?

McC No. Peace is a transitory condition. It is a (usually short) "era of good feelings" between nations. Continual peace is neither possible nor desirable because it is through conflict that ideals are tested and either reaffirmed or changed.

Conflict management, on the other hand, is a very realistic goal. It allows conflicts to develop and find resolution but directs them away from violence.

Our goal with the so-called McConnell network was to find strategies that would allow for conflicts of national interests, but keep them from erupting into violence. In certain instances we found that conflicts had to be encouraged in the short run to keep them from festering into total conflicts.

MN What is the meaning of "total conflict"?

McC It was a phrase we coined to describe those conflicts in which the only perceived solution is the destruction of the opponent. One of the most famous total conflicts were the many wars between Rome and Carthage which ended in the total destruction of Carthage. Our conflicts with the Soviets were at one time seen as total.

MN Returning to the McConnell network, please describe how it was formed, how it functioned, and some of the ideas it developed.

McC It began during the mid-1980s when there were serious questions about humanity's survival. I had been working for several years at the Russian Studies Institute of the University of Michigan and had published an article questioning our approach to relations with the Soviets.

It seemed to me that we were working backward. Our government was working very hard to make agreements with a government we didn't like or trust. This was bound to fail.

MN   This is what you called the "fallacy of legality."

McC   Yes. I had begun to look at the United States and the Soviet Union as partners in the survival of the world. When you have a partner you trust and respect, you can carry on your business on a handshake. On the other hand, when two partners have a poor relationship, when they are continually jockeying for advantage, then no contract is sufficient. Any agreement devised by the mind of man can be circumvented by the mind of man.

I suggested that we had to find ways to improve the underlying relationship between us. If we did this, agreements would be much easier to conclude—in fact, such an improvement would make many agreements unnecessary.

MN   How would it make agreements unnecessary?

McC   Well, for instance, we did not need agreements with France to limit their nuclear stockpiles because we were confident that they had no intention of aiming their missiles at us.

Our underlying relationship with France was one of sympathy and respect (although they often frustrated us). War between us was "unthinkable" in spite of frequent conflicts.

MN   What specific proposals did you make?

McC   The article contained about a dozen low cost steps we could make to improve our underlying relations. I listed them not because they were great ideas, but simply to illustrate that once you focused on the underlying relationship instead of the legalities, it was easy to find ways.

Some of the things suggested were the establishment of a joint US/USSR trade center with a database to aid in matching products and markets, a jointly financed and operated space station, diplomatic restraint when we were not directly involved in a problem created by the Soviets (we had a tendency at the time to take over other nations' problems with the Soviets and make them our own).

MN   What happened next?

McC   In spite of being a simple idea, the article was a success. It happened to get picked up by a couple of liberal senators looking for a new idea. Liberals were on the run at the time and fresh out of new ideas.

They liked it because it gave them an approach to the Soviet Union which was not belligerent, nor did it suggest sacrificing our national interest just to nail down formal agreements—something the conservatives had accused them of.

As a result of the article, I was asked to testify before the Senate Foreign Relations Committee and got some publicity. This helped me to make contacts which led to the formation of the New Relations Working Group, which the media called the McConnell network.

MN   How was it organized?

McC   I had some initial meetings with members of Congress and people in the administration who were interested in further discussions on our relations with the Soviets, but being busy people, no one had time for meetings so we formed a computer network to exchange views. That was not so common then as it is today.

MN   Did that mode work well for you?

McC   Yes. It was fascinating to watch the ideas develop—it worked almost as a group mind. It turned out that by using the computer network ideas were detached from ego. They were thrown into the database without anyone caring if they survived or not.

Ideas would build into theories almost effortlessly. Participants would come and go, adding their perspectives and experience. A kind of natural selection took place until we began to distill an approach to conflict which was unique and which worked.

MN   Please describe some of your conclusions.

McC   We began with Soviet/American relations because almost every national conflict at that time was cast in the light of the overall East/West conflict.

If Somalia was being armed by the Soviets, we would send arms to Ethiopia—if Ethiopia had a revolution and jumped into the Soviet camp, we would begin arming the Somalis. It was crazy.

Many leaders of Third World nations understood this, of course. They played off the superpowers to enrich themselves and were showered with an incredible amount of sophisticated weaponry. Our weapons and the Soviets' fueled every war during the last half of the twentieth century.

Moreover, every strategy tried since World War II to control this mounting conflict had failed. The United Nations failed—it became a forum that created and intensified conflicts, the arms-control process had failed—each new agreement left us with higher levels of armaments, détente had failed—each side was left feeling betrayed because there was never a common understanding of what détente meant. Nothing seemed to work.

MN   And yet solutions were there.

McC   Yes, they were. But at the time, the people who wanted a better relationship with the Soviets kept pushing the same failed solutions. They wanted a United Nations that "worked" or another arms agreement which would be obsolete with the next breakthrough or a freeze of nuclear weapons at ridiculously high levels.

Our group took a different tack. A consensus emerged that we should focus on measures that would improve the underlying relationship (as my initial article had). A second point was that America could take many steps without any formal agreement that would improve this relationship. We developed a strategy of "irresistible opportunity."

MN   What did you mean by that?

McC   We looked at actions we could take which would draw the Soviets into the world economy and world culture exchange without threatening their identity. Ways were explored in which the ruble could be turned into a hard currency, for instance, to facilitate their entry into world trade on an equal basis with other countries. We thought that this would be an irresistible opportunity for them because their economy was ailing.

We also looked at our own defense policy to find ways of improving our relationship. We suggested many actions which might make our defense posture less threatening to them without endangering our own security. There were a whole range of actions which we called by the name of "minimum assured deterrence." The basic idea was that we should have the minimum amount of force available to protect ourselves. Holding excess force in reserve tends to look threatening from the other side and draws a response which leads to escalation. We sought actions that we could take unilaterally to deescalate the arms race.

Eventually, as some of these proposals were adopted, they created an irresistible opportunity for the Soviets to lower their own spending on arms.

MN   What made your approach different from other groups that were making these types of proposals at the time? Why did your group receive a hearing and eventually have some of its ideas adopted?

McC   There were two ways in which we were different. First, we were an open group in which anyone who had access to a computer terminal could participate. All earlier attempts had been made by narrow, usually elite groups which did not build widespread support.

Second, we decided early in our endeavor that it was not enough to think up new ideas and make logical arguments for them. There was a wise old politician who joined our group, George Winslow. He continually asked of each idea, "Who has the power to implement this? How could they be motivated to do so?" It was fine to argue about what should be, but if no one could find an answer to George's questions, the idea was dropped.

MN   Was it Mr. Winslow who came up with the idea of "a program, a constituency, a coalition"?

McC Yes. After we had answered his questions about who had the power to implement the idea or program, we could ask what groups in our society would benefit by its implementation and what groups could influence the policymaker. We then searched for a way to create a coalition between them to get the job done. This approach worked very well.

We had to carry it one step further, of course, and ask which groups would be opposed to such a change and how their opposition could be dealt with.

MN Especially the armed forces and their suppliers?

McC The military-industrial complex is what we called it then. They had to be dealt with. In a pluralistic society such as ours, you could not simply advocate ideas which would put many hundreds of thousands out of a job. New missions had to be found for them. Luckily, there were many missions available for brave and dedicated people.

When you said that military budgets have dropped to one-tenth their twentieth-century level, you were technically correct. But as everyone knows, we still have a very large army. They are simply performing nonmilitary missions. Every school kid knows about President Andrews' West Point speech of 1993 in which he said, "For 200 years, you have defended the republic and the Constitution. Now you must defend the Earth itself."

The ecological disasters of the late 1980s were the main motivation in this change. And the reforestation of the Sahara by the American Army was one of its finest hours.

Today, the American services are widely respected and welcomed around the world for their contributions to preserving the ecosystem and aiding in the construction of transportation and communications systems. Their scientific work on the seas and in space is providing us with greater understanding of our world and our place in it.

MN How could a simple computer network gain so much influence?

McC Numbers. We simply recruited and recruited. At its height in the early 1990s, we had almost 20,000 active members who participated in discussions and the building of a database on conflict management. This in itself was a powerful forum for new ideas.

Equally important were the many groups which used the network. Many politicians (both liberals and conservatives) mined our database to find ideas and new directions. President Andrews' campaign statement that, "The Republicans have thrown money at our security problems, but have not made us more secure," was picked up on one of our online conferences.

Politicians are in the business of winning elections—maximizing their votes. When they joined our network, they had an important resource that they could use to find the facts they needed or test ideas (sometimes anonymously). Quite often they put out appeals for money on the network as well.

It also spawned many businesses. The conflict-management industry did not exist twenty-five years ago. Now, of course, there are thousands of firms offering conflict-management services and many of them began with conversations on our network. Now there are many conflict-management databases available, expert systems programs, consulting groups, conflict-resolution centers. They deal with anything from family disputes to labor/management problems, to international relations. Even the socialist countries have established similar institutions.

MN   Didn't the commercial nature of the network cause a split during the 1990s?

McC   Yes. Many of those who were grounded in the old peace movement felt that there was something immoral about making money on conflict management. I and many others argued that it was important for people to be able to earn a living in this line of work. After all, people had been earning a living on war for thousands of years. Why not on peace?

The dominant culture of America is business. It has been since the Civil War. We had to turn conflict management into a business or it would have remained forever on the sidelines.

Those who disagree formed the Satyagraha network, which

deals mainly with philosophical and religious approaches to peace. They perform a valuable function and most competent conflict managers keep in touch with their ideas.

MN   Where does the conflict management movement go from here?

McC   There is a growing awareness that we must move beyond conflict management. The companies which specialize only in conflict management are facing a shrinking market because their techniques are now so widely known and applied. People are becoming better managers of their own conflicts.

The most progressive companies are developing approaches to emphasize the constructive uses of conflict. After all, once the connection between conflict and violence is broken, it can be a very creative experience.

MN   Thank you, Dr. McConnell.

McC   Thank you.

(Thomas Fehsenfeld)

. . . I suppose that the seeds of change first began to take root in 1985 at the beginning of American President Ronald Reagan's second term of office. The confrontation between the two military alliances of NATO and the Warsaw Pact had never been more acute, and international scientists were claiming that the odds against a nuclear war breaking out had come down from 100:1 to 10:1. There had never been a more urgent need for new and imaginative initiatives in arms control and disarmament negotiations or a more crucial moment in the world's history for the superpowers and their allies to rethink their perceptions of peace and reshape geopolitical perspectives which had previously been based on the belief that each threatened the other with annihilation. . . .

It was therefore an encouragement that as 1984 ended, there were indications that America and the Soviet Union were seeking a rapprochement and a resumption of the arms control talks which had been in abeyance for nearly a year. It looked as if a first step in normalization was about to be taken; but, although on the surface some improvement resulted, the underlying fear and distrust remained, and until that had been removed or at least reduced, there seemed little likelihood of progress toward peace. By this time, political diplomacy at leadership level had been at a virtual standstill for a decade, and there appeared to be little chance of exchanges being renewed without confidence first being restored.

This vacuum needed to be filled. The initiative to do so came from the peace movement, which had risen from its dormant state in 1979 and had been responsible over the next five years for a marked change in public opinion which challenged the way in which international affairs were dominated by defense policies and the ever-escalating arms race. But after five years of demonstrations and protest, a new dimension was needed if the efficacy and credibility of the peace movement was to be sustained. It was this dimension which proved to be the inspiration for the new, imaginative initiative which was to become the cornerstone of the peaceful coexistence structure we know today.

This far-reaching initiative had modest beginnings. Small groups of people came together to promote what came to be called "people's détente." They were convinced that only by creating communication links covering the whole spectrum of society of both Western and Eastern Europe could there be any possibility of changing attitudes and perceptions. Reconciliation of differences can come about only through person-to-person relationships, and this was what a "people's détente" was all about. The groups recognized that ideological differences, more than anything else, posed the biggest obstacle to attitudinal change. Therefore, if there was to be positive dialogue, the differences had to be recognized and not allowed to obstruct the course of the dialogue. In order to avoid any possibility of the initiative foundering on the rocks of ideology, the plan was to develop an interprofessional, interdisciplinary, and "common interest" interaction. This provided a common base for working on specific projects, sharing expertise and experience which, in turn, created mutual confidence among themselves and the general public.

An international group of physicians set the example in 1981 when they shared their concerns regarding the dangers and effects of nuclear war. Created on the initiative of two eminent physicians, one American and one Russian, this group has continued to hold annual conferences which bring together an ever-increasing number of doctors. Following this example, a group of retired NATO and Warsaw Pact generals met in Vienna in 1984. They exchanged views on the growing threat of nuclear war and its consequences on East-West relations. Their exchanges dealt with confidence-building measures in both the military and political fields and the question of alternative strategies of defense as a move toward greater European security. They promoted the concept of Europe as a Continent of Peace for which all European countries would be responsible. This concept long outlived the "dialogue of generals" and became a major factor in achieving the peace we have today. Other interprofessional dialogues followed in which former diplomats, newspaper editors and their radio/TV counterparts, educational authorities, and many others met and interacted. Scientists and churchmen were joined by businessmen and industrialists in seeking common ground and developing common interests. In the last fifteen years of the twentieth century, the extent of the dialogue was far-reaching.

Besides these interprofessional and interdisciplinary exchanges, other common interest groups all over the world came together with practical projects which were to benefit many. A group of English psychologists successfully collaborated with the Institute for Conductive Education in Hungary in the treatment of spina bifida/spastic children and other victims of nervous diseases. The method was adopted in other countries and eventually was incorporated into the curriculum of the United Nations University of Peace as a new approach to cross-cultural understanding. Similarly with the environment. Guided by the UN Environmental Program, young people undertook a wide series of tasks: monitoring pollution, engaging in antierosion projects, planting trees, cleaning up rivers, coming to respect the environment and one another. It began in the International Year of Youth 1985 and has since become common practice. One might say in all truth that young people led the way. They set an example in an ongoing program of activity that continued through the 1986 Year of Peace and the 1987 Year of Shelter for the Homeless. Today we enjoy an environmental regeneration thanks to those initiatives taken twenty-five years ago which, as a result of international cooperation and coordination, saved our planet from an ecological holocaust.

This practical expression of concern and program of activity, which helped to build bridges of communication over a wide field of mutual interest, has been a triumph for holistic thinking. The United Nations in 2001 established a Program of Common Interests, which assists young people of all nations to benefit from these exchanges. Those of us who took part in the early years of this initiative can vouch for the fact that it was the "doing," not just the "speaking," which created the understanding and trust on which peace has been founded. . . .

(Brigadier Michael Harbottle)

Barry Jacobs was watching the evening news and opening the day's mail. He had a lot of reasons to be happy: The business was doing well, the renaissance was getting better and better, and his two children were happily planning their lives with confidence and enthusiasm. 2009 had been a good year. . . . One of the letters addressed to him was a dividend notice from Peace, Inc. He opened it and noted the surprising dividend amount and a short reminder that he was invited to a stockholders' celebration of the tenth anniversary of the nuclear-weapon-free world. He noted they still held special reservations for the First-Thousand Club. That was the first thousand stockholders to buy stock in that crazy company back in 1985. He was actually number 786, and his name is still on that slab of stainless steel on which they engraved the names of the stockholders. It was a crazy little gimmick that they used to get people to buy stock. They would engrave your name on a stainless steel block, so in case there was a nuclear exchange, at least the names of those who tried to prevent it were preserved for posterity. It's funny though; that little gimmick meant something to Barry. At that time the world didn't seem to stand a chance of survival. In fact, the odds were put at 8900 to 1 by a Swedish group for a nuclear exchange before the end of the century. . . .

It all began with a small company by the name of Peace, Inc. They were a small group of California businessmen who felt that when the masses dearly want something and that something is not being delivered to them, what you have is a market. In this case the world wanted some relief from the almost inevitable nuclear war. Carl Sagan's study on long-term biological effects of nuclear war had started a snowball of paranoia in the Third World. They too were going up in the pyre, or rather into the morgue freezer. So these California businessmen saw approximately 4 billion people desperately wanting something that meant their lives to them and the lives of their children, and in fact the actual, virtual life of the planet on which they all lived. They called it the "supermarket" because it was the largest market known to business history.

At this time the peace groups were stalled with a Congress that dithered away the better part of a decade, finessing to death any real arms agreements or weapons freezes. The military/weapons business was big business, and no one really knew who was running the Soviet Union. The world said its prayers every day, and the world sighed a sigh of relief every morning that some little computer thousands of feet under the ocean hadn't freaked out and let the whole thing go. It was indeed a supermarket.

In 2009, Peace, Inc. really seemed quite reasonable and logical, but in 1985 it was a wild idea. These California businessmen simply went into the business of delivering a world free of weapons of mass destruction and creating a working peace between the United States and the Soviet Union. The way they did it was fascinating, and they earned fortunes for themselves and their stockholders. Like Barry Jacobs.

They started simply enough . . . by offering people a chance to do something about the nuclear war threat by buying stock in the company. They said that if you really want to get anything done in this world, you need two things: lots of money and the best minds in the world. Simple. They began by hiring the best publicists and the best lobbyists in the business. They hired away the really outstanding names. They got them all. They went to Congress and successfully lobbied for a NASA-type funding agency they called the Conflict Prevention and Mass Destruction Weapon Elimination Agency. They lobbied Congress for a funding law that appropriated 10 percent of all weapons spending to this agency. They also sold to the public a "peace tax" surcharge of 5 percent for five years that created a superfund like the EPA toxic waste fund. Suddenly there was big money in disarmament and peace.

Peace, Inc. consulted the government in setting up this NASA-type agency with two goals in mind: eliminate, dismantle, and ban all weapons of mass destruction, and create and build a relationship with the Soviet Union that paralleled the United States/China relations of that time. Then they really got into gear. They looked at the problem this way. First, the world must survive long enough to grow up. The first order of business was a study of safeguards on both countries' weapons systems and communications. They discovered that the Soviet safeguards lacked adequate computer grids and operated on a series of subsystems with many daily failures. They convinced a wary Congress to provide the Soviets with a new safeguard system and modern computers and communication equipment to lessen the threat of accidental war. They studied the system of launch on warning used by both countries and found ways to double and triple the avenues of communication between the two countries.

Next, they hired Armand Hammer, Admiral Rickover, and Lee Iacocca to take on the big job: finding solutions to the political problems between the Soviet Union and the United States. . . . First, they conducted an exhaustive study of the postwar behavior and leadership of the Soviet Union and deduced that the Soviets had conducted their entire postwar policy from a position of isolation and deep-seated fear of invasion. The Nazi invasion had deeply scarred the Soviets and left them with a compelling need to maintain their country on a war footing through forty years of peace. . . .

The program began to take shape under the guidance of Armand Hammer and Lee Iacocca. The first phase of their plan had two important worldwide conferences: the Global Conference on the Long-Term Solutions to the Problems in International Relations between the United States and the Soviet Union, and the Global Conference on Plans to Dismantle and Ban Weapons of Mass Destruction. Both conferences were unique, because they were conferences on the solutions to these problems and offered for the first time a chance for the Third World to participate in the development of working solutions. Their fates were now inextricably tied with the fates of the combatant nations, and their voices and ideas were invited for the first time. . . .

(Dan A. Baker)

. . . Who was responsible for the change? Was it individuals like Mahatma Gandhi, the forerunner of resistance without violence? Was it Martin Luther King, who started the final steps leading to the solution of the world's racial problems? Or did it begin with the hundreds of grass roots (peace) groups that drew tens of thousands of followers into passive resistance to that maddening buildup of atomic bombs along the iron curtain in Germany and southeastern Europe? Was it the dedicated group of Warriors of the New World, who solidly implanted this then radically new mode of thinking about war and resolution of conflict in our midst? Or was it statesmen such as former US President Carter, whose vision led to the Camp David Accords—which were to become the model for other milestone agreements, like the Johannesburg accords, the Geneva treaties, and the Sao Paulo Convention? Or was it former USSR President Chernenko, who broke the ice that would eventually melt the antagonism between the two superpowers? It might well—and just as well—remain an academic question. Maybe all these caused the unprecedented shift in thinking, or maybe it resulted from the combination of any of these and the volatile world political situation of the late 1900s.

As late as the mid-1980s, the road led in one direction only—toward self-destruction of the human race and termination of life in general. . . . Increasing numbers of individuals tried to combat this seemingly inevitable fate by educating the public about the threat of nuclear destruction. . . .

Popular opinion began to change as people awakened to the imminent threat. The Beyond War movement started in the early 1980s in California and quickly spread throughout the world. This was probably the most effective group advocating the New Mode of Thinking, this now so seemingly self-evident, natural, logical way of interacting among peoples and nations. I vividly remember the evening when I was first introduced to the Beyond War movement. I was vehemently fighting the so "utterly idealistic" notion that there would be no more conflicts—until I realized that conflict as such would remain and that it was only the method used to resolve conflict that needed the new approach of thinking. . . . We now take for granted that an enemy exists only if proclaimed, that we are all living on one planet—in one interdependent physical and ecological system, and that we people must and will be able to settle our differences without violence.

An attitudinal shift of such magnitude can only occur in response to dramatically changed outer circumstances. This change in outer circumstances occurred in 1945 with the explosion of the first atomic bomb. Albert Einstein was among the first to acknowledge that "the splitting of the atom has changed everything—save our modes of thinking; and we thus drift toward unparalleled catastrophe." Previously, wars had been limited in time and space. There was a certainty that eventually peace and often better conditions would follow war. With the invention of nuclear warfare, man possessed the means of self-destruction. Warfare could no longer guarantee a "winner," and any sort of armed conflict among nations risked the survival of life after the war. People began to see that the world was—had to be—"beyond war." Any opposing viewpoints defied the fundamental principle that the goal of all life is survival.

Gradually people reached the necessary realization that war was obsolete—that war, used to resolve conflicts among nations, had to be replaced by other means. They began to see that their concept of an enemy needed to be revised. We could no longer permit ourselves to pose, to declare some nation or someone as an enemy. We could no longer defer the responsibility to our elected representatives; it was a personal issue. Either we would work to implement the "new modes of thinking" in our lives or we would all perish.

Increasingly, Americans began to alter their view of the Soviets, their historical enemy. In late 1984, the heads of the US and USSR chapters of the International Physicians for the Prevention of Nuclear War were presented with the 1984 Beyond War Award via a space-bridge joint telecast in Moscow and San Francisco (the first space bridge between these two cities). At about the same time, a team of researchers of the American Academy of Sciences confirmed the nuclear winter theorem proposed earlier by Carl Sagan and other scientists, effecting a major change in the US defense policies of the conservative Reagan administration which had until then considered nuclear retaliatory actions a feasible option. This and the general increase of public awareness about the consequences of a nuclear exchange brought the United States and the Soviet Union back to substantive negotiations on the limitation of nuclear arms in Geneva in early 1985.

The original buildup of nuclear weapons arsenals started slowly in the early 1950s and then increased exponentially. Similarly, the reversal of this buildup, its replacement with worldwide cooperation, began gradually and picked up momentum as the positive implications of the first steps became apparent:

May 1985: US/USSR agreement on a nuclear test ban.

October 1985: Formal signing of a nuclear test ban treaty and a freeze on all nuclear weapons developments by the United States, the Soviet Union, Great Britain, India, and Pakistan.

November 1986: US House and Senate ratify these treaties with two-thirds majority across party lines.

April 1986: The French socialist government, in defiance of its independent defense policy course established under Charles de Gaulle after World War II, joins the five statutory nations in signing the nuclear weapons freeze.

December 1986: China joins the above treaties, and the seven members of the treaty announce a new round of strategic nuclear arms reduction negotiations.

March 1987: US and USSR negotiators agree on a schedule to dismantle the Pershing II and SS-20 missiles deployed in Europe.

February 1988: First discussions among Soviet, American, German, French, and British negotiators begin, resulting in the late 1993 implementation of the European Demilitarized Zone.

April 1995: Reunification of the two demilitarized German states.

May 1995: Reunification of South and North Korea.

(Klaus Heinemann and Joerg Heinemann)

. . . As Professor Andrews mentioned in his introduction, I was chairperson of the Massachusetts League of Women Voters when the League sponsored a series of meetings known as "the dialogue." The dialogue gathered people in cities across America to ask "How will peace come about between the United States and the Soviet Union?" Following each dialogue, a Message to Washington and a Message to Moscow were sent to the major policymakers of the two superpowers.

Many believe that it was the mandate that was sent to American and Soviet leaders from these dialogues that catalyzed a dramatic change in the US/USSR relationship. This peace between the two nations not only reduced the risk of nuclear war but also allowed us to begin to address the very fundamental human concerns of our world: hunger, health, poverty, and the environment.

On the overhead projector I have put a time line with key events in US/USSR relations over the last twenty-five years. As I understand, you have already studied the history of this period, why don't we open up the session to the questions?

Student   Thank you. What I'd like to know is just how did the dialogue come about? What prompted the League of Women Voters to take the initiative they did?

Lecturer Well, if you remember, relations between the Soviet Union and America were at an all time low in the mid-1980s. In the fall of 1983, a Korean airliner with over 200 civilian passengers was shot down by the Soviets when it strayed into their airspace. Reagan denounced the Soviet shooting as an unprecedented military attack on a civilian plane. The Soviets denounced the plane as part of a spy mission because their radar showed them that a US spy plane was following in the wake of this passenger plane the day it was shot down. . . . The League, responding to the deepening rift in US/USSR relations and an increasing fear in the American people about the heightened risk of war, decided to take on this very issue.

Though not as widely known then as they are now, the League still held great stature as an organization. They had sponsored the presidential election debates every four years and were widely respected for their nonpartisan nature and broad reach.

It was particularly this nonpartisan nature which prompted them to see that the American people were deeply divided over how to deal with the Soviets. So in 1985, they sponsored the first national dialogue.

Student I've grown up hearing about the Great Dialogue. My mother was also an organizer with the League. But what I've never understood very well is how were the dialogues structured? How were they run?

Lecturer The pilot dialogue was run in 1985. On one day, in each of the seven cities—Boston, San Francisco, Washington, D.C., Los Angeles, Houston, St. Louis, and Atlanta—hundreds of people held a dialogue about how peace would come about between the United States and the Soviet Union.

The cities were linked by slow-scan television. There was an effort made to include all parts of the American community and an extraordinary mix of people was present: conservatively minded and liberally minded people, rich people and poor, bluebloods and recent immigrants, young and old. What was unusual about the dialogue was that not only were very different ends of the spectrum present, but also everyone had an opportunity to speak. Celebrities, local heros, the so-called common people talked.

What made this possible was that the large groups divided into small working groups of eight to ten people, each of which reflected the diverse mix of the audience. Every group had a facilitator and a person who had been to the Soviet Union. They ensured that each person had an equal chance to respond to the questions: What are the problems in the US/USSR relationship? What about the Soviets? What do they see as the problem? What could peace look like with the Soviets? What can I do to make that happen?

There was a climate created that day that encouraged understanding. The purpose was to spark dialogue and to explore differences rather than force consensus. In this atmosphere there were extremely divergent views expressed about peace between the Soviets and Americans. However, there was a surprising amount of commonly shared beliefs uncovered: that nuclear war is *not* winnable, that we don't understand the Soviets and they don't understand us, and that, given the current nuclear threat, we have to talk to the Soviets. There was the beginning of a belief that things *could* be different.

Each of the small groups in each city had time to tell the large group about their discoveries. After this process occurred in each city, various participating cities were able to share with each other via slow-scan video. The teleconferencing made the dialogue seem more of an all-American experience. People felt that their opinion mattered. Someone was listening. Each group drafted a Message to Washington and a Message to Moscow. The groups wrote about how they felt peace between the Soviet Union and the United States could be achieved. The different messages were unique, but all stressed the urgency of Soviet-American cooperation to lower the risk of nuclear war. People felt that they should and could be listened to by their policymakers.

Student   What was the Dialogue like which you organized?

Lecturer   To begin with, we weren't sure how it would work. There we were, in the Old State House in downtown Boston:

former Senator Tsongas and present Senator Kennedy, mothers with children, teenagers from the experimental high school, residents of South Boston, the CEO and founder of Digital, Olsen, members of the Local Associated Neighborhoods. People who were known as liberals were mixed with people known as conservatives: Kerry, the newly elected senator, who had in the 1960s founded Vietnam Vets against the War, was there, as well as his opponent in the past election, Shamie, a self-made millionaire and a strong Reagan supporter. Flynn, the current mayor, sat next to King, the first major black figure to run for mayor in Boston, next to White, a previous mayor of Boston.

I remember a moment when I thought the whole thing was going to break. One camp of participants said the Soviets were the evil empire. Others maintained, just as furiously, that the Soviets were like us; they cried and had babies, too. The tension in the room was palpable.

The president of the local AFL-CIO stood up. "You know," he said, "I hate the Russians. But more and more, it just seems to me that somehow we have to talk to them."

A woman, a factory owner in Roxbury, answered. "I've done plenty of political battle with you, Reilly, as many of you well know, but I have to say that in this case, you are right. We have to speak to the Russians."

From that moment something in the room changed. What had been an unbearable tension began to shift into a kind of positive concern. The Boston dialogue wrote a Message to Washington and a Message to Moscow that was simple but signed by the entire audience. The Message to Washington said something like:

Dear Mr. President, We the undersigned, sincerely urge you to reach beyond the partisan difficulties that have entangled us and define a way to sincerely speak to the Soviets to make the world safer for future generations and lower the risk that now exists for nuclear war between our two nations. We know that you, at least as much as any of us, want this. And we want you to know that we send you our sincere support.

When I saw this message emerge from the group, I knew we were on the right road.

Student   But when I heard about the dialogue, I heard that there were many that went on for a period of years. What happened after the first pilot in 1985?

Lecturer   In 1986 the League, in each of the fifty states, joined with associate sponsors to run the dialogue. Unlikely combinations of groups joined together: Lion's Clubs, universities, corporations, churches, community and activist groups, sports groups, and high schools.

During 1986, the dialogue was held six times throughout the year, and each time it occurred, it happened in twenty cities simultaneously. These cities were a mix of large and small, midwestern, southeastern, cosmopolitan, and small town.

Information was put together and a simple process developed so that people could run the dialogue themselves. A Speakers Bureau, which only sent out teams of two people of different persuasions to start the dialogues, was developed. In addition, teaching teams were sent out to train local leaders to be facilitators.

The major media picked up on the dialogue. It was reported on "60 Minutes," "The MacNeil/Lehrer Report," "Good Morning America," and "Nightline." "Face the Nation" did a special on "Face the Dialogue."

Late in 1986 the Soviets began to take note. Contact was made with Soviet groups interested in the dialogue through the "Sister Cities Program" (which already had twenty-four cities paired up by the early 1980s). In 1987, the dialogue was extended to our Soviet counterparts and held between eight Soviet and eight American cities.

Student   Given the intense control of information in the Soviet system and their strong distrust of America in those days, how could their bureaucracy have allowed this to happen?

Lecturer   Your concern is well placed. Americans were surprised at the time also. But because of the media, the Soviets were able to watch America talking about *them,* the Soviets. Americans showed they were deeply concerned about war. And they were saying that the way conflict will be resolved is through communication. From widely divergent camps, Americans were communicating with each other. Communicating with their leaders. People saw that human concerns for family and future generations reached across ideological differences. The Soviets saw, as did the world, that the Americans were trying to come up with a consistent and long-range approach to US/USSR relations.

This affected the Soviets. First, they could trust America to be consistent. With each turnover in administration in America before had come a new tack in relating to the Soviets. This was an anathema to the Soviets, whose bureaucracy changed players very slowly.

Along the same line, the Soviets had always found negotiating with the Americans difficult because of the divisions that had existed within the American political system. In the 1970s, SALT II had been signed by Soviet and American negotiators but then was not ratified by the US Congress. Within the American bureaucracy there have always been strong public fights over policy—a sharp contrast to the Soviet system where the public line is uniform and more constant. The dialogue opened the possibility that America could be trusted to act as one coordinated body.

Second, the Americans seemed genuinely concerned about preventing nuclear war. The Soviets considered themselves very serious about the issue. The legacy of World War II—20 million dead—left an irrevocable scar on the Soviet people. Soviet statements, beginning in the 1970s, emphasized that "victory" in nuclear war was "madness." Now America, as a united country, was echoing that belief.

Student Professor Andrews said that you were in one of the US/Soviet dialogues. What happened when the Soviets and Americans tried to talk to each other?

Lecturer In 1987, as one of the state chairs, I was fortunate enough to attend the dialogue between Seattle and its sister city in the Soviet Union, Tashkent. I remember the filled auditorium. Representatives from major media, the state and national Congress, men's and women's groups, schools, corporations, community, sports, religious and recreational groups all sat in nervous expectation. Technicians bustled about with the teleconferencing equipment.

The president of the League of Women Voters and a Russian scholar who was a visiting professor at the University of Washington opened the session. There was an awkward pause while the camera people adjusted the screen. Finally, the first image of the Soviet audience in Tashkent flashed across the screen.

The room fell silent. I remember feeling scared. We watched as the Soviets slowly began to wave. A few cried out, "Hello Seattle!" In our best Russian, we answered, "Dobriy vecher!"

Velikhov, Vice President of the Academy of Sciences, and a former physicist, had been invited to their province to make the opening speech. "I'm one of the people who helped to develop nuclear weapons," he said. "We believed then that they were like muscles that would make us strong, that would let us have our way in the world. The more the weapons grew, though, the more we saw them as a cancer, making this world unsafe for everybody. I am here today because I realize that we have to take a step to eliminate this cancer from the earth."

The American audience broke into thunderous applause. The Soviets joined us. We began to stand. The Soviets stood also. That was the beginning of the first US/Soviet dialogue.

Student   What then, was the reaction of the American leaders?

Lecturer   At first, not much. From 1985 to 1987, very little changed in the Geneva process. In 1987 and 1988, however, statements by President Reagan began to reflect more and more the statements that were emerging from the dialogues.

In 1988, the comprehensive arms control talks that had begun in Geneva in 1985 changed their name to the Common Security Talks and took on a new orientation. As you can see by the time line, in 1988 there were a series of previously signed agreements which were reaffirmed. I took a trip to the Soviet Union during this time, and I remember various Soviets stressing the importance of building a relationship first before moving to specific details. Soviets establish a relationship by beginning negotiations with broad declaratory principles, while Americans in the past had tended to focus in on practical details. . . .

Student Weren't there also some technical breakthroughs about this time that contributed to progress in arms control talks?

Lecturer Yes, there were. In 1988, there was a new unit to measure the destructive force of nuclear weapons that both Soviets and Americans could agree on. In the past Soviets were determined to limit launchers, while the United States was concerned about limiting warheads. The other change was a Soviet concession to a modified version of on-site inspection. This had always been a thorn in the side of past negotiations.

With this, Reagan took the cautious step of opening negotiations over reductions of obsolete weapons. Obsolete weapons reductions were a way to test the new verification method and, in effect, a way to test the new relationship.

Student In 1988, President Reagan was leaving office. Is this when he announced the goal of "peace in the year 2000"?

Lecturer Yes. I believe, in fact, that the breakthroughs on measurement of destructive force and modified on-site inspection were only technical tools and that it was the commitment to peace that he made with the bipartisan group "Peace 2000" that proved to be the true impetus to advancing the talks. Reagan set a tone that matched the mood of the country. Much like Kennedy's commitment to put a person on the moon in ten years, there was now a year by which people expected there would be peace between the two superpowers. . . .

(Mark D. Sarkady and Ellen G. Meyer)

In this year of 2010, Argentina and Chile celebrate their 200-year existence as independent republics. For this reason, the *Monitor* visited the nestor (ref. Greek mythology: a wise old man) of Latin American literature, Pablo Miguel Barajona, who in past decades has become an admonisher and leading thinker heard worldwide. His new novel, *Coronados de Luz (Crowned with Light)* is on the best-seller list in many countries.

We posed a single question to Pablo Miguel, and he answered it in a long talk, occasionally interrupted by pauses for reflection. . . . We asked:

Pablo Miguel, in your opinion how can it be explained that the world has become so peaceful, that we, in contrast to all historical experience are living in a peaceful era, which has lasted for decades, and it appears that war is completely a thing of the past?

The last bit didn't seem certain to him, he began cautiously.

It assumed a complete transformation of man's nature. That would no doubt rather be the work of eternity. But the era of peace had certainly begun with the Writer's Congress of 1985, which I participated in as an already successful author at the time. The Congress was called at the time because there were concerns about a feared decline in the book culture. Mankind's necessity for stillness and independent mental labor, which books encouraged, was underestimated at that time, and the intensity of visual and acoustic information was overestimated. The assembly, meeting in Mexico, in which the most important writers from all countries participated, decided nothing about the current crisis in literature (which in reality did not exist), but on the other hand, by and by it would take up another, absolutely unforeseen topic.

Perhaps you remember. Three Latin American colleagues, Barquez, Nerida, and Varas, made a resolution concerning "R" thoughts. The resolution alluded passionately to the danger of another world war, as the tensions between the superpowers, the United States and Russia, had reached the boiling point at that time and both were threatening to use atom bombs. From their point of view all other endeavors were secondary to this danger. They proposed a collective decision by all authors present to oppose the danger of war with their literary works, to consciously serve peace and nothing else.

Pablo Miguel continued:

In my opinion absolutely nothing up to that point merited the decisive consequences proceeding from this suggestion. It was really revolutionary, for it is surely an axiom for a writer that the admonishing finger is the death of literature. A good story, written well, is what brings success, and at the very most a moral might be packed into the action or embodied in the characters. Now, however, they wanted everyone consciously to write instructively. Even at the conference the term had been introduced:

"R" literature. "R" stood for responsibility. Artistic primacy should be insignificant in comparison with conscious servitude.

For the Western writers, this above all seemed an almost unfulfillable demand, but they yielded to it. The Congress decided they would write instructively with the goal of saving world peace.

The idea caught fire immediately. Naturally, many literary critics set up a hue and cry as to how anyone could postulate such an unaesthetic writing principle, but to a certain degree they were swept aside. On the contrary, critics very soon began to review books according to the presence of the "R" factor, an entirely unique situation, for it is really an unliterary principle.

As in all times, good books and bad books were written in those years. Some were celebrated that today are forgotten. But the "R"-factor idea succeeded powerfully, and after a certain delay in time, it succeeded in totalitarian countries as well. It was so forceful that nothing could oppose it. I would say that obligation doesn't necessarily have to harm literature, and so there were also very good books written in those days. . . .

We journalists may have looked down on this a bit skeptically, for the patriarch of the scholarly novel came to thought with the remark that books alone naturally could not fundamentally alter the course of history. However, these books were the initiators. The "R" idea was swiftly carried further and spread to all mediums. Journalists, commentators, film producers, newspaper publishers—all sorts of opinion makers, and not lastly politicians, took hold of the idea to stand up in an instructive way for peace, to demonstrate "responsibility." Then came an ecumenical idea of it.

Ecumenical spirit is an important point. Just one year after the Writer's Congress, there was an ecumenical world conference for peace, at which practically all the religions of the world were represented. In those days it was not easy to find common ground until it became clear from the collisions of the many truths that this was not the point. Furthermore, each one should renounce the desire to force "his" truth on another. Today, what in those days seemed to be a sheer impossibility seems to us self-explanatory: to respect the truth of others. Christians remembered Jesus' words: "Do unto others as you would have them do unto you," the old golden rule. It was decided not to do any more missionary work. How difficult that was for the Christians! At that time I had made a contribution to "R" literature, my book *Many Houses and One Spirit*. Do you know how offensive that was? It was a saying of a Hindu representative: "We want to respect the spiritual house of others." An important chapter in my book was dedicated to the explosion of religious hatred in India. In those years there was a bloody persecution of the Sikh minority. Can you really imagine what it means that the "R" factor even liberated India? . . .

It's an idle question to ask what the impetus was: blind anxiety of a weapons arsenal that could destroy the entire globe or mankind's spiritual progress which crossed the threshold, or both. The fact is, after a centuries-long era of wars and power struggles, mankind had reached a turning point. . . .

(Bruno Leuschner, translated from German by Heather Frederick)

It began when one woman in America, who could not sleep at night, wrote this letter to another woman on the other side of the world.

My dear Russian sister:

You do not know me, yet perhaps you do. I hold in my heart the dream that you do know me, as I believe I know you. I am an American woman. When World War II was raging, I was five, six, . . . and nine years old. Your people and mine were friends—allies—then. I remember my parents weeping at the siege of Leningrad and at the news of millions of your people dying and dying. I merely had nightmares about the bombs coming. Your nightmares were real.

The sons of my parents' friends hated what was happening in Europe and Asia and they left soft, comfortable homes to fight it. They did not wait to be drafted into the service. Many did not return. There were always red-eyed mothers in our neighborhood who had lost their sons, women who never again slept without crying first.

We did not suffer the war as you and your people did, but our lives were not untouched.

Those of us who remember that war believed that after it was over, there would be peace forever. The world could not be so stupid a third time. Did you, at the end of that war, doubt that there would be lasting peace?

With that naive belief, as a young woman growing up I dared to dream dreams. Did you not dare to dream, too? Mine were that I would marry a good man whom I would love and that I would have healthy children. I also dreamed of being a writer.

This is what I think you dreamed. That you would know a world without war, that you would marry a good man, and that your children would never experience the horrors you knew. Perhaps you dreamed of being a writer, or an actress, a mathematician, or a doctor. But I do not believe you dreamed of another war in your future.

This is what happened to my dreams. I did marry a good man whom I love deeply. In my thirtieth year, our first child came, a son whom we named after an American-Russian writer who celebrated life and the truth.

Four years later our daughter was born; we named her after her German-American grandmother. In their faces is the miracle of life: expressions and features of my family and my husband's that run generations deep. Have you not noticed that in your children's faces?

The dream about peace in the world never happened. Wars and killing began almost immediately, for which our leaders—yours and mine—gave valid "reasons." The Berlin blockade, Korea, Hungary. With Vietnam, I knew that the people who remembered World War II were no longer in charge. Today, hundreds of fires smolder everywhere in the world, ready to erupt at a misunderstood word, a misplaced sentence, a breach of thought.

I look at this tall son of mine who has jokes in his eyes and fierce loyalties to his friends. I see this slim daughter who makes music at the piano and who tends wounded birds. I wonder if they will live to know the joy of their own children. I don't sleep much at night.

Russian sister, did you not celebrate your child's first step, first word? Didn't your heart stop when a sudden fever hit your child without warning? Did you not laugh at your daughter's outrage when she learned that yes, she must indeed do chores and homework? Did you not marvel when your children began to read, to think, to learn?

I cannot believe as you walk in the world, as you shop for your dinner, that you do not notice spring come or the sweet smell of summer, leaves falling, or the new gray hairs on your head. Don't you enjoy a soft bed and a warm drink when it's cold and jokes and someone you love rubbing your back after work? I cannot believe that we two do not love the same exquisite blue planet the cosmonauts and astronauts see from outer space. I believe you are as frightened as I am that all we know will be extinguished by our leaders who refuse to dismantle the machines of war.

Please read this and know that, on the other side of the world, I am your friend and that I love you. I wish you well and a long and happy life doing whatever it is that brings you joy.

One thing I ask. Please copy this letter and give it to your friends. And please write me back to tell me if I am wrong about you or not.

The woman signed her name and address. Then she went to a Russian man she knew and asked him to translate her letter into Russian. Afterward, she took the translation home and made copies of it in her American-learned script. Night after night, she painstakingly copied the originals.

When she had fifty copies, she went to a Russian Orthodox church near her neighborhood where the old, wrinkled women spoke little English.

She gave a copy of her letter (in Russian) to one of the women and watched while she read it. When the old woman had finished (it took her quite a time), she stood up and embraced the American woman. Tears streamed down both their faces. Until that moment, the two had been strangers.

The Russian woman asked for copies of the letter to send to friends in Russia. Other women in the congregation asked for copies, too, to send to their friends.

In about a month, the American woman began receiving replies to her letter. A trickle of them came in at first. Most of them were in Russian. The woman took them to her friend, the Russian man, for translation. Slowly, he did this for her. She gave these translations to her friends.

The letters made the American woman sing. Russian women wrote and told her of their lives in the war and of hopes and dreams they had had for the future. They told how their lives had turned out, too, with sadness and humor and finality. Above all, the letters said one thing clearly. The writers of them, mothers all, hated war and wanted peace in the world.

A newspaper in America wrote a story about what the woman was doing and printed some of the Russian letters. Suddenly, hundreds of letters from Americans came to the woman to be sent to Russia. All of them spoke of a fervent desire for peace and of love for the Russian people. Soon there were too many letters to translate into Russian. Then the American woman began to forward them to the postmasters and postmistresses of Russia. All over the Soviet Union, the men and women who processed mail were confronted with bags of letters addressed simply to "our Russian brothers and sisters."

The American woman, who was becoming quite well known in the United States, appeared on national television shows to explain what she was doing and to read some of the letters. Experts in Soviet/American relations were asked to comment on the phenomenon of strangers writing to one another across the world and were at a loss to explain it.

The American woman next suggested that people begin writing not only to others but to the leaders of America and of the Soviet

Union. Two million letters arrived a few days later in Moscow; three million the next. Canadian film crews covered the news and satellite photos of truckloads of mail being unloaded in Red Square made network news all over the world.

Six million letters from Russia, perhaps seven, were deposited on the White House steps, stacked neatly there by the US Postal Service.

Schoolchildren in each country took up the practice of writing letters to each other. Soon, plans and dreams and fledgling romances were flying across the world. American children began learning Russian words and soon demanded school courses in the language. Russian children, who were already reading and writing English, were delighted to practice their skills with the Americans.

Television networks in the United States, quick to spot trends, began airing specials on Russian culture, Russian history, and Russian cuisine.

It was not long after the woman had begun her letter writing, perhaps a year, that the governments of the United States and the Soviet Union sat down together at last to speak of peace. They could no longer ignore the mountains of mail that blocked their respective doors of government. In a new spirit of humility, the leaders of both governments began painfully to dismantle and destroy the machinery of war.

Seated prominently at the tables of peace were dozens of Russian and American mothers.

And peace finally happened.

(Joan Kufrin)

8

Getting to Know You: Exchanges

Getting to know you,
Getting to know all about you;
Getting to like you,
Getting to hope you like me.

We have now passed from the threat of nuclear holocaust through various emergencies caused by economic disasters to more normal diplomatic and military developments that can aid peace, all the way to the strains of that lovely lyric from *The King and I*. Student exchanges, or any kind of exchanges, are built on the idea that if we can just get to know each other, things will be better. They belong at this point in the book because they certainly are a piece of the "change of consciousness" approach as well as one kind of specific action group, the subject of the two previous chapters.

It may be inconceivable that any kind of mass exchange is possible until a better relationship has been established between the superpowers. Yet it is possible that a breakthrough could come through some kind of startling, "break the ice" proposal, such as the one the president of the United States makes in *Jerome Pressman*'s essay. Sent up as part of the White House mail by the president's staff, Pressman's fictional letter suggests the serious notion that a way has to be found around the impasse over weapons and their control. "What is needed is to jump out of the vicious cycle (the only way to resolve it) onto a new, fresh level which can reach out and energize the latent shrunken pockets of goodwill."

As Pressman's essay points out, an exchange does not require disarmament as a quid pro quo. An exchange can take place without prior agreements on other matters. Whether the Soviets would allow an exchange on the scale Pressman writes about is a moot point; no one has ever before had the temerity to suggest it. He asks for a million exchange students going each way each year, arguing that in this case quantity would change the quality of the interchange. The Russians might think so also, for Pressman wrote that, in agreeing to the exchange, they had already tacitly underwritten a change in their own system.

The intelligence reports read that, while it had been the new young premier who had initiated the policy review, it had been the residual gerontocracy who pushed the hardest for acceptance. The old men must have known that agreeing to the Sophomore Exchange was more than that—they were voting to change the Soviet system (just as the American posture would change).

This idea of a massive exchange has two main elements in it. The "visitors" become hostages in each other's countries, thus drastically reducing the likelihood of direct confrontation. But through tasting of the other's culture, a new basis of understanding is built that carries positively into political and economic life.

E. Grey Dimond, of Kansas City, Missouri, pictures a Peace Army in his essay. It all begins with President Reagan, who "could go down in history as having bankrupted the country or, even worse, having blown us off the map or [who] could take his remarkable ability to charm people to the conference table." Reagan brings the Soviet foreign minister to a Santa Barbara high school, whereupon the foreign minister invites 600 graduating students, their teachers, and the Reagans to come to the Soviet Union for a month. The visit is so successful that it is followed by a 20,000-per-year student exchange through a draft system. Only those students in the upper third of their class are eligible for the draft (the rest might get drafted into a *real* army).

The essays that emphasize exchanges also at least imply that through better understanding both superpower systems undergo substantive change. This at least implies that both systems are willing to change somewhat in the interest of world peace. On the basis of the past forty years, there is little evidence to suggest that the Soviet leaders would willingly become involved in any process that would lead to their relinquishing the kind of control they now exercise over their own people. And many thoughtful Europeans feel that America's leaders likewise would not knowingly give up the position the United States occupies in the world.

Yet no configuration of political relationships lasts indefinitely. The rise of Japan and China, for instance, is already changing the outlook of both the United States and the Soviet Union—Japan mainly through its economic might and China through its political cohesiveness almost forty years after the revolution and its experimentation with elements of capitalism. In her essay, *Nancy Perry,* of New York, suggested that it was change around the world that in fact made life most difficult for the superpowers and led them to try some joint initiatives. A project whose acronym is PEACE, begins at a grass roots level to promote better global understanding. One of its early works is a major teacher exchange program around the world.

Children, one step in age below the teachers, become the catalyst in another essay, by *Katharine Emsden,* of Castle Rock, Colorado. Again, some suspension of belief is called for to envision how a grass roots movement beginning in the United States could spread to the Soviet Union. In any case, the enthusiasm and natural innocence of children infects teenagers in many communities, who in turn "launched into discussion of how to spread a desire for peace to those currently fighting in other lands. By the end of 1991 several foundations organized groups of twenty-five teenagers to walk and talk their way across a particular country during their summer vacation." Emsden's essay echoes a thought in many other essays that did not find their way into this book—namely, that much of the public apparently thinks peace is never going to be achieved by the politicians but will come about only if the people find some way to take their interest in preserving humanity around the globe as their own responsibility. Emsden says:

Perhaps we were unrealistic ever to have expected men of state to resist temptation by the fruits of power and knowledge as they tried to solve deep-seated conflicts we ourselves had allowed to take root. Peacemakers must have childlike perspective, as the Beatitudes of Christ Jesus suggest . . . . Here at last the biological hypothesis of the psyche's potential for change was being actualized from within the heart of a child.

Patricia Overby, of Fullerton, California, had an idea that belongs in the same genre as Kenneth Boulding's new region of time, discussed in chapter 6. Her idea is called the Decade of Human Heritage, from 1990 to 2000. It belongs in this chapter because it is one form of exchange. A new US president, aware of the deterioration of superpower relations and feeling that any solution must deal in some way with a recognition of the worth of all human beings and *cultures,* proposes a decade in which the United States would sponsor family exchange trips "in which citizens of the United States and of other countries would be invited to discover their family roots by visiting relations in their countries of origin." Moreover, the United States agrees to match the money spent anywhere else in the world on similar projects. The Soviet Union does not accept matching funds, but even there and in its satellites the visits and looking into the past become popular.

Threads of human heritage, developed independently all over the globe, were brought together and woven into a splendid, multicolored cloth that represented the sum of all human life, past and present. This converging of separate human paths brought out more than the obvious universals of human creativity and intelligence. It produced a new and keenly felt awareness of man's common aspirations for self-fulfillment.

Did this have an effect on the ultimate power relationship? Overby certainly believes it did.

Although nothing in the world was changed by the Heritage Decade but humankind's view of itself, that was enough. The old ways were fading, and all the strategists had to reckon with the new.

Finally, this chapter ends with an essay by *Stephen E. Silver,* a New London, Connecticut, doctor whose idea of exchanges is as large as Pressman's. Silver's numbers are smaller (3000 the first year), but they are all the children of prominent persons. We must add the proviso that to first agree to such an exchange, there would seem to have been a major improvement in relations over what they are today. Yet the reason for this program was a joint attempt to get around the massive suspicion that exists today—what Silver calls "the insoluble riddle of distrust." The exchange program does not of itself solve any of the problems between the two countries. But because it results in a merging of interests on the personal level, it provides the rationale for getting on with resolving political differences.

Silver's essay is written in the form of a guest address to the US Congress by the then (2010) Soviet premier, who ends it with an invocation of God's protection over the joint work of the two superpowers, Such invocations are commonplace in the addresses of American presidents, but to date we have not heard such a reference from Soviet leaders. But, if exchanges can work, it is not too large a miracle to hope that the religious fabric could again be restored to a nation in which religion held a large position before the Bolshevik Revolution. It is also fitting that the essays included in our book, which began with those in which peace was found through common catastrophe, should end with those appealing to the idealism present in all mankind and to those common threads of humanity that in the end must be found if peace is to become reality.

The vigorous hatchet-faced man with the close-clipped gray hair surrounded by half-a-dozen blue-suited staff moved rapidly out of the elevator. It was a large oblong room filled with electronic equipment and blinking lights that they stepped into. One complete wall was covered with a televideo, marked in large letters, President of the United States, and at the bottom of which was the date, November 2, 2010.

"Let's get the premier now," he said.

The screen flashed on displaying the visage of a square-jawed bald man who smiled and waved his hand.

"Hello Alexii. How are you?" The president said. "Remember, you and your wife are coming over this Joint Thanksgiving." The concept of Thanksgiving had been broadened into an American-Soviet joint holiday when two years after the signing of the agreement the initial bombs had been destroyed. "This year it's my place again down at the Cape at Orleans. We'll have lots of that clam chowder that you like. And congratulations, your grandson made the dean's list at the University of Chicago. He's a bright boy."

The premier, with a laugh, responded, "Thank you, John. We are coming of course. But first an important political favor to help me in the coming elections. Kurchyatov, my Minister of Heavy Industry, who has his own constituency, is upset because one of his granddaughters, Natasha, has fallen in love with a fellow student at Yale. She doesn't write her mother, her grades are terrible. Can you not do something?"

The president reflected that, while he was a Stanford man, Yale owed him for some past discrete favors and indeed his secretary of state was a Yale man. "Alexii, leave it to me. We'll settle this matter rapidly." In an aside he motioned to his personal aide. "Get on it now. Whatever it takes. I want action within the hour. Wrap it up." As the premier began addressing other agenda issues in this weekly televideo conference call—the further strengthening of the United Nations, the residual Irredentist movement in Ethiopia—the president thought, "All minor issues, not hot war issues as in the old days." Somewhat bored he drifted away in memory.

It had begun in the summer of 1984 with that badly written, mistyped letter that his staff had sent up to him in an effort to lighten his then dark mood. He could see it before him word for word:

September 13, 1984
President of the USA
White House
Washington, D.C.
Dear Mr. President:

I propose a strategy and a program, entitled Sophomores For Peace (SOPH) for resolving the current nuclear war stalemate between the United States and the Soviet Union. In this program each year the *entire college sophomore class* of the United States would be exchanged for that of the Soviet Union. Consequently, there would be a constant population (although each year the individuals change) of a *million* or so American sophomores in the Soviet Union and vice versa.

The argument is that with the cream of our youth exchanged, there would be two major effects. The first is that such a population exchange would constitute a more effective deterrent to nuclear war than the current balance of terror. Such population exchanges between warring tribes are not unknown in history. The second effect is that the major problem between the United States and the Soviet Union is really that of *goodwill* not nuclear weapons. The impact of a million American sophomores on the Soviet Union and vice versa with the myriad of individual human emotions, feelings, and relationships that would ensue deals with the source of the problem and cannot help but create a sense of greater cohesiveness and friendliness between the two countries. True, exchange programs between the two countries have occurred before, but these have had little impact because they were too small. It is a case where adequate quantity makes a change in the quality of the total interaction.

It would seem that the present irreconcilable nuclear confrontation between the United States and the Soviet Union is locked in and exacerbated by all attempts at communicating on the level of reduction of these weapons. Given the amount of ill will and bad feelings and the vicious cycles of action (cruise and Pershing missiles) and reaction (iron curtain emplacement) such negotiations seem interminable if not hopeless. There are too many dimensions to argue about: throw weight and number of missiles, land- versus sea-based, American high accuracy versus Soviet low accuracy, missile systems behind or in front of the Urals, past nuclear agreements, counting British and French missiles, etc.

What is needed is to jump out of the vicious cycle (the only way to resolve it) onto a new, fresh level which can reach out and energize the latent shrunken pockets of goodwill. Such an approach must be dramatic, massive, abrupt, and preferably *naive,* and yet not be vulnerable to existing paranoic fears.

The present sophisticated, technological, and highly intellectually balanced technocratic approach has proven sterile.

Let's stop focusing only on weapons; let's talk "sophomores." The sophomores would love their Russian year abroad. The Russians might be intrigued with such a proposal.

Jerome Pressman

Perhaps, the president reflected, that was how history was made—the right thing at the right time. The readiness was all. In the first half of the 1980s the nuclear freeze movement had achieved legitimacy and political acceptance. This had left in place an existent infrastructure of organizations, the peace movement, the women's groups, the European Green structures, etc., all fundamentally waiting for the next step. There was also disseminated throughout society this great emotional need for action and for dedication to something larger than the individual. It was a compulsion to do it themselves—they, the grass roots, not the political leaders. There was the feeling that enough was enough; there were too many bombs, too many missiles—the next step was necessary. Consequently the Sophomores For Peace (SOPH) program found ready-made the vitality, the tension for action, the leaders, and the organizations with the requisite communication channels open for coordinated action.

The SOPH letter writer, a retired physicist, had circulated some hundred copies to magazines, newspapers, technical societies, individuals prominent in the peace movement, as well as government officials, for example, the president. The initial meager response was the publication in a few technical journals, such as *Physics Today, Bulletin of Atomic Scientists,* and several college newspapers. However the turning point came when a copy fortuitously came to the attention of the Harvard Negotiation Project (HNP), who saw, subsumed in SOPH, some of the aspects of the HNP method of principled negotiations, viz, "separating the relationships from the problems" and "recognition and understanding of their and your emotions," etc. It was the national broadcast on the Public Broadcasting System by HNP of a seminar on SOPH which first brought the plan to national attention and debate.

The churches supported SOPH even more quickly than the peace organizations, just as they had been in the forefront of the nuclear freeze movement. The college students, suddenly excited at the prospect of significant action, switched from their dominant conservative stance and presented a united front, backing SOPH. The university administrators supported SOPH as having a high moral and educational purpose and recognized it as being a focusing of many "year-abroad" programs then in existence with a generalization to all sophomores. The economists pointed out that, fiscally considered, the educational costs of SOPH balanced out at an even swap and that the only cost was that of transportation. At discount rates of $200 each and one million students, the cost was equal to the price of one B-1 bomber or one-fifth the price of a guided missile destroyer. Cheap enough. Soon, responding to these many large and rapidly growing constituencies, a strong congressional bloc had formed.

When the then president of the United States made the SOPH offer to the Russians, it may have been a purely political move for domestic consumption or a move to embarrass the Russians. Perhaps he did not even believe in SOPH. No one will ever know if he felt surprised or even trapped when the Russians accepted the proposal. But why did the Russians buy into such a concept? Why had they accepted the president's offer? The American think tanks, east coast and west coast alike, who had secretly vetted the concept had said to a man, "They will laugh at you, they will think you are crazy." Again, was it that the timing was right? A "new" scientific fact of a nuclear winter had just been supported by a consensus of American and Soviet scientists, including both national academies. The question arose repeatedly: Why use weapons which inevitably would react back on the users to destroy them by blotting out the sun for protracted periods of time? But still the distrust remained; arms reduction negotiations were perpetually stalled in a quagmire of subtle and detailed analyses of competing advantages on a myriad of tactical and strategic levels. A new idea was needed or, as the intellectuals would say, a new "paradigm."

When the then president of the United States in a Christmas address to the nation carried overseas and to Russia by every satellite and European communication channel proposed SOPH, public opinion in the United States had already been prepared, whereas in Russia SOPH as a formal proposal came as a surprise. The Russian censorship system had always been erratic and inconsistent. . . . As the SOPH ideas began to move throughout Russia through unjammed radio, through visitors, through word of mouth, through the iron curtain countries, there was incredulity, then amazement, that the Americans, that the American president, had actually proposed sending each year a million young Americans to Russia and taking similarly a million young Russian students into the American schools. Slowly the belief spread that the Americans were for real. A new focus, a new consciousness, a new way of thinking began to establish itself in the Russian mind.

The Russian people responded in a spontaneous surge. SOPH tickled their sense of fun, their imagination, and their repressed need to dare to go beyond their daily lives. Soon the composers began to write SOPH songs. "The Sophomores Are Coming" sung to the accompaniment of a balalaika became a favorite in the cafés. The poets began declaiming their SOPH poems. "On Airplane Wings of Love" was chanted in all the parks. The teenagers and many a gray head began wearing T-shirts with SOPH emblazoned across their chests. The favorite phrases became "Why not? It is possible." The movement in the United States had been spearheaded by the middle class. In the Soviet Union it was driven forward by the masses—a truly proletarian movement. The sociologists would analyze the differential pattern for years.

The Soviet bureaucracy was at first confused. Its initial response had been to ignore SOPH, to laugh at it as another temporary, decadent capitalist import. At the same time their geopolitical theorists attempted to calculate on their out-moded computers its significance in the cold war with much difficulty. As the SOPH movement became stronger and the calculations proved recalcitrant, a policy foray into repressive measures was initiated, involving the arrest of a few bolder poets in conjunction with a counterpropaganda program launched in the Soviet media. However, this proved already too late and already a mistake. The Soviet people had seized on SOPH with a spirit of fun and almost a dadaistic bravado. The repressive actions made SOPH "real and serious" and added a deep tonality of stubborness to their already complex feelings. By then SOPH had become a movement clever enough to mimic the Polish Solidarity movement, with its strength through passivity and its submerged leadership.

It was at this juncture that something truly remarkable, something perversely human, something truly worthy of a Dostoevsky happened. The newly appointed Russian premier, the former ascendent star as picked by Western pundits, announced that the Politburo had accepted the SOPH proposal. The intelligence reports read that, while it had been the new young premier who had initiated the policy review, it had been the residual gerontocracy who pushed the hardest for acceptance. The old men must have known that agreeing to the sophomore exchange was more than that—they were voting to change the Soviet system (just as the American posture would change). But, then, they must have believed that Russia needed to change, that nothing was forever, just like their own lives. Perhaps the grand and naive American gesture—it was more than a signal—had penetrated the layers of Russian paranoia (as the Americans saw it) or the legitimate fears of attack (as the Russians saw it). The Russians ran no military risk since their missiles were still to be in place, and there were no requirements for gutting their defense systems. Perhaps even in as strongly centralized a system as the Soviet one, even those critical decision neurons at the top had to respond to overwhelming signals from the body proper below. Or perhaps deep in their hearts the old men had somehow really wanted peace.

This simple announcement, with details to be worked out at staff level, that Russia accepted SOPH, was the key that opened the door to a multiplicity of cascading events at every level. As the secretary of defense, a Catholic from Georgetown University given to theological statements, put it, "Now all things are possible, for now the United States and the Soviets are on the same side. Not capitalism or communism, but 'communion,' that magical word, has won out." The Allies and the iron curtain countries and dependents supported the New Alliance vigorously. Realistically, they had no choice, but it was also true that their humanity was stirred by a sense of great vision, for it was One World now. Negotiations that had been blocked for years—trade agreements, cultural exchanges, scientific projects—all became suddenly possible.

At the time of the first sophomore exchange (now known in history as the First Exchange), before the long-term nuclear disarmament agreements had been formally signed, the Soviet Union and the United States agreed as a symbolic act to exchange and destroy ten nuclear weapons. The United Nations was given control of the nuclear material. Each Russian nuclear bomb structure transferred to the United States (vice versa in Russia) was assigned to a large stadium with a group thematic leader and supporting artists to create a "celebration of joy" within which the bomb was to be "destructed." Michael Jackson was the theme leader at the Pontiac Silverdome, the Rolling Stones at the Los Angeles Coliseum, Bruce Springsteen at the Hoosier Dome, etc. In the Soviet Union the leading artists from the Bolshoi, the Opera, the Circus, all the conservatories performed in the major sports stadia and cultural houses. As the first airplanes left the ground and the ocean liners their docks, carrying their sophomores in both directions, the Celebration of Joy began. Never so much joy! Never so much fun! Never so many fireworks! Never such as auspicious beginning! Never so much Beethoven!

How to describe the actual exchange? Can it be done mathematically? A million American students each meeting approximately one thousand Russians and vice versa in one year (some casually, some deeply) is a billion new relationships. How many megatons does this balance? How do we calculate the number of Soviet-American meals shared—365 times 3 times 1 billion? In what units do we calculate it? In decimals? In bits? In bytes? Or in bites? How many handshakes or smiles nullify one high-power neodymium laser beam? What is the exact point in the continuum of irrational numbers at which distrust turns to trust? Perhaps the discursive approach is best. Simply assessed, almost everybody, students and friends, had some fun, and an amazing amount of affection found its way about. Some learning also took place! And changes occurred.

As the agreements were signed and the large-scale dismantling and destruction of all American and Soviet nuclear devices moved rapidly into the post-sophomore era, the nuclear proliferation period was brought sharply to heel. With the joint Soviet-American demand, in concert with their allies and the United Nations, that all nuclear weapons be destroyed, no third country could claim any rationalization or justification to keep them. Nor did they have the strength to withstand the enormous pressures brought to bear. Moreover, worldwide verification and an in situ inspection system was put in place in all the countries of the world. With the universal act of nuclear disarmament well under way, conventional disarmament was easily the next step. With Russia and the United States as honest brokers, there began a rapid resolution of regional and local conflicts on the basis of negotiations. Differences and honest disagreements remained, but now they were insulated and smothered by Russo-American economic and moral pressure in a rapidly disarming world.

With the large-scale disarmament changes began in the world economy. . . . Unlike the OPEC shock this was due to the injection, annually, of literally a trillion dollars of freed up capital for investment and the creation of new wealth. These changes locked disarmament irreversibly in place.

Organic microprocessors and computers, hyperintelligent robots, the completely automated factory, the cornucopia results of biotechnology, new energy sources—all moved rapidly into everyday practice and use with this enormous infusion of capital. The beginning widespread utilization of not only the automated factory but also the vertical automated farm tower created two major changes in society. First, the automated factory decoupled income from labor so that a labor theory of value and its accompanying income distribution system was no longer valid. Second, with the vertical farm tower any land was suitable, so that the Sahara, with its copious solar energy and recycled water, was more advantageous for crops than verdant farmland. Consequently a worldwide rationalization and equity in the distribution of wealth began to come into being. More ingenuity had to be shown in the invention of new social and economic forms than even in the technical changes. It represented a new stage in the evolution of man's consciousness and . . .

At this point the president woke from his dreamlike scan of the events of the past several decades and looked at the screen. The premier was still there. "Well Alexii, that finishes it. The last nuclear bombs were destroyed this year. The world is safe from what we feared, the mass destruction of a nuclear holocaust. We are entering the New Phase and the world has the Soviet Union to thank for it."

"Thank you, John. You are most gracious as usual, but we did it, our two countries working together, the United States and the Soviet Union. You know, John, with the nuclear warheads and their missile carriers destroyed we no longer need the Sophomores for Peace program; our youngsters can stay at home now."

"Alexii, true, but the world still needs some fun! Let's keep the program going. Do svidaniya, and of course we'll see you on the Cape soon."

As the president leaned forward to switch off his screen, his aide came forward rapidly and whispered in his ear. The president smiled, looked back at the screen and spoke, "Mr. Premier, tell Kurchyatov that his grandaughter married the Yale boy two weeks ago and that her grades are picking up. I hope this helps your political position in the coming election. So long, Alexii."

(Jerome Pressman)

. . . The distrust and hostility which grew between the East and West, as they came to rely on a strategy of deterrence during the forty-year period following World War II, was exacerbated by an ill-informed and increasingly insular public. The Russian people, owing to government paranoia, couldn't get information about the outside world; Americans didn't want it. Lulled into a false sense of complacency as decades passed free of the long-awaited nuclear holocaust, most felt no compelling drive to follow closely what was happening in Libya or the Punjab.

Driven by the demands of a country afflicted with myopic vision, the American mass media saw little incentive for presenting a detailed picture of what was happening faraway. No one, it was assumed, would be interested. Thus developed a vicious cycle, as ignorance of foreign issues and events blossomed into outright xenophobia.

And so it went. Isolation. Intervention. Insulation. Always, the basis for relations between "us" and "them" began with "I."

As we ventured gingerly forward—striving to preserve the status quo, knowing we couldn't—the world was changing of its own volition. China was developing into a superpower in her own right; Japan became an industrial power to reckon with; Eastern and Western allies grew more independent, and Third World nations began asserting themselves.

Meanwhile, advanced communications and transportation systems brought faraway countries ever closer together, creating an interconnected global society. America and the Soviet Union suddenly found that around the world events and attitudes were taking shape which would have an increasingly direct impact on their people, even as their power to control those attitudes and events diminished.

As the number of people and nations in the world multiplied, so did our problems. The number of absolute poor increased to approximately one-fifth of the world's total population. Natural resources dwindled—while international debt swelled to crisis proportions. Terrorism flourished; nuclear weapons began to proliferate. And, as always, governments, races, and religions struggled for power and independence—in the Middle East, Central and South America, Africa, and Asia.

All of which made life increasingly difficult for the superpowers, but in the end actually might have saved us. Heated up by world events, a kettle of simmering interest and half-baked ideas finally came to a boil. Governments stopped talking and started acting. Long-discussed plans to stabilize the world community became reality.

The result was Project PEACE, a five-point program initiated in 1985 to address on a global level the key areas of *P*ower/Politics, *E*conomics/Environment, *A*rms Control, *C*ommunications, and *E*ducation.

Project PEACE started at the grass roots level with the largely uninformed mass public, whose involvement and understanding was vital to the success of the plan. To promote a global perspective, schools and the media launched a dual drive to expose more citizens to foreign cultures via news and education. As growing numbers of individuals around the world gained access to and awareness of each other as people, Project PEACE took on a life of its own.

Today's children are tomorrow's leaders; hence teachers—with their power to shape young minds—became an integral element in the formula for long-term peace. Prejudiced educators beget prejudiced students. Thus a program was set up to promote a greater exchange of teachers between East and West, North and South—not only to learn but also to teach.

This Educator Exchange Program not only exposed vast numbers of teachers to foreign people and cultures, thus encouraging a more sympathetic global viewpoint when they returned to their classrooms at home, but also exposed students to foreign lands via the exchange teachers who were visiting and teaching in their countries.

Cultural exchange programs of all kinds were stepped up, with massive numbers of private citizens traveling between East and West, as groups such as the Citizen Exchange Council gained prominence.

Top level politicians spent more time living and working in nonallied countries, observing firsthand the problems facing other governments. This was instrumental in giving world leaders a view from the other guy's shoes and was imperative if countries were to stop the destructive practice of assuming they knew the motives of others. . . .

(Nancy J. Perry)

. . . Almost imperceptibly during the 1980s the United States came of age and, like her individual immigrants, began to realize the grave responsibilities implicit in being a leader of democratic freedoms. She had fought her own revolution to procure those freedoms. She had fought for the survival of her unity as a republic, and she had helped other nations against their aggressors. Now the stakes involved the future of mankind, and the world looked to this country to discover what was expected of it.

Only where love and need are one
And the work is play for mortal stakes
Is the deed ever really done
For Heaven and the future's sakes.

—Robert Frost, "Two Tramps in Mud Time"

Surely here was the ultimate cure for boredom in the Western world. Having lost the ability to feel human, many American people had begun to withdraw under a cover of powerlessness. Elsewhere, however, citizens fearful of nuclear war and of a planet exhausting its nonrenewable resources at an alarming rate turned to America for the meaning of it all. Was our country up to the task of answering for its own attitudes? Accepting responsibility, possibly admitting mistakes, is the highest sign of strength on an individual or national level, and it is the vital corollary to freedom. Yet it would involve a major change from the then prevalent macho diplomacy wherein superpowers were vying for supremacy. What happened in the decade of the 1990s reads now, in the year 2010, like the cosmic legend of good against evil within the human spirit. . . .

Aware of the possibility for actual genetic changes, reflecting new attitudes, and eager to fulfill expectations held by the rest of the world, communities in the United States began meeting to set the stage for peaceful cooperation. To these meetings came all facets of the neighborhood: traditionalists, pessimists, professionals, and children. It was the last who kept reminding their group of its basic purpose: sharing and ensuring life, be peaceful and in harmony with nature.

Being at peace with themselves was far more natural for the children than for most adults. . . .

They pointed out that being satisfied with who you are, clearing your mind of thoughts of revenge, trusting, and making an extra effort would prepare the whole world for putting peace ahead of all other wants. They drew connections between peace and every human activity. Much to each community's surprise, it was the children who dominated these meetings in their own quiet and uncomplicated way.

Following their lead, many teenagers launched into discussions of how to spread a desire for peace to those currently fighting in other lands. By the end of 1991, several foundations organized groups of twenty-five teenagers to walk and talk their way across a particular country during their summer vacations. Each child was matched with one from the country visited, and within two years a reciprocal program had begun so that the United States could host teenagers from fifty other countries.

Most of the original community meetings included adults in various communication fields. The media soon aired the ideas conceived in different neighborhoods, satellites transmitted programs around the world, and by the mid 1990s this grass roots beginning had become a worldwide phenomenon. Schools picked up on the new international concerns, and added interest in becoming a diplomat for world peace replaced the old verbal games of carving up the globe and canceling the human race.

The year 2000 had been considered by many a likely time for nuclear holocaust. Instead it was the year of documenting economic and social needs around the world. A newly organized United Nations took on the mission of distributing task descriptions to fifty nations, mandating that men and women aged twenty to twenty-five carry out the jobs for six-month periods. Serving in love proved far more popular than serving in war.

The true direction behind our recent world unity came not from the politicians we had chosen as peacemakers but from a new spirit among our children. Perhaps we were unrealistic ever to have expected men of state to resist temptation by the fruits of power and knowledge as they tried to solve deep-seated conflicts we ourselves had allowed to take root.

Peacemakers must have childlike perspective, as the Beatitudes of Christ Jesus suggest. . . . Here at last the biological hypothesis of the psyche's potential for change was being actualized from within the heart of a child.

(Katharine Nicely Emsden)

Although fear and frustration were pervasive, they were directed mainly at the superpowers. People resented the devotion of so much wealth to the manufacture of nuclear weapons. They also felt a deeper, almost instinctive fear that the very number and global distribution of these weapons would somehow draw everyone into the nuclear madness. . . .

All this was fully appreciated by the winning candidate in the

US presidential election of 1988. A moderate hawk by reputation, he admitted many times during his campaign that he was coming to fear the awful inevitability of nuclear weapons more than the enemy against whom they were supposed to defend. Every increase in their numbers made him more uneasy, not more secure. Driven by these misgivings, he proposed to search for new solutions to the world's dilemmas "before frustration and fear turned to despair, and humankind lost control of its destiny." . . .

Once established in office, the president set up committees and began inviting people to the White House to make their recommendations. Each visitor had a different perspective and probed the problem from that direction. Most of the early witnesses proposed changes of a technical or systematic nature—supporting their ideas with models, flowcharts, and statistics. They produced better designs for the world's economic and financial systems and bold new frameworks for world government. But as time went on, the character of the testimony changed subtly, so that the management of human relations was more often reviewed in historical and psychological terms than through the medium of models and charts.

At this point, the president began to meet regularly with his working committee. He knew he would have to pave the way for technical reforms with a bold, leading idea, and he hoped this new emphasis on psychology and history would spur some creative thinking in that direction. It did. The committee's list of essential program elements reflected its newly enlightened perspective on the human side of the problem.

First, an appropriate program would have to address the world's fear of nuclear weapons in some substantive way. Second, it should incorporate at least one element that could be interpreted as representing the nation's faith in basic human decency. This was necessary to counteract the cynicism and distrust that had become epidemic in the world. Third, whatever was done had to look more like an offer than an appeal. In an atmosphere almost devoid of goodwill, an appeal would be suspect. Fourth, there should be an element of challenge in the proposal, an element which could draw a cautious world into the project by providing an opportunity for safe response. Fifth, the proposal had to be ideologically and economically neutral, so that it could not be attacked as a political end run around the superpower conflict. Any trait of selfish political motivation would doom the project from the start. Sixth, the solution should address itself in some way to the fundamental core of resistance, evident in all peoples, to accepting other cultures, nations, races, and creeds as equals. . . .

The committee recognized that the brotherhood of man was a powerful concept not always accompanied by powerful feelings. And powerful, positive feelings were desperately needed to counter the strong negative emotions at large in the world. So they determined that a key objective of their project should be to nurture and encourage such feelings—to educate human feelings to human reality, just as human reason is educated to physical reality. They, like the president, were convinced that lasting technical reform of the world's management systems would be impossible to implement without an almost revolutionary improvement in general human relations.

Although the committee's insights were not all new, their willingness to address the world's problems in terms of such insights was a significant departure from the conventional wisdom (which states that a show of force is the only way to get people's attention). There was a risk in their approach, to be sure. But war and threats of war also produced risks, and in light of world circumstances there seemed to be no alternative.

By year's end, the public announcement was ready. The years from 1990 to 2000 were declared a Decade for Human Heritage. It was to be a time set aside for improving man's understanding of himself and for calling on the world to celebrate the heritage of humanity's achievements. The United States proposed to kick off the decade by offering to sponsor cross-national family exchange trips in which citizens of the United States and of other countries would be invited to discover their family roots by visiting relations in their countries of origin.

Money to support these "heritage journeys" would be taken from a nuclear weapons program by deauthorizing some $2 billion worth of planned nuclear missiles. The journeys would continue to be supported for the remainder of the decade on a challenge basis: In each succeeding year, the US government would match every dollar spent on heritage projects, anywhere in the world, during the previous year. To secure future funding, corporations, associations, and other government bodies were encouraged to establish additional exchange programs, for example, among members of worldwide professional organizations, among artists in the same medium in different cultures, or among parties linked by agriculture or business.

Traveling the country in support of the project, the president asked would-be participants to plan wisely and to take only what they needed of the precious resource so that as many as possible could be served. He made public the guidelines his planners had laid down to ensure respect for the laws and sovereignty of all nations and called on all participants to pledge to abide by them. He pledged in turn that the heritage process would be as fairly and effectively managed as was humanly possible.

Buoyed by high enthusiasm at home, the president and his planners took their case abroad. "We have a decade," he said, "enough time to plan and to learn. We shall try to see to it that every country that wishes to participate can do so. We want the heritage process to succeed and will do our best to see that it does. Please help us." . . .

Throughout the first two years of the decade, public interest in all subjects relating to the theme of human heritage grew steadily. This interest stimulated the production of numerous books, films, classroom materials, and (most profuse of all) television programs—the latter designed as often as possible with world distribution in mind. Whatever television's limitations as an artistic wasteland, it was still the best tool available for worldwide communication. Information concerning the varied histories and habits of the human race was now coming apace, often through the medium of old familiar formats. Nature lovers were tuning in to human nature, arts fans to cross-cultural comparisons, and history buffs to sagas which traced ancient human migration routes and the flow of cultures. New formats were also created, especially through the agency of closed-circuit international television hookups. These were used to bring ethnic and interest groups from all countries together for talk and sharing and celebration. . . .

By the middle of the decade, nearly every village and hamlet in the world was involved in some sort of heritage project. The Soviet Union and its East bloc partners were well into projects of their own—and refusing to hear of matching funds from the West. Although decidedly less comfortable and less accustomed to such an open approach, the Soviet Union had nevertheless made some progress toward exchange with the rest of the world. The bloc nations, however, were openly enthusiastic, and the melting pot of Central Europe was having itself a small renaissance.

The decade ended with a burst of activity and enthusiasm, and with great celebration. Threads of human heritage, developed independently all over the globe, were brought together and woven into a splendid, multicolored cloth that represented the sum of all human life, past and present. This converging of separate human paths brought out more than the obvious universals of human creativity and intelligence. It produced a new and keenly felt awareness of man's common aspirations for self-fulfillment. Looking back at human history from this new perspective, it was easy to see that man's search for social customs to serve his needs was an inevitable part of the human experience. From this perspective, those heretofore troubling differences among nations and cultures—always so cherished and now more appreciated than ever—could be seen as separate elements in a vast and marvelous repertoire of uniquely human values and customs, all of which had risen, inevitably, in response to different human environments. . . .

But the most significant thing about this view of man, this new and growing consciousness of an all-embracing human identity, was that it was not simply understood but felt. It was felt because it had come, as all human values must come, from the realm of everyday human experience—from human contact with human reality. The heritage process, with its emphasis on simple communications, familiar activities, and ordinary human relations, had stimulated the growth of human feelings among people who had not shared them with each other before. It had forged the new worldwide network of human connections that fostered these feelings. And because of them, those who shared the new consciousness of human identity were able to strengthen one another and support one another in the usual human way. Standing together, they felt obliged to demand that this great history of learning and achievement not be sacrificed to the cause of petty human weakness. Standing together, they became a force to be reckoned with by those who still persisted in defense of the old strategies and old habits of thinking. And they made the difference. Although nothing in the world was changed by the heritage decade but humankind's view of itself, that was enough. The old ways were fading, and all the strategists had to reckon with the new.

(Patricia Overby)

Mr. President, Members of Congress, and all American people everywhere—Comrades:

My presence here before you in your national Capitol is surely the greatest honor ever bestowed on me, so if my delivery this morning appears at times strained and halting, you will please realize that it is not due entirely to my inadequate English. It is with some trepidation that I find myself the first Soviet premier to ever address this august body. It is a historic occasion, but it is not nearly so historic—or important—as the event whose anniversary we are today commemorating. . . .

Twenty-five years ago today, in Helsinki, the Joint Commission on Peace formulated a bold and entirely new proposal for establishing peace. The plan was designed to circumvent completely the insoluble riddle of distrust. Difficult questions of nuclear strategy and arms control would likewise become irrelevant. In short, what the commission proposed was the manufacture of a situation which in and of itself *commanded* the establishment of international trust. Since the negative attitudes of rivalry and distrust which had fueled the arms race for so long could not be quickly dismantled, they would simply have to be allowed to remain in place—while a parallel countervalent structure was constructed, one which generated positive attitudes.

The commission found few guidelines. There was, however, a historical precedent in one of the elements that had maintained the Pax Romana. You will recall that the Romans held young princes of conquered nations in Rome as further insurance against foreign uprisings. Besides, properly nurtured, these youths would eventually return home—romanized. If this system could work with subservient nations, why should it not work, with adjustments, between equals?

From a theoretical perspective, as early as 1966, Thomas Schelling, in *Arms and Influence,* had pointed out that war, like diplomacy, involved a bargaining process. In this process, force could be used not only to achieve military objectives but also to inflict national pain. In fact, the character of war had been changing over the years so that the coercive effect of civilian violence had become an important part of modern warfare. Conceivably, war might even be fought entirely in terms of exchanged pain. Furthermore, this pain, to be effective, need not be actually delivered but simply threatened. Consequently, the bargaining of international conflict might be conducted to a large extent in terms of reciprocal *threats* of *civilian* violence. . . .

Previous experience in Western nations had already demonstrated the coercive political power of holding even a single hostage. Aware of this, the commission reasoned that an exchange of key hostages from each nation would not only be relatively humane, but would also work as well or better than a threat to the lives of millions. These exchanged hostages would exert their deterrent force in that they would be among the first casualties of any attack by their own nation. It was proposed to utilize a limited number of hostages and, in order to increase their leverage, they were carefully selected with regard to their emotional significance to the nations' policymakers. After all, those who needed most to be deterred were not the rank and file of the nations but their leaders—and those were, in fact, the ones who would be most particularly deterred. Any deterioration of the international climate would now be felt as a *personal* threat. Any destruction would now entail an unacceptable *personal* loss. In short, it would be of infinite *personal* concern for policymakers to ameliorate tensions, since it would be primarily their own children who were now in the most exposed positions.

Besides, it was felt by the commission that from a symbolic point of view, the sending of one's own children to live in a foreign country would represent an undeniable act of collective faith, so dramatic in its impact that it would immediately provide a major impetus for lessening distrust.

Limited student exchanges had proven successful, and there was no reason to expect that these exchangees would not be well received. It has always been the governments that were the objects of mistrust; by contrast, there was a strong tendency toward the establishment of warm and friendly relations between our peoples. No one ever doubted the sincere desire of our *people* for peace. They would now be given the opportunity to prove it. After all, our nations were composed not of communists or capitalists but simply of Russians and Americans, with many shared values and traditions. The truth of this was to be exploited to its full potential.

Once instituted, the plan would tether our two nations together, not by the reciprocal trajectories of missiles but by strands of the purest and strongest substance—family love. There would arise a mutual commitment to peace in which the two nations, albeit reluctant at first, would be forced almost literally to become brothers.

The initial response to the proposal was stunned silence. However, so desperate had the international situation become and so fervent was the worldwide desire for peace that within a matter of days there was an overwhelming ground swell of acceptance. The very novelty and strangeness of the plan gave it an unexpected power to inspire optimism; for the first time in decades there appeared to be a real hope for peace.

At first it was feared that many families might refuse to expose themselves to these personal risks. Fortunately, strong leadership in both the United States and the Soviet Union was instrumental in emphasizing the patriotic duty of families to voluntarily participate in the program. Of course, general humanitarian obligations were also stressed. Those chosen were, for the most part, eager to participate in the adventure of this grand experiment.

The first group of exchangees consisted of 3000 young people ranging in age from fifteen to twenty-five. All came from families of at least local prominence; the parents of the Americans were heads of major corporations and industries. They included the children of your senators, governors, and presidential advisors. The Russians sent to live in the United States were of comparable age and background—sons and daughters of commissars, generals, scientists. The period of sojourn extended uninterrupted for three years, during which time the exchangees lived in their host countries with carefully chosen families who cared for them as their own children.

As anticipated, these families developed warm feelings toward their "foster" children. Each was the main anchor for a child in an otherwise alien world and thus provided a true sense of home. To the credit of those early pioneer families, they did everything possible to make the stay of their guests rewarding and enjoyable. . . .

The commission predicted that the original hostage-holding aspect of the exchange would be of paramount importance only in the beginning. Later on, once the immediate danger was over, the program, although unchanged on the surface, was expected to generate a completely different set of benefits and take on an altogether deeper significance. This is in fact just what happened. The participants began to develop a degree of affection, understanding, and even a certain sense of identification with their hosts. Through firsthand experience, Soviet citizens learned about America and American ways. Such experiences were a useful corrective to whatever propaganda and prejudices they had been exposed to at home. Once returned, the exchangees proved to be enthusiastic advocates of the program as well as of their host countries. Many of the friendships formed during those three years were durable and resulted in continued visits. As is evidenced by my own American brother-in-law, there has been much intermarriage, and I believe that at last count there are twenty members of Congress with Russian spouses. This has been all to the good. . . .

Over the years we have seen the exchange program grow enormously in prestige. We recall in amazement the days when exchangees were regarded as "hostages." Now, on both sides of the Atlantic one has to apply for admission to the program, and selection is regarded as a high honor.

The program, as you remember, was not launched in a vacuum, but was accompanied by a tremendously augmented cultural and economic exchange. International travel among businessmen, diplomats, and tourists was greatly encouraged. Also, each government instituted at home an unprecedented educational program designed to foster better understanding. The Russian language is now commonly taught in America as an integral part of secondary school education, and Russian history is a required subject. Most of your young people are as familiar with Pushkin and Tolstoy as our schoolchildren are with Whitman and Melville.

Consequently, there has been both an intentional and an unintentional interpenetration of cultural elements. Certain aspects of Russian culture have found acceptance on these shores while, conversely, certain aspects of the American way of life have met with a warm reception in the Soviet Union. The reawakening of religious feeling in my country is but one example.

A particularly incisive feature of the Joint Commission's proposal was its insistence that no conferences be held initially to deal with underlying causes of international conflict. Once clearly identified these might still prove to be next to impossible to eradicate, even with prolonged negotiation. Rather than labor to untie that Gordian knot, it was decided simply to cut through it with the exchange program. Only after the program was securely established would such conferences be permitted. However, once begun, they continue to take place at frequent intervals. The exchange has undeniably provided a cogent incentive to achieve progress at these meetings. Important agreements have already been reached on the subjects of space exploration, global ecology, and ocean bed resources. . . .

In summary, the exchange program did not in itself solve any of the international problems that had beset us. Rather, by adding a new element, it provided a necessary impetus for us to work out our differences by peaceful means. Once in place, the program fostered the achievement of other preconditions for lasting peace. Although more than a mere catalyst, the program served as a necessary first step in the right direction. . . .

Look at the world about us today and contrast it with the one of twenty-five years ago. I am referring not to the material advances, which we knew to expect and which somehow seem to arise unbidden as years go by. Rather, I am talking about the spiritual progress that has taken place. The world in 1985 was on the brink of annihilation. There was a widespread sense of fatigue and hopelessness for the future. In a healthy society, if anyone should have an optimistic attitude, it should be the children; yet in a survey of American schoolchildren undertaken in 1983, nearly 40 percent of them felt that a nuclear holocaust would occur in their lifetime. Shocking—that things should have come to that! No future? And what of Homer, of Tolstoy, of Mozart? Civilization reaching a dead end?

No, it did not happen that way. We did not let it happen. Look about you. Pinch yourselves; this is no dream. The world is still here and is better than ever. More importantly, talk to your children; listen to them. The striking feature of the present when contrasted with 1985 is not just that we are still here. We have been given back our future.

Peace is not merely the fortuitous absence of war. There is nothing that says that peace is the natural state of mankind, and that war is a hideous temporary aberration. On our tiny crowded planet where nations constantly jostle each other, peace does not come easily. We have learned that peace, like war, is a struggle and that victory is represented not by a triumphal arch but by villages intact, cities thriving, and children who expect simply to grow old.

We have not arrived safely at our final destination. Even at this time of commemoration, we must be aware not so much of past accomplishments as of the future, always uncertain, which awaits us. We have work before us—and always will have. However, let us be eager to do it, for it is holy work. May God provide us with the patience and wisdom to succeed in this vital and sacred endeavor.

The preceding is a transcript of an address by Sovier Premier Andrei Simonovich before the US Congress on December 22, 2010.

(Stephen E. Silver)

9

Imagination and Responsibility: Dilemmas in Translating Creative Ideas into Action

Lincoln P. Bloomfield

Defining "Peace" and "Realism"

One of the many fascinating aspects of *The Christian Science Monitor*'s Peace 2010 contest was to show how extraordinary a storehouse of "peace energy" lies beneath the surface of our society. One would have to live on Mars not to sense the powerful yearnings of citizens everywhere for a world at peace. Indeed, President Eisenhower once foretold the day when governments would simply "have to get out of the way" of the people's desire for a more peaceful world.

The flow upward of policy proposals is a key strength of democracy, but there are also negatives to be aware of. Some passionately advanced ideas for international reform rest on a weak information base and connect badly with reality. Others arise from such hostility toward authority ("You can't trust the Establishment") as to render them useless as policy prescriptions. Mark Twain spoke volumes when he said that it isn't ignorance that causes the trouble, it's that people know so very much that isn't true.

One thing that distinguished the contest essays from other views of a better future was the requirement to tell *how* peace came about. That was the catalytic agent that released the surge of creative energy. The essayists had to confront today's world, warts and all, as the starting point for their flights of imagination. Imagining the future is, by definition, a mind-bending task. Imagining it as a *coherent process* that takes us from here to there embeds ideas in the context of reality. The Peace 2010 contest was a kind of hotbed that both clarified and legitimized inchoate ideas by requiring that they be brought to life in a dynamic scenario possessing an interior logic.

Definitions of "peace" vary widely, as the previous chapters attest. Peace is what you think it is (or want it to be). At the modest end of the definitional spectrum, an experienced diplomat's goal is to see international conflicts negotiated before they turn into wars and small wars ended before they become big ones. The reductio ad absurdum at the opposite end would be what Galgacus said of the Romans: "Where they make a desert they call it peace." In my liberal Unitarian church we rather abstractedly sing Tennyson's vision of "the Parliament of Man, the Federation of the World." But to some fundamentalist ideologues, whether Western, Soviet, or Islamic, peace can come only with the total defeat of one's enemies.

A more usable definition speaks of attitudes, in the spirit of President John F. Kennedy when he said, "Peace is a process—a way of solving problems" (American University speech, June 10, 1963). My own working definition is not nirvana but what might be called "minimal peace." It assumes the empirical reality of disputes, conflicts, and occasional outbreaks of violence. But to me, peace must irreducibly mean that armed aggression by a people, tribe, country, nation, or state against another is systematically averted. Such a condition requires the means to both deter wars and secure justice for grievances. Above all it means preventing nuclear war.

Pyrrhus could have been speaking of thermonuclear weapons when he said of a costly win over the Romans, "Another such victory . . . and we are undone."

Avoiding nuclear war, as the sine qua non of minimal peace, logically assigns finding a more stable way to coexist on this shrinking planet to second place. All else is overshadowed by tension between two great antagonistic systems of economic and political rule, each animated by a belief in the rightness of its prescription and each capable of unwittingly incinerating the world. As potential sparks for igniting a wider conflict, the dry tinder of the Middle East and the threat of race war in southern Africa cannot be excluded from a definition of minimal peace.

This is not to ignore other urgent problems that make life unpeaceful for so many. There is no excuse for inadequate attention to the rest of the exigent global agenda—poverty, trade and monetary imbalances, resources, environment, indeed all major sources of injustice and misery. But true peace will come only on the day that the following two conditions are met: establishment of a rule stating that whatever their ideology or grievances, countries will leave their neighbors alone, and implementation of effective procedures for equitable conflict resolution. If not only wars but also everything else has the same priority, then peace has no real meaning.

After saying what one means by peace and suggesting appropriate action, another core question must be confronted: Is it realistic? Particularly in America, where so many become involved in foreign policy concerns, the challenge for bureaucrats to be more imaginative is a constant counterpoint to the plea for outsiders to be more realistic. The twin qualities in the title of this chapter—responsibility and imagination—are a metaphor for the very real gap that exists between those inside and those outside government.

The future is unknowable to us, and that which is "unrealistic" and even unimaginable at one time may become commonplace at another. We can nevertheless exclude some utopian thinkers who practice full time what Sir Halford Mackinder called "the impact of wishing on thinking." John Adams was an eminently practical president yet only a few years out of office he could write to Thomas Jefferson that "our pure, virtuous, public-spirited federative republic, will last forever, govern the globe, and introduce the perfection of man." At the other extreme we can discount inveterate cynics and professional skeptics who, like Gilbert Chesterton's anarchists, are disappointed with the future as well as the past.

The Peace 2010 contest produced a unique distillation of the ideas of hundreds of people in varied walks of life who combined their hopes for the world with their knowledge. They provide a summation of some imaginable ways in which the world situation might be constructively altered in the decades ahead. It may be that their contribution constitutes, to paraphrase Arthur Koestler, not so much the literature of prophesy as the literature of warning. But as imagined pathways to a more secure peace, the ideas presented here are all plausible to a degree, given their premises, whether passage of time and generations, a harrowing scare, or the access of greater wisdom through painful experience.

Imagination in Government

It is important to dispose of the notion, entertained by some among my academic brethren, that the intellectual and moral capacity of those people who think about foreign policy outside the government is somehow superior to that of those inside. Historian Barbara Tuchman strikes me as excessively unkind in her conclusion that "wooden-headedness, the source of self-deception, is a factor that plays a remarkably large role in government" (*The March of Folly* (Knopf, 1984), p. 6). Expert bureaucracies must deal full time with issues on which the outsider only occasionally focuses. One weakness of governmental machinery is the chronic shortage of philosophizing and future-oriented planning. But that does not mean that practitioners of foreign affairs are innocent of such thoughts or lack such capacity. It does nevertheless highlight three qualities that distinguish insiders from outsiders.

First, bureaucratic officials play a different role from that of the academic theorist, the critic, or the interest group. Second, their role is played within a time frame that insistently demands short-range decisions, regardless of whether adequate thought has been given or alternatives sufficiently considered. Third, the need for stability in large institutions fosters a conservatism toward alterations in the framework of policies and procedures. Pressures also come from political leadership for career professionals to "get on the team," and proposals for significant policy change may be regarded as unacceptable dissent.

These characteristics, although understandable, tend to stand in the way of timely policy changes. Secretary of State Dean Acheson was fond of quoting an unidentified old lady who said, "Always remember that the future comes one day at a time." The aphorism is usefully tranquilizing, so long as it is not an excuse for neglecting the longer time cycles of economic, military, and technological phenomena that serious planning must comprehend.

Another quality of officialdom differentiates even more sharply the universes of thought and action: *responsibility* for the results of ideas, proposals, or plans. Pressures, limitations, and consequences are realities of official life that inescapably bound the imagination while draining creative energies. (One unhappy side effect is the tendency to label as *ir*responsible potentially useful ideas that come out of the outsider's less bounded thinking.)

It is worth identifying the channels through which policy ideas are communicated to top decision makers. One obvious source is the expert consultant. Another is a small number of influential newspapers (such as the *Monitor*) and journals (such as *Foreign Affairs*). These publications are widely read by professionals (though not necessarily by the political leadership). But it might come as a surprise to learn how often seemingly novel ideas for policy already exist somewhere in the governmental apparatus. The bureaucratic culture may inhibit their consideration and perhaps even their ventilation. When policy is genuinely controversial, however, as during the Vietnam War, people in the middle levels of the bureaucracy, both civil and military, begin to open up to each other with their private doubts. The groundwork is laid for major policy change when top leaders also become convinced (or, as with President Johnson in 1968, give up their fight as lost).

Thus a consultant to government may be surprised to discover that all the pros and cons of an argument, including even far-out options, have already been advanced internally in one way or another. The consultant's role is sometimes simply to bestow legitimacy, so to speak, on an already simmering idea, or to lend weight to one side of an argument in order to help it win the day. At its best, outside advice will, as biologist Albert Szent-Györgyi von Nagyrapolt said of discovery, "consist of seeing what everybody has seen and thinking what nobody has thought" (quoted by Lewis Thomas in "Scientific Frontier and National Frontiers" (*Foreign Affairs*, Spring 1984)). The downside is that consultants may suppress their private doubts about major aspects of current policy in order to look "relevant" within the officially-defined framework of "realism."

Obviously the most effective source of policy inspiration is the president or other topmost official, although even then action does not necessarily follow. (President Truman commiserated with President-elect Eisenhower, saying "He'll sit here and he'll say 'Do this! Do that!' and nothing will happen" (Richard E. Neustadt, *Presidential Power: The Politics of Leadership From FDR to Carter* (Wiley, 1980), p. 22). Eisenhower himself is credited with the axiom that nothing is impossible so long as one doesn't care who gets the credit. Perhaps so. Certainly one of the least painful costs of good citizenship is to see one's idea announced by high officials as their own.

To know where ideas come from can be instructive, despite historian Lord Acton's axiom, which holds that "few discoveries are more irritating than those which expose the pedigree of ideas." Without inserting radioactive tracers into the bureaucratic bloodstream, the genealogy of ideas is particularly hard to trace in the realm of foreign policy, strategy, and international relations generally. But it is not impossible, as a few examples will demonstrate.

One of the best known examples is the analysis of US missile strategy concluded in the late 1950s by Albert Wohlstetter and others in the Rand Corporation. Early ICBMs were powered with liquid fuel that took several hours to load. Emplacing missiles in the open meant not only that they were vulnerable to physical attack but also by that token that they looked like first-strike weapons that invited elimination in an intense crisis. The Rand recommendation was that strategic delivery forces emphasize in the design a secure second-strike retaliatory capability as the heart of deterrence. Future land-based systems were thenceforth emplaced in hardened silos, along with a commitment to build submarine missile-launching platforms to reinforce crisis stability.

Another example was the Washington-Moscow hot line, stimulated at least in part by Harvard professor Thomas Schelling's scholarly analysis of the value of good communications among adversaries to minimize fateful misunderstandings at times of tension. In the same period, highly influential books by Harvard professor Henry A. Kissinger and MIT professor William W.

Kaufmann elaborated the basic doctrines (and problems) of limited warfare in the nuclear age.

In the diplomatic realm, a 1976 Brookings Institution report detailed the essential components of a just and durable Arab-Israeli peace. It was not the first (or last) such report, but its drafters included numbers of prestigious analysts outside the government, several of whom (such as Zbigniew Brzezinski) would shortly enter government in positions of authority. The terms of the report are recognizable both in President Carter's Camp David efforts and President Reagan's 1982 Peace Plan.

Policy in the Reagan administration was strongly influenced by a pair of magazine articles, one in *Foreign Affairs* by Professor Chester Crocker urging changes in US policy toward South Africa, the other in *Commentary* by Professor Jeane Kirkpatrick arguing that US human rights policy should differentiate between potentially reversible authoritarian regimes and irredeemable totalitarian ones. Both professors moved into positions of power where, for better or worse, their concepts could be implemented.

In the international economic area, a virtual blueprint for development strategies was laid out in a report prepared by the MIT Center for International Studies under the direction of the late Max F. Millikan, Walt W. Rostow, and others in the late 1950s. The primary consumer was the Senate Foreign Relations Committee, in particular then Senator John F. Kennedy. That their blueprint, like some of the others cited above, turned out to have defects does not detract from their strong influence on policy.

It will be noticed that all these instances involved private citizens who were known to government, trusted by government, in some cases recently out of or about to enter government. But what about the anonymous or unconnected citizen or group with a proposal of merit? Examples are harder to find. One early instance is the notion of citizen exchanges between the United States and the Soviet Union to both improve understanding and place what would be in effect mutual hostages in each camp, presumably making conflict less likely. Credit for the constructive innovation that is the Peace Corps is also widely shared.

It is easier to document waves of changed citizen attitudes that become political forces that the government cannot ignore. In this category the Congress has generally transmitted ideas to policymakers in the executive branch. One clear instance was the gradually organized opposition to an earlier version of an antiballistic missile (ABM) system. First, communities normally indifferent to experimental weapons systems (such as Lexington, Massachusetts) discovered with alarm that their town was being considered as the site for an ABM battery. Next, citizens knowledgeable about such matters became involved, mobilizing academic and scientific expertise to analyze, publish, and testify before congressional committees. The pressures contributed directly to the ABM Treaty of 1972 as part of SALT I.

Some years later that same combination of citizen concern and expert backup developed in Wisconsin, where the Navy planned to install underground a very low frequency radar array to facilitate communication with nuclear-powered submarines. It was the same story in the late 1970s in the western states, where even deeply conservative citizens and legislators mobilized opposition to deployment of MX missiles in their region.

No successful example of outside input was more vivid than the drive in the early 1960s to end testing of nuclear weapons in the atmosphere. The detection of the poisonous radioactive element strontium 90 in milk that children were drinking created overwhelming pressure on Washington (and evidently the Kremlin as well) to conclude six years of desultory negotiation, occasionally broken by massive nuclear explosions, with the landmark

1963 Limited Test Ban Treaty forbidding tests in the atmosphere, underwater, and in outer space.

On at least one occasion (never repeated so far as I know), the process itself was deliberately restructured in an effort to make officialdom more responsive to citizen concerns, attitudes, and recommendations for policy. From 1975 to 1976, the Department of State collaborated with the Charles F. Kettering Foundation in organizing an extraordinary series of so-called town meetings in five US cities—Pittsburgh, Portland, Oregon, San Francisco, Minneapolis, and Milwaukee. What was so novel was that high officials, *before* being permitted to speak their piece, were required to sit and listen while citizens stood up and expressed concerns, views, and ideas. (The departure from the normal format was sufficiently traumatic that a state department psychiatrist accompanied the Washingtonians on at least one of the trips!)

It might be concluded from these cases that influential outside proposals typically come only from experts with an "in," leaving only a kind of undifferentiated mass sentiment as the stimulus for other major policy shifts. But the Peace 2010 contest has shown the extent to which innovative policy ideas and scenarios can come from the lay public, as it were, *if* sufficient stimulus is provided.

In its various expressions and through its varied channels, the tradition of private sector policy initiatives is uniquely strong in the United States—that "nation of joiners" observed by de Tocqueville a century and a half ago. Something of the same sort happened in the early 1980s in Western Europe, with hundreds of thousands taking to the streets to protest the deployment of US intermediate-range missiles. Even in tightly controlled Eastern Europe, the mass movement represented by the Solidarity workers' union shook and, for a brief time, shaped government policy. In Western Europe the protests proved insufficiently representative, with majorities in the end supporting deployment. On the other hand, in Poland the protests were excessively representative, frightening Moscow and its Polish agents into new repressions, including martial law and the outlawing of Solidarity. In the Soviet Union itself, not only is open dissent a punishable offense but there is also a long cultural tradition of noninvolvement and passive support for government policy.

Mass sentiment is not always correct, and Foreign Secretary George Canning of Great Britain eloquently warned against "the fatal artillery of public excitation." In America, Walter Lippmann was an influential spokesman for the proposition that governments should hang tough and avoid being stampeded by the mob into, say, an ill-advised war. Today the problem has changed. On superpower relations, polls uniformly show the public to be tilted toward peace rather than toward war, regardless of (or perhaps particularly) when government is talking tough. (On nonnuclear issues, such as terrorism and hostage taking, when the majority understandably wants retaliation but government, despite muscle flexing, does nothing, Lippmann may still be correct.)

Official conservatism is not often shaken by popular feeling or unorthodox logic to the point of altering the course of the ship of state by more than, say, five or ten degrees. Strategist Herman Kahn once allowed that a plan for world government would most likely be implemented when, right after an unwanted exchange of nuclear weapons between the superpowers, the leaders of both sides would agree over the telephone to sign the Clark-Sohn Plan for disarmament plus limited world government.

Most policy and strategy changes are, however, modest and incremental rather than drastic and of the "root and branch" variety (the essay by Charles Lindblom making these distinctions was significantly entitled "The Science of Muddling Through" (*Public Administration Review,* Spring 1959)). Yet events sometimes short-circuit the process, catapulting officialdom into a rare posture of radical leadership. Following the trauma of World War II and the revelation of the power of the atomic bomb over Japan, the US government in 1946 put before the United Nations an astonishing blueprint for limited world government that became known as the Baruch Plan.

Far from reflecting a sudden presidential or other top-level impulse, the plan for veto-free international control of atomic energy moved systematically upward through the system, starting with internal technical studies—notably the Acheson-Lilienthal report—and finally emerging as a formal initiative that the overwhelming majority of UN member states voted to accept. It represented a rare example of direct linkages between analysis and action and, rarer still, willingness by a powerful country to forego short-term unilateral advantage for longer-term global security. We can speculate on how different the world might be today if the Kremlin had not rejected the Baruch Plan while racing to acquire its own nuclear arsenal. (We can also speculate on the possibilities if the Soviets had, like the British, openly shared in the US wartime atomic bomb development.)

Signposts to the Future

The tension I have described between official responsibility and private imagination appears to be a constant in organized life. Nor is it all bad to want our leaders to stay in touch with tough reality. The trouble is that the normal process of policy adjustments at the margins, though it can get us through this week, this month, even this year, is simply not sufficient for the flexibility and responsiveness demanded by daunting problems.

A fascinating deviation from that pattern is President Ronald Reagan's call for a program to substitute strategic defenses for offensive nuclear systems—the so-called Star Wars plan, officially denominated the Strategic Defense Initiative (SDI). There is much to criticize in both concept and execution, but SDI reflects a widespread human uneasiness about having a sword of Damocles permanently suspended overhead and about a deterrence strategy grounded on potentially genocidal retaliation. (As the SDI program surges forward, private analyses and public pressures might fruitfully be focused on fleshing out the casual but crucial presidential afterthought that antimissile defenses be developed *collaboratively* with the Soviets to avoid perilous destabilization of the strategic balance.)

Official awareness may also be starting to catch up with some fallacies in the "development strategies" that drove American and multilateral aid programs for several decades. Official wisdom came only after frustrated rural populations swelled the new urban superslums and after it became glaringly obvious that steel mills were no substitute for a decent diet in impoverished, often illiterate societies. But of course some outsiders have labored for years to point out fallacies in aid policy and urge midcourse corrections.

Other important foreign policy sectors remain virtually impervious to innovative ideas that might help all parties to break out of depressingly familiar molds. A follow-up essay contest could profitably invite creative ideas for solution of regional issues, specifically encouraging policy deviations that "practical" people presently deem unrealistic. Let me take an obvious example: South Africa careens toward catastrophe, but the only available choices appear to be a never-never white program of "reform" and a precipitate black demand for total "equality." Escaping the trap of unattainable alternatives will require those free to do so to think through blueprints for other solutions, such as a real partition or a "cantonization" that gives the black nations of South Africa some of the best rather than some of the worst of that fertile land while allowing the "white tribe" its dream of living alone—but no longer able to have its heavy lifting done by an unenfranchised proletariat.

Other time-urgent situations are deadlocked by a mix of intransigence, fanaticism, political cowardice, and bureaucratic inertia. Before it is too late, someone should be mapping the West Bank in a way that sets before all parties a concrete blueprint that is demographically fair and strategically reasonable. Neuralgic situations in Lebanon, Ulster, Central America, the Philippines, Eastern Europe, and Afghanistan all resemble Greek tragedies in that their probable fate is painfully obvious but the available "heroes" seem powerless to prevent it. Fair solutions, however unorthodox, need to be fleshed out, if not by governments or the United Nations, then by someone else.

The American tradition of citizen involvement is virtually unique, even in comparison to other Western democracies, in which party organizations are the usual vehicles for "outside" policy initiatives. Yet another typically American quality is optimism about the future, also not matched in older cultures with a tragic view of history. The enthusiasm and commitment shown in the *Monitor* contest supplies additional confirmation of anthropologist Clyde Kluckhohn's bon mot that "America's golden age has been located mainly in the future rather than in the past" (*Mirror for Man* (Fawcett, 1957), p. 189). The Soviet Union's uniqueness lies in virtually total governmental control over all information flow, a fact sometimes poorly understood by Westerners accustomed to access to a wide spectrum of opinion.

These broad differences between open and closed societies raise a final vexing question: Is it worthwhile for people to press the far more accessible US government to undertake policy initiatives that may require action by the Soviet Union as well? Or does this mean *both* US and Soviet leaderships must be persuaded? The answer can only be "it depends."

Three US administrations from 1961 to 1972 borrowed from outsiders a range of arms control ideas ranging from aborting ABMs and limiting missile launchers to cutting off the production of fissionable material. The Soviet Union was ready for major agreements, but its subsequent behavior put in question whether Moscow was really prepared for what the United States conceived as the follow-up stage of implementation. Washington expected Moscow to cut back its drive in the Third World for influence by means of indiscriminate support for those in rebellion. And Washington did not deliver on Moscow's expectation of credits, trade, and high technology. The United States and the Soviet Union had two very different agendas for "Détente I," and each was disillusioned by the other. Their deep differences render problematic many proposals for independently mobilizing world public opinion.

Having said that, of course, there *was*—and is—a common item at the top of both the US and Soviet agendas: the powerful desire to avoid a catastrophic war, along with growing pressure to cut costly arms budgets. If there is to be a "Détente II," both can use all the ideas inventive people can think of.

In diplomacy, timing is everything. On the eve of the October Revolution Lenin said, "Yesterday it was too early; tomorrow it will be too late." In a slightly more spiritual vein, Bismarck, the German Empire's "iron chancellor," observed that "history advances in spurts, and then with irresistible force . . . all that is given to the statesman to do is to listen prayerfully whether he can dimly perceive the footsteps of God amidst the flux of history, then grasp a tiny corner of God's cloak as He goes by . . ." (as translated by one of Bismarck's intellectual descendants, Henry A. Kissinger).

If the iron chancellors of today's world are to be responsive rather than reactive, far more imaginative thinking by concerned men and women is required. This is the time to multiply efforts, such as the present one, in the quest for a more peaceful world.

Contributors

The Editors

The editors of this book have written chapter 1 and the introductory text appearing at the beginnings of chapters 2 through 8.

Earl W. Foell is editor-in-chief of *The Christian Science Monitor.* A native of Houston, he graduated with honors in mathematics from Principia College in Elsah, Illinois. Except for a few years with the *Los Angeles Times,* Mr. Foell has spent his entire working career with the *Monitor,* serving as managing editor and editor before being named editor-in-chief in 1983. He was for many years the paper's UN correspondent. Mr. Foell has been president of the UN Press Corps and is currently on the board of the World Peace Foundation and the Japan Society. He is chairman of the Third World Journalism Exchange Program of the American Society of Newspaper Editors.

Richard A. Nenneman is managing editor of *The Christian Science Monitor.* He graduated magna cum laude from Harvard College and later received an M.A. degree in International Studies from Harvard. He served with the US Army Counter Intelligence Corps in Germany for two years. Following a brief career in banking, he became the *Monitor's* business and financial editor. After serving nine years in that position, he rejoined the banking community and became the chief investment officer at the Girard Bank in Philadelphia. He returned to the *Monitor* in 1983.

Both Messrs. Foell and Nenneman wrote chapters in the book *Understanding Our Century,* published to commemorate the 75th anniversary of *The Christian Science Monitor* in 1983.

The final chapter of this book was written by Lincoln Bloomfield, who is a professor of political science at MIT. Professor Bloomfield received the S.B., M.P.A., and Ph.D. degrees in political science from Harvard and was the recipient of the Harvard Chase prize in 1956, as well as a Littauer fellow (1952) and Rockefeller fellow (1954, 1975). Professor Bloomfield served as director of global issues in the National Security Council during the Carter administration. The author of several books, the professor has also written numerous articles, that have appeared in such publications as *Newsweek* and *Foreign Affairs.* Professor Bloomfield is also a trustee of the World Peace Foundation.

The Essayists

Douglas D. Alder is a professor at Utah State University in Logan, Utah. He also is director of honors programs at the university. *143, 159–164*

James Andrews is an editorial writer for the *St. Louis* (Missouri) *Globe-Democrat* newspaper. *113, 135–138*

Robert Aronstein is a communications systems engineer working in the Washington, D.C., area. He has also been a free-lance writer for the past ten years, producing among other things the unpublished novel *Witness,* about a nuclear attack on Chicago, from which his essay is derived. *16, 27–32*

Dan Baker is president of Eurocalifornia in Escondido, California. The firm is an importer of European products. He has also produced films and is currently in the process of forming a corporation like the one starred in his essay. *169, 186–189*

Laura Bernice Barker is a free-lance writer from Wichita Falls, Texas. *84*

J. Edward Barrett is a professor of religion and philosophy at Muskingum College in New Concord, Ohio. *17, 145*

Paul Basile works for the International Energy Development Corporation of Geneva and holds two graduate degrees (in astronautics-aeronautics and business) from MIT. He previously worked as program officer in the energy section at the International Institute for Applied Systems Analysis at Laxenburg, Austria, and was on the staff of the House Energy Committee in Washington. *54, 57–64*

Louis René Beres is a professor of law at Purdue University in Lafayette, Indiana. *18*

Kenneth E. Boulding is an economist who is perhaps best known for his work as an environmentalist. He is currently living in Boulder, Colorado, where he is distinguished professor of economics, emeritus at the University of Colorado, Boulder, and research associate and project director at the Institute of Behavioral Science at the same university. *144, 164–167, 209*

E. Grey Dimond is provost emeritus of the health science schools and distinguished professor of medicine at the University of Missouri, Kansas City. *207*

James W. Eaton, of Orem, Utah, has worked in the labor relations field for more than sixteen years in both the public and private sector. *112*

S. Edward Eaton, of Hingham, Massachusetts, is a physical chemist who worked for the industrial consulting firm of Arthur D. Little as a group leader and was director of new product development at the USM Corporation. *112, 128–135*

Katharine Nicely Emsden has taught at the university

level. She is currently living in Castle Rock, Colorado, and is a teacher at the Colorado Academy in Denver. *208, 222–224*

Thomas Fehsenfeld lives in Grand Rapids, Michigan, where he has an oil products service business. He has had an active interest in conflict resolution groups for several years, particularly in how the West can adapt the non-violence principles of Gandhi. *4, 50, 168, 175–183*

Dietrich Fischer is assistant professor of economics at New York University and author of *Preventing War in the Nuclear Age. 110, 121–128*

Randy Fritz is a graduate student writing a thesis on medical malpractice at the Lyndon B. Johnson School of Public Affairs at the University of Texas. *56, 68–73*

Fung Waiman, from Hong Kong, is secretary for evangelism on the staff of the World Council of Churches in Geneva. *75*

Geoffrey A. Grimes is an English professor at Mountain View College in Dallas. He is also founder and chairman of the board of Hands Around the World, International, an organization that facilitates the exchange of children's art from seventy countries. He lives in DeSoto, Texas. *141, 146–149*

Edmonde A. Haddad is president of the Los Angeles World Affairs Council. *78*

Brigadier Michael N. Harbottle is director of the Centre for International Peacebuilding in London. He served the British Army in Africa, Cyprus, Europe, India, the Middle East, and the Near East and was chief of staff of the multinational UN peacekeeping force on Cyprus (UNFICYP) from 1966 to 1968. *81, 169, 183–186*

Klaus W. Heinemann is president of Eloret Corporation in Sunnyvale, California. A physicist, he runs a small research institute that does government-sponsored research in surface physics at NASA. *170, 189–192*

Joerg Heinemann is the son of Klaus W. Heinemann

and is a sophomore at the University of California, Los Angeles. *170, 189–192*

Toby Herzlich has worked as a producer for a television station in Connecticut. She is currently special projects coordinator for Project Victory (see Craig Schindler) in Santa Cruz, California. *141, 149–151*

Steven Horowitz is a free-lance journalist in Milwaukee, Wisconsin. For several years during the 1970s he and his wife lived on a kibbutz in Israel, where he practiced sheep farming. From this experience evolved his strong interest in a Middle East peace settlement, the theme that forms a major part of his essay. *79, 90–99*

Rudolf Jäckli, of Zug, Switzerland, is a member of the International Committee of the Red Cross who before retirement served as a geologist and general manager for European Shell Petroleum. *18*

Nabil M. Kaylani is a professor at the College of Liberal Arts, Rochester Institute of Technology, Rochester, New York. *51*

Erazim Kohák is professor of philosophy at Boston University and a fellow of the Institute for Human Science in Vienna. He is author of *The Embers and the Stars* and other works on philosophy in Czech and English. *80, 99–102*

Joan Kufrin is manager of corporate communications for Leo Burnett Company in Chicago. *172, 202–205*

Richard D. Lamm is serving his third term as governor of the state of Colorado. He has written extensively and often controversially on major issues facing US society. Houghton-Mifflin will publish later this year his latest book, *Megatraumas: America in the Year 2000. 15, 20–27*

Bruno Leuschner is a Chilean who has lived in the Federal Republic of Germany for the past fifteen years. He lives in Schwenningen, where he works for an export firm. He has traveled extensively in South America, the locus of his essay. *171, 199–202*

Ellen G. Meyer is a master's and Ph.D. degree candidate in public policy at Harvard's Kennedy School of Government. At the time she wrote her essay, she was coordinator for public education for the Nuclear Negotiation Project at the Harvard Law School. The project explores how negotiation can prevent and control crises in order to lower the risk of nuclear war. *171, 192–199*

Robert Muller is assistant secretary-general of the United Nations for the commemoration of the UN's fortieth anniversary. *109, 116–121*

Michael N. Nagler is a professor of classics at the University of California, Berkeley. He is also a director of the Marin Experimental Teaching Training Advising Center in Tomales, California. *142, 151–159*

Patricia Overby has been a teacher of music theory. Her home is Fullerton, California, but she is presently pursuing a Ph.D. degree in political science at the University of Michigan. *209, 224–229*

Torkel L. Patterson is a Lieutenant Commander in the United States Navy who served in Japan for four and a half years and specializes in northeast Asia security matters. *113*

Nancy J. Perry lives in New York City, where she works for Time Inc. *208, 220–222*

Jerome Pressman is a physicist and laser scientist who lives in Lexington, Massachusetts. *206, 211–220*

Barbara K. Rossiter is a Christian Science practitioner in New York City. She has traveled several times to China, a country that has a major role in the essay she has written. *76, 86–90*

Mark D. Sarkady lives in Littleton, Massachusetts. He is a mediator and organizational consultant to business and public interest groups. *171, 192–199*

Craig Schindler is the holder of both a law degree and a Ph.D. in ethics and psychology. He has taught at Harvard and the University of California, Santa Cruz. He is currently president of Project Victory, an organization that aims to bring together people with diverse viewpoints on the subject of peace. He lives in Santa Cruz. *141, 149–151*

Stephen E. Silver is a physician living in New London, Connecticut. *210, 229–235*

Robert Sprinkle is a physician living in Dallas. *19, 38–45*

Godfried van Benthem van den Bergh is chairman of the Netherlands Association for International Affairs and senior lecturer in international relations at the Institute of Social Studies in The Hague. *48*

Richard K. Wagner, of Los Gatos, California, is a long-time manager at IBM who has worked twenty-two years in the computer business. *113*

J. Tayloe Washburn is a partner in the Seattle law firm of Roberts & Shefelman. *84*

James Werner, of San Diego, holds a law degree from the University of Chicago and is director of the San Diego County Law Library. *55, 64–68*

Morley G. Whillans is a retired medical doctor who was involved in various fields of medical research and university teaching. *83*

Vernon F. Wilkinson is a retired schoolmaster in Christchurch, New Zealand. He has just written a book, *After the Bomb: Flight to Utopia. 16, 32–38*

Douglas H. Young specializes in the practice of international law in Fort Lauderdale, Florida. He has also had two novellas published. *114*